PRAISE FOR *BLACK BIRD IN A PEAR TREE*

ᚷᚤᚢ

Emperor Hadrian deified his deceased beloved Antinous and built a city in his name Antinopolis, and centuries later the Mughal Emperor Shah Jahan built the Shalimar Gardens and the Taj Mahal for his beloved Mumtaz Mahal and today, following their footsteps, Birnbaum has written ... black bird and a pear tree ... a family tree [where] names, countries, epochs, and politics all collide. This book, Birnbaum's second dedicated to Wally, is a love story that transcends place, space, and time ... one thing is clear, roots of the pear tree stand firm and grounded, watered by love and compassion for all.

Black bird and a pear tree ... memoir to her beloved and to her family ... well-constructed within the pages of a historical autobiography ... love-letter to Wally and the family they created as a couple—children, grandchildren, great grandchildren, and their respective partners ... nieces, nephews, cousins ... memoir traced through historical violence against the many others of the world ... tracing the meaning and significance of names—first, middle, and last.

These names illustrate the intersectionality of race, class, nationality, gender, language, and religious identities from the East to the West, from the global North to the global South ... in a dialogue between science, religion, and [wordless] mysticism ... What does it mean to write in a time of crisis? In Birnbaum's case, it means writing with love, compassion, kindness, non-violence, and a vision of the future where the past gives clarity and foresight bringing new ideas into being, new understanding and new meaning—hermeneutics ...

Black bird and a pear tree is an ethnography of the soul through an excavation of the self (great grandmother, feminist cultural historian, nonviolent revolutionary) genealogically tracing family names through world stories to understand the present political climate and to welcome the future. This book is a gift.

——Atiba Rougier, New School for Social Research, New York City, January 2018

ᚷᚤᚢ

Atiba Rougier's review of *black bird and a pear tree*. Convergence of a contemporary third world Caribbean male, three generations younger, and me, a ninety-five-year-old great grandmother, evoking Atiba's great grandparents who survived slavery and exploitation ... one of his grandmothers was blind.

——Lucia

The personal is political is spiritual is historical is magical is cosmic. This is what Lucia Chiavola Birnbaum rightly and fascinatingly demonstrates in her evolutionary memoir *black bird and a pear tree*. Hers is a culminating life history swirling together maverick academic discoveries, compelling personal stories, goddess-given insights, and enlightened values. In sharing her knowing in this way, Lucia shows us how everything in our own lives is intimately related and can never be torn apart, despite our efforts to present ourselves in logical and linear ways. While teaching us so much about the histor(ies) she relates, she offers us an innovative and feminine form of writing based on the spiral – or perhaps the weaving shuttle. Lucia returns us to compelling themes again and again, always on a new rung, a new level, inviting us to reflect on old events from ever-deeper perspectives. A much welcomed, right-brain stimulating and heart-opening missive for our time.

——Marguerite Rigoglioso, Ph.D., *The Cult of Divine Birth in Ancient Greece* and *Virgin Mother Goddesses of Antiquity*

Lucia offers us pulsating threads – history, personal story, signifiers in names and locations, and serendipities – as we follow her spiral weaving encompassing a timeline that stretches from the paleolithic to the present. *Black bird and a pear tree*, a story of love between Lucia Chiavola and Wally Birnbaum, traces ancient lineage roots in African origins and in the branches that emerge, cross, take disparate routes and on a fated night, meet in Lucia and Wally with almost instant recognition of connection.

The Red Hot Radical, as Lucia named herself to her students, and the peaceful nuclear physicist forged a lifelong amalgam of love grounded in what Lucia considers the legacy of our primordial African mothers – caring and sharing. Wally and Lucia worked, lived, loved, and played in partnership beyond conventional strictures. Mutually supportive, mutually nurturing. Partnership in educational pursuits, child rearing, and careers. Together as "passionate political activists," they created the enduring Peace and Freedom Party.

Lucia and Wally "lived their deep beliefs," imbuing their children and grandchildren with a sense of social justice as well as a sense of their deep history and connection to living beings through shared origins. Lucia also imparted this gift to her students, me among many.

black bird and a pear tree is a testament to a woman of expanded consciousness. Lucia reaches into our ancient past. She reaches to our primordial African mothers who she deeply believes have blessed our DNA with a way forward for our species. Whether in our "unconscious, preconscious, or consciousness," there is profound knowing of the caring and sharing imperative. At 96 Lucia continues to be an inspiration, asking us to think with heart about our connection to each other, to understand the implications and responsibilities of our shared DNA, to work for a just, sustainable future for all beings and the planet.

——Annette Williams, Ph.D., Chair, Women's Spirituality Program, California Institute of Integral Studies

With this extraordinary memoir—poetic, profound, political and personal—Lucia's truth-telling gives us an essential perspective in these uncertain times. From the heart of a great grandmother and the mind of a brilliant historian, Lucia's message vibrates with clarity in its call for values of sharing, caring, and healing. Acknowledging dance as a joyful presence throughout her life, as well as a meaningful metaphor, Lucia observes that, "keeping our deepest beliefs and acting on them to make the world better is like dancing." This remarkable love story of Lucia and her beloved husband Wally is a most beautiful dance of life.

——Mary Beth Moser, Ph.D., scholar of the Black Madonna (*Honoring Darkness: Exploring the Power of Black Madonnas in Italy*) and Italian folklore studies (*The Everyday Spirituality of Women in the Italian Alps: A Trentino American Woman's Search for Spiritual Agency, Folk Wisdom, and Ancestral Values.*)

Inviting us to shed old silencing skins to sashay onto lava-transformed and rose-infused dance floors reverberating with riff-gifts of prescient knowing and heart-full, insight-brimming, and transporting poetic prose, the great Strega Nonna—lover and godmother to us all—calls us here into concert with her name-sakes from so many spirals ago. Emerging from the dark subterranean sea of simmering chaos, she bears light-filled buried maps of shimmering suppressed wisdom from our African ancestors. With an authenticity that only someone who has risked both career and cash flow can fully embody, Lucia's visionary recovery of the seed-carrying legacy of caring, sharing, and healing—toward regeneration of life-sustaining and celebratory culture—offers both inspiration and practical guidance at this most auspicious and perilous time on the planet: to embrace Other as kin is to nurture and cherish the diversity that is portal and pathway to the flourishing of all sentient beings. To read these stories is to be expanded into vistas of new possibilities by a heart broken wide open to the deep generativity of love.

——MaryClare Foecke, Ph.D.(c), "Wandering Spaces Between: Wondering Gift Culture"

There is nothing I like more than page-turning books of love and revolution. Lucia's book quells my hunger and lust for those stories enlightening many realms of life's mystery. As if she was a story teller out of an ancient cave painting, Lucia tells stories in the liminal state of knowing, and the story itself becomes a spiral dance of her/history and reality that is at once an epic saga of Lucia's family and that of the human species. Written in zoom in and fade out film technique, Lucia's story takes me to times and spaces where I feel bedazzled and hallucinated as if in augmented reality. History, mythology, archeology, science, religion, spirituality, geopolitics, revolutions and family stories spiral in a whirlwind that sometimes blows me away and other times sucks me in.

Entwined in their "deep story" of a passionate love for each other, studying and traveling together in intellectual endeavors and enterprises while tracing their ancestral origin in Sicily, Wally and Lucia enlighten us about who we are and show us how to live and how to make the world better. For this, Lucia sends her piercing laser sharp light, scorching layers of deceptions overshadowing us. At the same time, her stories bathe us in the warm light of loving, caring, sharing and healing for green earth.

I will not hesitate to say that this is the ultimate saga of the Godmother of Sicily, juxtaposed to the Godfather of Sicily. Praises to Cara Lucia, my mentor, my role model, my light in these dark Trumpian times, from a very grateful student and your favorite anarchist.

———In Hui Lee, mentee

Bless you Cara Lucia. Bless your dedication to understanding, your courageous true storytelling, and your ever-more-complexifying "survival hypothesis"—to the tune of Ravel's Bolero—which states that, no matter who or where we are, all of us live in, and out, the same Pear Tree Spiral: birthing, blossoming, harvesting, dying, and seeding.

Cara Lucia, you have sought shards of light in our shatterings and you have emerged with pure revelations. Straight from the core, you say, come the submerged human wisdoms, zooming in and out of the fire like immortal, mythical black birds scatting Love, Peace, and Freedom.

Pilgrim Lucia, we are reaching the paradigm of caring, sharing, and healing that you and Wally dreamt of and helped us to conceive. We are going green, Peace Girl is here to stay, and, like Atiba said, "I think we are on the cusp of something good."

Thank you and bless you, Cara Lucia, for your lifetime of great works, global sisterhood, and for four decades of ineluctable friendship set in motion by common cause.

———Pamela Eakins, Ph.D., *Tarot of the Spirit*

black bird and a pear tree
the story of Lucia & Wally, 1945-2019

❧

by Lucia Chiavola Birnbaum

Printed in the United States of America
ISBN: 978-1-7333866-1-6

Cover: Lucia's original maiden surname, Chiavola, means black bird. African owl/Sicilian black bird … hearts pierced embracing on bough of pear tree. Barbara Ardinger, who calls herself a Pagan crone, came to visit in a rainstorm, and afterward gifted Lucia & Wally a moon-dipped, hand-sewn tapestry inscribed in mirror image to "cara" (dear one).

Back Cover Credit: Angelo Romano/Public domain, "Flag of Sicily"

Permissions:

Mary Saracino, "Subterranean Rage," www.newversenews.com, May 23, 2008. Reprinted by permission of author.

Louisa Calio, "Signifying Woman," first appeared in version first appeared in an anthology Sweet Lemons 2 published by Legas Press, 2010. Reprinted by permission of author.

DEDICATION

꧁꧂

For Vivian Deziak, pilgrim, we live in mysterious times~encounters~emergencies~emergence of timeless mysteries~feelings~memories~beliefs:

> The terrain of the mysteries is the edge where power encounters power,
>
> for mystery is arising of powers that are timeless uncharted and untamed,
>
> that will not follow the logic of naked force,
>
> and so act in unexpected ways.
>
> Mystery is surprise.[1]

PROLOGUE

꧁꧂

Lucia Birnbaum:
Great Grandmother ~ Peaceful Revolutionary
African origins, migrations out of mother continent
Birthing, blossoming, harvesting seeds, renewal

T his is the story of Lucia & Wally—as told by Lucia—who met at the
end of world war II one late November night in 1945, instantaneously
bonded, and lived thereafter with kids and kindred spirits, resisting
USA devolution to empire threatening nuclear bombs on challengers of USA
white supremacy by never-ending wars.

Signifyers of Lucia & Wally's deep story ...
encouraging you to find yours

Lucia Chiavola Birnbaum

"Signifyin' Woman"
Italian American Jazz Poem by Louisa Calio[2]

⟶⟶⟵⟵

Rumor has it she was born a gypsy on the streets of Palermo, Sicily
Then again some say, it was on the bay of Naples
while others claim I was made in New Orleans
under one of those giant trees
with roots that go down so deep, they reach into the earth's center.
Trees with arms so long, high and wide,
they reach out and grab you like the Great Mama.

The dark bark betrays our true origins.
Straight from the core I've come
with silvery lips, wide hips, menstrual blood and Oracular Visions.
Part witch and bewitching, I refused to be from one place or one race.
I travel in any skins, many skins,
black like the panther, spotted as a leopard.
White as the milk in her mama's red-rosy breasts.
I am red tongues licking fire, a bold soul, an old soul
backyard worshipper, gypsy wanderer.
Sicilian queen, a dew's drop on mint green
pure, liquid mercury, the sharp in turns,
the quick in glances, the dirt in between cracks of concrete.
I am the wave length Green
a fish-bellied, crab-crawling, moon-child, secret reptile
Virgin & Mean… the final curtain call before the Great Silencing…
Global-eye, a spy, the rhythm and the drum-beat of eternity

black bird and a pear tree

The curse of blessedness, all female feminine woman, pure and simple,
Madonna, puttana, the funneling that germinates Seeeeedzzzz.
The veiling revealed!
Unsettling, rumbling, pulsating, earthquaking rumblings,
I shake the earth when I walk and sway my hips
I am an instrument of the divine …
"mercy, mercy, mercy /me /" mus i cal gal
Louis Prima's sista, an Italian American Signifyin' Woman!

Lucia Chiavola Birnbaum

"Subterranean Rage"
by Mary Saracino

Deeper than bone
deeper than muscle or sinew
or tenacious tendon
this howl of ages
rivers through bloodlines, ancient as oceans
salty as the primeval seas
this is what happens to women who
out-step their bounds
dare to be bold, brazen
speak up, name the subterfuge
women who grit their warriors' teeth
fight on, for their children
their lovers, their nation
their homes, their hearts' desires
branded as heretics: witch, bitch, cunt, whore
they race through forests and fields
trying to outrun the acrid scent of their own sweat
running from the hellish hounds
the priestly proclamations
the wrenching bite of the strappado
running for their lives
caught between sinner or saint
rarely allowed sovereignty over Self
over mind & womb, over laws meant to undo them

Thousands of straggled cats launched the Plague
tender necks swinging from tree limbs
flaccid, cold paws an omen: the rats will have their day

Crucibles of change, cauldrons
of sorrow, voices stymied for eons by the threat of extinction
womb-wisdom silenced by public outcry
burned at the stake of cultural conditioning
the subterranean outrage
seeps out, sharp as knives
sharp as memory
sharp as justice denied
sharp as the bloodied knives
eviscerating their midnight powers

Deep is this grief
Deep this anger
A dirge of rage lost to the winds of time.
The weeping memory wails, still.
Hear it the moonless night sky,
touch it in the hot light of noon
smell it in the poisoned soil
taste it on your remembering tongue
see it in the burning irises
that bear witness to this unyielding genocide.

"I Believe: declaration of a migrant feminist from Germany to USA last quarter century"
by Renate Sadrozinski

❧

Women's rights are human rights.
Black lives matter.
No human is illegal
Love is love.
Water is life.
Science is real.
And kindness is everything

❧

Spring 2019 brings a converging looming climate catastrophe and violent USA white supremacist culture challenged by resistance of colonized of the earth: Climate Justice (young and everybody else) / #MeToo / Black Lives Matter (colored peoples of south of the world) / Dakota Resistance (indigenous peoples of the earth) / supporters of Medicare for all, free education preschool through college, abolition of gun violence, living wage, accessible housing for everybody—paid for by stopping all wars and preparations for war and redirecting energy helping to create green nurturing planet. Case in point: story of Wally & Lucia, told by Lucia.

On May 11, 2019, Lucia was asked to say a few words at the wedding of her eldest grandson Josh and timeless granddaughter Whitney. Struck by similarities of grandparents' bonding, parents' wedding, promise of kids, and expecting a baby Summer 2019, Lucia spoke of the simultaneity of past~present~open-ended future …

"Your Light"
By Annette Lyn Williams, grateful student and mentee

༺⸱༻

Lucia,

Your intellect is a laser
boring through patriarchal detritus
championing re-imagined yesterdays
advocating grandly envisioned tomorrows.

Your courage is a beacon
guiding those of tremulous voice
unearthing our skeletal truths
putting words to feelings and gut rememberings.

Your encouragement is sunlight, balm
melting away the icy encasement of fear …
burning times, hanging times, flesh lashed from the body times
when seeing meant witch and speaking meant death.

Your heart is radiant, Strega Nona
warming your children with its glow
giving us strength and conviction
as we pick up the standard, walk our talk in the world,
follow the paths of our highest destinies.

Like Yemọja you are Yéyé Ọmọ Ẹja "mother of children of fish."
Illuminating particles of light disseminated in your writings touch
thousands.
As we, your students, honor our beings,
the light you nurtured within us will go forth in waves
as we in turn nurture others.

Thank you, Lucia.

CHAPTER 1
Story of our deep story

꿔꿔

40,000 BCE: Paleolithic Africans, in the contemporary land mass today called Sicily, migrated to Marina di Ragusa where the ancestors of Lucia & Wally may have met … intersecting with other African migrants from Levant of West Asia where Judaism was founded in 5000 BCE.

1200 BCE: Canaanite Semites, hypothetical ancestors of Lucia & Wally, founded trade settlements throughout the ancient world, including on the island of Sicily in 800 BCE.

Year One CE: At the end of the Punic wars, Romans subjugated Jews, Gauls (Celts), and early Christians.

1060 CE: Scandinavians settled in Normandy, France—subsidized by the pope of Holy Roman Empire to Christianize Pagans. Normans conquered Sicily in 1060 CE and Britain in 1066 CE.

Late November night in 1945: Wally & Lucia met at a dance in Kansas City, Missouri, instantaneously bonding, marrying nine weekends later on February 3, 1946, migrating in September to Berkeley, California, where we lived our deep story for sixty-six years, leaving a still unwinding legacy …

꿔꿔꿔

Lucia, searching for signifyers of this story, comes across the advice of Heide, gardener: "Never underestimate the regenerative power of nature." Lucia adds: Never underestimate the ability of dominant elites to suppress the truth nor the persistence of conquered peoples to keep the truth in unconscious feelings, suppressed historical pre-consciousness, and glimmerings in consciousness signified in names, timeless chronologies, suppressed traumas coming to awareness, lightning shocks of truth … and signifyers.

George Santayana, USA philosopher of Spanish inheritance, taught at Harvard University in the early years of the 20th century: From whom I learned "Science and religion are both myths, but myths are far from signifying nothing."

Luca Cavalli Sforza, geneticist of Muslim inheritance, migrated to USA, married a Jewish woman from a nonviolent northern Italian aristocracy, named their son Francesco, researched at Stanford University: From whom I learned genetics history of Africa, inspiring me to write the story of African descendants, with this story of Lucia & Wally as case in point.

⚜

Excavating suppressed stories of our kin in the Mediterranean region, we found Jewish Semitic Canaanites… Jewish Christian Semites… Moors/Muslims from Africa… Saracens/Muslims from Asia… who shared Jewish~Christian~Muslim prophets Abraham~Isaiah~Joseph~Jesus~Muhammad (messenger) and signifying women Inanna, Astarte, Isis, Cybele.

A jingle from my Sicilian American childhood unlocked gates of suppression: "In 1492 your father was a Jew. Your mother was a jumping jack, and so are you."

Gifts illumine our story:

Our eldest grandson Josh gave us a "roots" journey to Sicily, and a trip to Mexico. The wedding of Whitney & Josh gifted us a trip to New York: on-site learning of our primordial ancestors/contemporary descendants/legacy…

Gift of our grandkids navigating contemporary cultural swerve through the dark night to shore where great grandkids~kindred spirits give glimpses of an emerging paradigm.

Gift of kindred spirit Jan Parker, *Culture of Rape. Classical Greece to Hollywood USA* provides a cultural backdrop for this origin story: the dominant paradigm of Western civilization in classical 5th century Greece BCE, an imperial culture of raping/killing/enslaving vanquished others.[3] Hermeneutics of raped goddesses/violent male domination are exemplified in the life story of motherless/fatherless Norma Jean Baker who became Marilyn Monroe, sex goddess of the West.

Truthful story of USA needs to be known before we can heal. Kidnapping Africans, stealing/enslaving them in the already inhabited land of Natives whom European invaders killed/raped … followed by immigrants from Europe and elsewhere, who came to USA, experienced bigotry, and brought up kids …

New immigrants—Lucia's Sicilian and Wally's Jewish kin—descendants of Africans who came to USA.

Today, in Spring 2019, we live in converging crises … with glimpses of possibilities. Including crises of people in 150 countries—unacknowledged economic/political colonies of USA in Africa, Asia, the Caribbean, South America, Pacific region, and Europe. Crises of climate, environment, politics, constitutional, and spiritual crises of the unacknowledged USA empire: 800 military bases, 19 aircraft carriers equipped for battle, "black holes" for torture, uncounted surveillance facilities throughout the world, preparing for endless wars benefitting 1% of world billionaires controlling wealth and power of other 99% of peoples of the earth.

In October 2015, two weeks before All Hallows Eve (Halloween), lying on a hospital gurney waiting to be wheeled into surgery to remove extra eyelid folds interfering with my vision, I watched a nurse decorating for the holy day. Underneath a clock ticking conventional time, she put a sign: "Haunting Season."

⚜⚜⚜

Evoking my African/Sicilian/Italian/American context for this manuscript, Louisa Calio's first name is a variant of mine. Her jazz poem, Signifyin' Woman, inspires me to look for signifyers for my deep story … hoping to inspire you to find your own signifyers. Mary Saracino's poem dives into our mutual suppressed story of Sicily: persecuted Jewish/Christian/Muslim sister carrying subterranean rage at power-over vulnerable peoples epitomized in bodily and spiritual rape of beliefs of all those historically vanquished. Renate Sadrozinski's statement of belief of our kindred feminist sister born in Germany, today living in USA, conveys her riff on women's story: her father killed while defying Nazis, her mother punished in patriarchal German society, and her name Renate pointing to rebirth of suppressed others. Atiba Rougier surprises, invoking simultaneity of past~present~future in his story of coincidence of this ninety-five-year-old great grandmother (me) and his story of a three-generations-younger Caribbean scholar awakening in a world of "woke" youth.

My major signifying experiences include meeting Wally, love and light of my life, traveling the world together, personally confirming on-site scientific truth of African origins and human migrations out of Africa … explorations across the world spiraling toward contemporary cultural~spiritual crises~possibilities …

The itinerary of our deep story may be tracked in my books: *Liberazione della donna. Feminism in Italy* (1986). *Black Madonnas* (1993, 1997, subsequent editions), *Dark Mother: African Origins and Godmothers* (2001), *La Madre Oscura* (Italian edition, 2004), *La Mere Noire* (French & African editions, 2007), International Valetutti New Left Award for Black Madonnas, Salerno, Italy, 1997.

In 2011, while caring for Wally who was dying, I wrote *The Future Has an Ancient Heart: Legacy of Caring, Sharing, Healing, and Vision from the Primordial African Mediterranean to Occupy Everywhere* (2012). After he passed, I wrote a revised edition with a new subtitle: *The Future Has an Ancient Heart: A love story, a vision, and a prophecy* (2013).

Black bird and a pear tree: story of Lucia & Wally, 1945-2019, was written September 2014 to Spring 2019.

CHAPTER 2
Story

꘎

began writing this story after Wally passed away on September 4, 2012 at high noon when there is no shadow. Initially intending to keep a journal that might be found in the ruins of our civilization that destroyed itself, this story was manifested in subsequent downward spirals of my life.

Yet … courage of our kids in a bleak world, cool of our grandkids navigating contemporary swerve, chortles then laughter of our infant great grandkids, unexpected gleams of light while writing/watching life and work of kindred spirits … are traumas/illuminations/life giving glimpses of possibilities …

Birth names—carriers of submerged meaning—intrigue me.

Wally, born of Jewish parents who migrated to USA from Ukraine (Poland), gave him signifying birth name: Shia Welvel (Isaiah Wolf).

Welvel, wolf, remembers our animal grandparents … awe-struck watching dark of night becoming light … every day.

"Shia" in Yiddish, the everyday language of Jews, transmits a message of prophet Isaiah of Judaism~Christianity~Islam: beat weapons of war into plowshares of peace. The 1960s, a signifying decade for Wally & Lucia and a great many others around the world, resonated to Isaiah's prophetic message "ain't gonna study war no more."

Wallace, his Americanized name, refers to Wales, an African migration path in Britain where Gauls (Celts) conquered by Caesar fled, where ancestors of Thomas Jefferson walked then migrated to colonial USA. In 1776, Jefferson was living with an African woman slave, and in the founding document of USA, penned "All men are created equal."

Lucia, my signifying birth name, in Latin means light—lux, lucis—transmitting the story of healer Lucia of Syracuse in Africa, today's Sicily, blinded and killed by Romans in 304 CE for her Pagan visionary beliefs. Teresa, my middle name, conveys my suppressed conversa historical story.

1960s and thereafter: Lucia & Wally, political/cultural nonviolent revolutionaries, worked for a better country and world.

1970s: Lucia, feminist cultural historian, looked for women left out of histories written by dominant males, uncovering females who preceded Lucia of Syracuse: Inanna, signifying woman beating a drum honoring the sun, migrating to pre-Judaic Sumer in West Asia. Astarte—woman star to whom Jews migrating out of Sumer—looked. Cybele, oldest goddess of Africa ...

Drawn to art, my 1960s generation of feminists, looking for precursors, found paleolithic rock sculptures of women in Old Europe. Marija Gimbutas, mother of Archeomythology, located Old Europe in south and southeast Europe, countries lapped by the African Mediterranean Sea.

In religious art during the first years CE depicted Lucia of Syracuse with candles on her head in dark subterranean caves carrying food to early Christians hiding from soldiers of the Roman empire sent to kill them.

Folk stories pull me. Once upon a time during a very cold winter, Lucia of Syracuse, at the prow of a ship without helmsman nor sails, brought wheat to famished people so they could survive until spring.

A dominant story tells of Roman emperor Diocletian. Upon learning that the visionary healer Lucia of Syracuse had gathered a popular following in Judea, the Roman province where Jews were considered trouble-makers, he branded Lucia a Pagan and ordered his soldiers to gouge out her eyes. When she resisted dying, in a signifying act of sexual violence, a Roman soldier thrust a sword down her throat.

During the first years of CE, Lucia's killing, along with murders of other dissenters, were attempts to silence heretics. Nonviolent trouble-maker, "Jesus of Nazareth, King of the Jews," was crucified by Romans in 33 CE. Patriarchs of Judaism and early Christianity divided uncodified beliefs of Jews into Judaism and Christianity. Many Jews aligned with the Holy Roman Empire that was allied with Christianity.

In the 7th century CE, Moors—black Semitic Muslims out of Africa and dark Semitic Muslims out of West Asia—sharing ultimate beliefs with Jews and Christians, simplified their common Jewish/Christian/Muslim faith emphasizing shared prophets: Abraham, Isaiah, Joseph, Jesus, and Muhammad.

In the 9th and 10th centuries CE, Roman emperors/agents of Christianity, trying to unify heterogeneous peoples, proclaimed Jesus the incarnate only son of God and incited violence against Pagans, dissenting Jews/Christians/

Muslims, and suspect women, giving them a choice they could not refuse: convert to the version of imperial Christianity established by fathers of the Holy Roman Catholic Church—or be killed.

⚘

Trying to figure out how I became an outlier, I thought about my Sicilian Catholic childhood in Kansas City, Missouri. Curious questions prompted nuns to rap my knuckles. A Catholic priest, fixing his beady eyes on me, scared the hell out of me. For forty years he had offered Easter mass for his dead mother, that year he would offer Easter mass for me. This power-over vulnerable people—I was ten years old—became a major signifier in my life journey: I was an outlier identifying with others who were killed for questioning the established truth.

Ten years later, at the end of world war II, Wally, at our third weekend meeting (he was still in the USA Army) asked me to marry him, saying he would give up Judaism for me. I reached for his hand and said, "Yes"—but I did not want him to give up his faith. On February 3, 1946, a county judge in Lawrence, Kansas married us. On April 2, 1946, prior to our Jewish wedding ceremony in New York, a rabbi told us something that, somehow, I already knew: Jesus, the central figure of Christianity, was a Jewish rabbi (teacher) whose mother Mary and father Joseph were Jews, as were the early disciples of Jesus.

The 1960s rising tide of suppressed world beliefs converged with my studying the writings of Karl Marx on dynamic economic determinants of history and of Sigmund Freud on the power of sexuality in the unconscious. Wally's belief (similar to Albert Einstein's) was that science and religion are different yet compatible ways of knowing.

Einstein expressed: God does not play dice with the universe. Wally did not like to discuss ultimate beliefs, yet when confronted by an ethical dilemma, indicated he knew the difference between right and wrong; he would say two wrongs do not make a right. For both men, human knowing is relative: cosmos is spinning ~ while earth is spinning ~ while each of us spins different riffs ~ encountering others spiraling on their own journeys.

In the late 1950s/early 1960s, while writing a doctoral dissertation on the intellectual history of the West (USA and Western Europe), I studied the origins of the dominant paradigm of Western civilization whose violence Wally and I opposed: elites with power of life and death over vulnerable dark others, inciting perpetual wars sustaining power over elite hegemony.

Wally, a nuclear physicist, tried to keep violent uses of physics out of the hands of militarists/imperialists. Lucia, a feminist cultural historian, taught truthful stories of non-white-washed history. Both of us politically opposed violent USA domestic and foreign policies sustaining unequal and unjust relationships—called white supremacy—raping women into submissive silence and killing others suspected of subverting the hegemony of elite white male culture.

I was early drawn to Protestant scholars of dominant USA culture who molded my study of religious beliefs. First, Perry Miller who emphasized Puritans.[4] Then Henry Farnham May.[5] In the late 1950s, I was May's teaching assistant in history classes at the University of California, Berkeley (UCB), conveying story of Puritans to founding fathers to transcendentalists to abolitionists against slavery to civil war to industrial revolution to Protestant social gospel to progressive reform to world war I. My own research focused on what then was called Intellectual History of the Progressive Era, 1900 through 1920s.

In the early 1960s, as a doctoral student in History at UCB, I was invited to teach a course in the Department of Social Science, called "Marx, Weber, Freud"—as well as an honors course in primary sources of USA history. I was then a teaching assistant for Robert Brentano's graduate seminar in world history. I was impressed by Brentano's methodology: a Jew hermeneutically studying world history.[6] In 1964, Free Speech demonstrators at UCB were arrested. Bailing out our students from the Santa Rita jail, Brentano and I looked at each other and simultaneously said, "What are you doing here?"

In 1964, graduating from the University of California, Berkeley with a doctorate in History, I was given the choice of teaching at Saint Mary's College of California or at San Francisco State University, where a campus revolution ignited by African American students had begun. I chose San Francisco State (SF State). My emerging perspectives are evident in the article I wrote about my students in the Free Speech Movement at UCB: "Unkempt Prophets of Berkeley."[7]

During the summers of 1966-67, Wally and I traveled to Europe. Wally spoke to European universities on his research findings of measuring the mass of the meson with oil emulsions... meeting me in Rome where we participated in Italian feminist demonstrations, then danced in the afternoon.

In Summer 1968, Lucia, in a car of Berkeley radicals on our way to Ann Harbor, Michigan, to the nominating convention of the Peace and Freedom Party to support nonviolent Dick Gregory's presidential candidacy, hit a wall in the desert. I was given up for dead. Wally, at my bedside death watch, later told me I ranted in a coma for more than two months about Lucia of Syracuse.

I recovered. Returning to my post as Assistant Professor of History at SF State, the campus revolution led by African American students was surging. I immediately joined the strike; shutting down classes, demanding a department of African Studies, and opposing USA imperial war in Vietnam.

In the 1970s, in the summers between our intense nonviolent political activities at home, Wally and I traveled to my ancestral Sicily, considered the most invaded island of the world. Drawn to the southeastern Sicilian triangle fronting Africa and Asia (today a part of Europe, we wondered if this intersection place of African migrants was where our ancestors met.

Exploring the suppressed story of Sicily, I came across Muslims whose emphasis on prophets hit a chord somewhere in my bodily knowing. Muslims out of Africa were called Moors—meaning "black" for English writers after the Norman invasion in 1060 CE—which premise absorbed into the dominant northern European paradigm. Conquered Sicilians interpreted this differently, calling Muslims out of Asia "Saracens," children of Hebrew matriarch Sara(h).

Traveling the world together, beginning with our journeys in 1959, 1968, 1969, and during and after the 1970s, Wally and I counted forty-six journeys—exploring hypothetical sites of our ancestors in Africa, migrants out of Africa into Asia, Europe, Australia, the Pacific region, and the Americas—before he passed away on September 4, 2012.

In this period of intense political activism, I was invited to speak to many groups in Europe, Africa, Australia, and USA.

At the end of the 1970s, Wally, president of Physics International, was kicked upstairs to the Board—in effect fired—by business investors intent on the bottom line of profits. Lucia, Assistant Professor of History at SF State, was denied tenure—in effect fired for joining students on strike for a department of African Studies and opposing USA imperial war in Vietnam.

In the 1980s, an invited Affiliated Scholar in Stanford's Institute for Research on Women and Gender—today's Clayman Institute—I gave up my scheduled time to discuss my research with a colleague. She criticized the woman director (a medical doctor) who advocated drugs to remove women's bodily experience of menopause. In traditional cultures, menopause is considered a "change of life" when women enter the stage of life after bearing children. As dissenters from the prevailing paradigm—in which students/lesser professors did not challenge superiors—our contracts were not renewed.

In the 1990s, as first a visiting, then a full professor at innovative (aligned with Asian Hindu founders) California Institute of Integral Studies (CIIS), invited by Women's Spirituality program founder Elinor Gadon, I taught women's story with optic of others. I took students on academic tours to origin sites—migration places out of Africa. While Wally tried to democratize capitalism with employee Stock Ownership Plans, and looked to peaceful international uses of physics (Technology Transfer projects), he arranged the logistics for these CIIS tours—whose itineraries I wrote with genetics/archeological/historical/cultural information.

On our tour buses, everybody's questions became rolling seminars in the many ways of knowing. Lucia, outlier feminist cultural historian; Wally, independent scientific experimental physicist; kindred students with different experiences; local guides and bus drivers contributing local folklore ... all of us listening to each other, and looking with unblinkered eyes at primordial sites of human origin and migration paths out of Africa.

Learning~teaching~writing, I constantly returned to what Antonio Gramsci called subaltern beliefs of vanquished people: slaves of imperial Greece, slaves of Holy Roman Empire, tortured/killed suspects of Inquisitors enforcing doctrinal Christianity, subjects of European Catholic and Protestant states colonizing the world ... institutionalizing killing and raping in all their lethal bodily, psychological, economic, and political forms.

CHAPTER 3
Story of our story

❦

Recovering my deep story has not been an easy excursion. During most of my early life I knew nothing about the historic heretic whose name I carry: Lucia of African/Asian/Greek/Jewish/Christian/Muslim inheritance from Syracuse, Sicily. When my mother enrolled me for kindergarten, she replaced my birth name Lucia with Lucille, which was considered more American. Years later, I learned Lucille is the French diminutive affectionate form of Lucie.

In the early 1970s, I rescued my Sicilian name Lucia. In the 1980s, trying to understand the deep beliefs of Italian feminists, Wally and I went to their home villages. Their passion for black madonnas startled us ... followed by searing experiences when black madonnas became my uninvited signifyer ... simultaneous with learning my maiden surname Chiavola means black bird.

I thought about the long story of my signifying birth name Lucia ... beginning with awe felt by our animal grandparents in primordial Africa watching dark become light when the sun rose every morning. Dinosaurs evolved into black birds sixty-seven million years ago ... becoming hominid Lucy, whose two-million-year-old skeleton was found in Africa in the late 20th century by archeologists listening to The Beatles' ballad "Lucy in the Sky with Diamonds."

During Easter week in 1988, on a Friday in west Sicily at Trapani, a town pervaded by ghosts of persecuted dark others of Sicily, I watched an icon of black madonna carried all over town in a nurturing rocking movement—two steps back, then forward—to a tent where, with other women, the black madonna mourns the crucifixion of her son.

On the Saturday of Semana Santa, a black madonna is carried from church to church looking for her son. At the last church in town, the icon wavers in agonizing doubt before she is swiftly carried inside.

On Easter Sunday, in an interior town of Sicily, Caltanissetta, where persecuted Muslims historically fled, I watched a sensual encounter of icons of mother and son, *L'Incontro*: an icon of the crucified Jesus meets an icon of his mother and the son lifts a corner of his mother's diaphanous gown. A local woman (working elsewhere, home for the holiday) watching me, said this was *la fantasia meridionale*: a Sicilian/south Italian fantasy in which the word fantasia connotes sensual desire in noonday heat.

Three days later, on my return to my post in Rome (Writer in Residence, American Academy), I was jolted awake by an apparition of a Tamil (Hindu) woman of south India, the first migration stop out of Africa. After the fall of the Roman empire, a Hindu Tamil woman became Byzantine queen at Constantinople. In the apparition, her face was that of my mother.

In 1989, on a late November night, my mother died.

On October 19, 1991, our grandson Jake's birthday, our Berkeley home and garden died by fire ... I had a feeling that the black madonna had burned them down. Fleeing the flames, Wally grabbed the computer hard drive holding my footnoted manuscript *Black Madonnas*. I snatched a pot of succulents. In separate cars we lost/found ourselves.

After the fire, we first stayed at the home of our kids Marc & Nancy in Albany, where we watched on television the home next to ours burn down ... then we sheltered in Oakland at the home of our elder kids Naury & Barbara.

By 1993, the ashes of our burned down Berkeley home transformed into a radiant Mediterranean home and garden where icons of signifyers live harmoniously together: Black Goddess of Many Names of Africa; Buddha, sage of Asia; St. Francis of Italy; Green Man of England called "bocca della verita" (mouth of truth) into whose mouth Italians put denunciations of injustice; Einstein, scientist beaming on all the signifyers; shadows of black madonnas everywhere.

Spiraling back to January 1, 1925 when, belatedly Christened, I was given the middle name Teresa ... honoring my mother's aunt (Za Teresa) who brought my orphaned maternal great grandmother (Giuseppina) from Palermo, Sicily to Kansas City, Missouri ... simultaneously honoring my mother's little sister (Teresa) who died in USA at the age of four. Not until the 1980s did I learn, while closely reading the historical Teresa's writings, that my middle name transmits signifying historical information of Teresa's grandfather shamed as a Jew in the streets of Inquisition Spain ... as well as wordless feelings (*duende*) she evokes in art and poetry felt ... not reducible to logical prose.[8]

During Inquisitors' persecutions of Jews and others, Teresa escaped being killed by taking vows of a Christian nun. With St. John the Divine, she reformed Christian convents and monasteries that had become corrupt in the late middle ages. She taught nuns to keep their ultimate beliefs in silent prayer, expressing them by dancing. Closely reading her writings, I learned Teresa considered Jesus her brother.

Participating in Italian feminist cultural/political activities, I learned Sicily's first people were Sicani (originally spelled *Sikani*) of Africa. The subverting dominant Western narrative that Sicels, white people from the north, were the first Sicilians thereby transmits the historic white racism of the dominant Western paradigm.

Closely studying the whole story of Sicily, I realized others—Jews, Christians, Muslims—were the Semites. My ancient name Ciavola (even after Normans mutilated it with an un-Sicilian "h" to Chiavola), kept its Muslim pronunciation: "shahvola" (flying angelic leader).

Very late in our lives, when my mother and I spoke to each other beyond family roles, she told me I was born with a caul. Studying folk beliefs, I learned babies continue to receive the mother's in-embryo nurturance when born with pieces of the placenta (the caul) on the new-born infant's body. In folklore of suppressed people, infants born with a caul are believed to have the gift of prescient knowing.

Learning my deep beliefs has not been a linear journey, but an unplanned spiral journey. In France, where we were drawn to look for black madonnas (more than in any other country), we uncovered the story of heretic Cathar women.

In the 13th century, Christian Inquisitors, searching for heretics, came across Cathar weavers and healers (mostly women) in the south of France. Their deep beliefs included Jesus counselling nonviolent resistance to the empire. For Cathars this meant living in accordance with their deep beliefs: no killing ... making their own decisions about whom to invite to bed ... sharing their earnings as weavers with those who needed help ... healing the sick with mud poultices created by rain revivifying the dry earth ... giving last rites to the dying.

The Christian pope, learning that Cathar women were bypassing church intermediaries (male), declared a crusade against them: "Kill them all!" They almost did.

In the 1970s, while trying to understand Italian feminists (so familiar yet different), I encountered Cathar descendants, among them, my mother whose birth name was Catarina ... yet as far as I know, she (consciously) knew nothing about the Cathars ... yet she spontaneously (unconsciously) gave last rites to a young neighborhood rebel who died on Wabash Avenue in front of our home.

Remi Omodele, signifying kindred spirit, was born in Africa, educated in Europe, living in USA, fell in love and married Ric, a Jew. Their kids—educated cross-culturally/internationally—already live in the new paradigm. In 1994, Remi and I first met at a University of Virginia conference where I gave a paper on African origins. Later Remi was invited into our feminist group Women & Work (oldest in Berkeley), where she immediately understands/encourages my research on African origins and migrations.

At the public memorial for Estelle Jelinek, pioneer in the African American struggle, Remi was the only sister in Women & Work who had the strength to speak about Estelle (whose name means "star") ... about her early participation in the African American struggle for justice ... about her last years in despair at the condition of women and other dark others in a deadly world. Estelle had committed suicide.

Remi & Ric and Lucia & Wally ... kindred spirits ... tracked mutual origins in Africa, migrations out of Africa to Levant in West Asia then to Andalusia in Spain, particularly to Granada, where Moors of Spain were conquered by Christian Crusaders in 1492. Today in USA, Ric heals the earth with solar panels, while Remi (and I) heals earth inhabitants with truthful stories about Africa and migrants out of Africa.

After 1970, Wally and I tracked our ancestors' migrations out of Africa, traveling to sites where they may have met. In 2003, we took students on an academic tour to Andalusia (N.B. this is the African spelling of Lucia) in Spain while USA invaded Iraq with the official lie: Iraq had weapons of mass destruction. We explored Cathar sites in France, and chased after black madonnas in Europe, sending us into spirals of our deep story.

In the triangular Sicilian region in the southeast of the island, place of my signifying woman, Lucia who lived in the Greek capitol Syracuse of a colonized island where Normans, subsidized by the pope, invaded and took Sicily, mutilating my ancestral name Ciavola for black bird to Chiavola. A nearby town kept the name of West Asian woman divinity Cybele in the suffix of town name: Ragusa Ibla.[9]

⸎⸎⸎⸎

Turn of a new millennium marked the end of Punic wars when Rome defeated Carthage, while Semites—Jews, Christians, Muslims—settled all along African Mediterranean littoral in Spain, Italy, France, Africa, as well as islands, notably Sicily, Sardinia, Corsica.

In 1492, when Christian Crusaders conquered the Moors at Granada, Spain, emerging nation states of Europe, allied with resurgent Catholic papacy, sought to explore/Christianize the world. The king and queen (of Aragon and Castile) in Andalusian Spain sent Christopher Columbus to test the hypothesis—heretical round-earth theory—by sailing west to India. The expedition of Columbus touched Caribbean islands in the region later called America.

"Discovery of America" became a major premise of the Western paradigm, omitting salient datum: discovered lands of the Americas were already inhabited by Natives. Columbus' son, Diego, became a slave master in what dominant paradigm of the West called the "New World."

⸎⸎⸎⸎

Since the 1960s, suppressed stories of Jews and Muslims of Sicily and south Italy are being uncovered by Italian Catholic women, second- and third-generation Italian American Catholics and Jews, among others.[10]

All this has formed my spiral view of history: two steps backward—energized by knowing true stories of our past—before walking/dancing forward, accompanied by music. Ravel's Bolero sounded louder and louder to me in 2017 before Winter Solstice/Lucia Day on December 12 ... Jewish festival of lights at Hanukkah ... Christmas December 25 birthday of Jesus, light of the world ... January 6 end of Solstice season celebrated in Italy by arrival of La Vecchia (Old Woman) or La Befana, personifying/changing the meaning of the church doctrine Epiphany.

The popular story/festival of La Befana replaces church doctrine: divinity of Christ is proven in arrival of three kings of Orient bringing gifts to the Jesus child on January 6. La Befana is a popular female version of Epiphany: Old Woman puts gifts in the shoes of all kids.

⸎⸎⸎⸎

I confirmed my Sicilian ancestors by going with Wally to Ragusa Ibla in Paleolithic Africa where, in 10,000 BCE, heated waters rose thereby separating the island from the mother continent Africa. After a Norman invasion in 1060 CE, for the next five generations to the present, my paternal Chiavola grandfathers were born. They worked as falconers/game wardens in the Norman (then Angevin) castle in Ragusa Ibla, in close quarters with the ladies/lords of the castle, up to my own paternal grandfather, Luigi Chiavola, who could not come with the rest of the family to USA in 1912 because he was ill. In 1920, he was brought to USA by my Uncle George ... passing away just before 1924 when Wally and I were born. Nannu Luigi's portrait, gift of my Uncle George, hanging on a wall of my study in our Berkeley home, looks at me while I write this on January 6, 2018.

The name of my ancestral town Ragusa Ibla remembers Levantine (later Yugoslavian) Cybele—shortened to Ibla—persisting in Iblean mountains where my Nanna Lucia and her six kids (including my father) lived in their cave home where Nannu Luigi, who lived in the Norman castle, visited his family once a week.

In 2017-18, exploring the many layers of meaning of icons of gods and goddesses, I replaced nouns with verbs ... loosening our imaginations to envision nurturing beyond species, beyond gender, beyond family roles, beyond division of women into good/bad ... envisioning whole women and whole men relating to each other equally in love.

Art, I keep discovering, is a major transmitter of our deep story. The city emblem today of my ancestral Ragusa Ibla is a black bird: a falcon, holding in one claw caduceus (signifyer of healing), and in the other claw a sheaf of wheat (signifyer of nurturing) resembling a writing quill. I interpret this image to mean the healing and nurturing of everybody.

Subaltern history, the story underneath the dominant story of vanquished raped humans, points to knowing the whole story of humans, and offers possibilities of transformation. Stories of the oppressed, often officially suppressed by agents of the dominant culture, remain alive in names transmitting preconscious memories in dialect of historical subaltern peoples, in everyday/celebratory rituals—notably food and housekeeping rituals—in profanity/subversive festivals—notably *carnevale* in Latin countries—and are bodily felt at liminal times of spirals of life: birthing ~ blossoming ~ harvesting seeds ~ dying ~ renewing life. Subaltern history is explored by Antonio Gramsci in his *Prison Notebooks*.[11]

My signifying case of subaltern beliefs is the CIIS doctoral dissertation of Mary Beth Moser on the everyday rituals of the Trentino, whose beliefs the Inquisition at the Council of Trent in northern Italy tried to suppress ... yet persisting in water rituals remembering earliest life in the sea before global heating lifted submerged continents ... persisting in subsequent Christian epoch in our daily housekeeping rituals.

CHAPTER 4

Different forms of deep beliefs,
many kinds of gifts, many forms of nurturing

※⟡※

On the night before Valentine's day February 14, 2017, during a popular festival in the West honoring the Christian heretic saint whose message is love, I found a lost gift. Reaching to the back of my chest of drawers across from our bed, I touched a box, finding in it a silk shawl Wally gave me on our last journey together to the African Mediterranean in 2010. The valentine gift is a large silk square depicting a black cosmos illuminated by humans, with embroidered red roses.

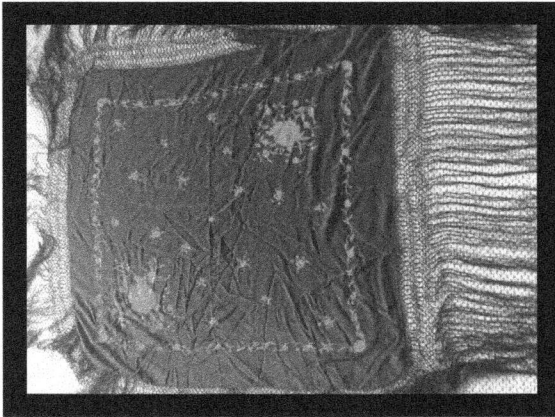

On March 5, 2017, my granddaughter Stefanie Rose came to help me format this manuscript. A gifted teacher of second and fourth graders, her mother's DNA report revealed highly multicultural genealogy of her Catholic beliefs: African ~ Semitic ~ Celtic ~ European ~ Asian ~ Native American.

Stefanie Rose, daughter of Linda Susan & Stefan Anthony, granddaughter of Lucia & Wally, offers a case of African ~ Asian ~ Semitic ~ Jewish ~ Pagan

~ Celtic ~ Christian ~ Muslim nurturing beliefs persisting through the generations to 2019.

Consciously, we gave our third son the name Stefan, honoring Wally's ancestral Poland, and from Stefano, remembering my ancestral Italy. At the outset of the Christian epoch, his Greek name was Stephen, a Greek Jew who was stoned to death for criticizing Jewish elders of the Sanhedrin … about the same time as Stefan's mother's namesake, Lucia of Syracuse, was branded a Pagan and blinded then killed by Romans.

An associated signifier—perhaps emerging from our preconscious: every time Wally and I traveled to Italy, we visited the sanctuary of St. Francis at Assisi, patron saint of Italy. Adjoining the sanctuary was the best bookstore in Italy for liberation theology: beliefs of early Jews labeled Pagan by Romans (later called Christian), associated with writings of secular heretic of Jewish inheritance, Karl Marx. Writings of Marx have been studied by revolutionaries, violently suppressed by reigning authorities, yet persistently unsettling the sleep of bosses to this day.

In his 1844 manuscripts, four years before issuing the Communist Manifesto, Karl Marx poured his ultimate beliefs into the concept of Nature … serendipity striking me, students of theology, historians of science, matristic scholars, and anybody who desires an equal and just world.

Also drawing us to Assisi were local shops offering folklore calendars transmitting folk beliefs enacted in everyday/celebratory customs, notably saints' stories recounting popular (non-doctrinal) stories of Christianity.

Wally and I loved staying at the Franciscan sanctuary in Assisi where we joined pilgrims from across the world—eating and sleeping communally, folk dancing together, and sharing political hopes for a peaceful green world of justice and equality of all beings.

Our son Stefan's middle name Anthony carries mystical-egalitarian beliefs of St. Francis and his contemporary, St. Anthony. In folklore, Anthony helps us find lost items and protects us on our travels. Stefan, whose Bar Mitzvah at age thirteen confirmed him a Jew, married Linda in a Catholic ceremony followed by the celebratory folk ritual of all Jewish weddings: dancing the hora—two steps back before dancing forward … everybody holding hands, dancing in concentric circles.

Today Stefan calls himself a Taoist. An inclusive believer, he considers particles (Newton) and waves (Einstein) equally signifying, considers established and heretical beliefs equally valid. I am reminded of the belief of St. Francis and his colleague St. Anthony: the holiness of all creatures.

In his childhood, Stefan identified with our inherited feral cat, George. After catting around all night, the untamed feline would come home bruised and bloody. Wally and I would catch him in a pillowcase and take him to be repaired at the veterinarian. Gift of George today are his descendants on our Berkeley hill: black cats with white markings.

Stefan advises I did not understand George. I would put out his food, but cat George would not eat until I left the room. Stefan today identifies with those left out of the dominant Western political economy of neo-liberals, which is based on the established piety that Wally and I considered blasphemous: "God shed his grace" on USA whose elites perpetrate raping and killing.

Our granddaughter Stefanie Rose, calls me Nanna Lulu, pronounced with Celtic broad "a" ("Naana"). Stefanie's Uncle Marc (Wally's and my middle son) suggested the name Nanna Lulu to the grandkids in our family—associating Inanna, our pre-Judaic Sumerian ancestor with the word for grandmother, Nanna (pronounced "Nahna" in Italian), and associating grandmother with the French/Italian popular name for Lucia: Lulu.

In my childhood, Lulú, was the name my paternal Chiavola uncles called me. Lulu, without a French accent, was the name my maternal Cipolla aunts called me, persisting to today when my cousin, Jack Lombardo, calls me Aunt Lulu.

❦❦❦❦

Stefanie Rose modeled the gift shawl from Wally. Wally's gift depicts a black cosmos illuminated by two large roses, with smaller roses embroidered in a galaxy fringed by long black strings connecting heaven and earth. This cosmology, bordered by embracing dancing roses, reminds some feminists of the embracing yonis (genitals) of the six-pointed star of David of Judeo-Christianity.

"Gift heirloom!" I exclaimed. The shawl will be for our grand and great grandkids named Rose. First to Stefanie Rose, our granddaughter, who will give it to our great granddaughter Isabel (Izzy) Rose, whose familiar name Izzy mysteriously remembers her paternal Semitic great grandfather Harry's red-haired brother (looking very Asian) Isidor, as well as her Scandinavian/Celtic maternal grandmother Marcia, were two great grandmothers named Rose. Stefanie's grandmother (me) dreamed she would gift the shawl to Stefanie … which I did on her birthday August 19, 2018. Stefanie will gift it to her niece

29

Izzy, who will gift it to her Rose signifying descendants … keeping our family's deep story spiraling …

✤✤✤✤✤✤

Italian writer Umberto Eco's book, *Name of the Rose*, considers the rose a signifyer of the Christian madonna, inheriting numinous meanings of names of signifying women who preceded her: African Isis, pre-Judaic Inanna, Semitic Jewish Astarte, Asian Cybele, Jewish Miriam, and Jewish Mary (the Christian mother of Jesus).

All of these names live in Lucia & Wally's deep family story of kin and kindred spirits. In addition to human mystical identifications with Nature, and nonviolent scientific investigations of Nature, liminal knowing is located in-between humans where human transformation may happen.

Cultural meanings are continually changing. African Sekhmet—daughter of sun god Ra, who destroyed his enemies—in her transformative role is a serpentine solar goddess who is the ultimate female source of power of all male rulers.

Twentieth century feminist mystic poets, Adrienne Koch and Gertrude Stein, tapped deep beliefs suggesting the rose as signifyer for women's womb—a portal of life. Transmitting deep poetic wisdom, they penned the perennial truth "a rose is a rose is a rose."

A flower with thorns, the rose is found in the wild as well as in gardens. When our house burned down in late 1991, Stefanie's other grandmother Marcia (Catholic with Scandinavian/Celtic ancestors) gifted us a rose bush for our renewed garden. In Spring 2017, the gift rose bush outside my kitchen door bloomed when Marcia's and our mutual great grandkids—Andrew Ellis and Isabel Rose—came to play at my house.

On August 29, 2018, the gift rose bush outside my kitchen bloomed in anticipation of the imminent birth of our mutual great grandchild. Flash! On August 30, 2018, Emma Lia—Marcia's and my great grandchild, child of grandkids Abi & Jake—arrived. In early 2019, we learned that a baby boy of our grandkids' Josh & Whitney will arrive Summer 2019!

Suggesting constant interplay of signifyers, proliferating/deepening human meanings/possibilities, Kathy W (extended family) during Winter Solstice gave me documents of oppressed Jews in Italy and a gift of an herb culinary/healing bush.

Matriarchal Studies, founded by Genevieve Vaughan, given scientific imprimatur by Heide Goettner Abendroth, and widened to an inclusive international meaning in the journal *Return to Mago*[12] ... strikes me in the many ways humans nurture ... mothers & fathers, grandmothers & grandfathers, sisters & brothers, aunts & uncles, nieces & nephews ... all the many ways we nurture in the once and future paradigm where nobody is othered ... where everyone cares and shares ... where everybody heals everybody on everybody's renewed green earth.

CHAPTER 5

Wally & Lucia—Jews & Sicilians—
poetically traversing terrain of the mysteries 1945-2019

᪨

W ally and I met at the end of world war II, on the night after Thanksgiving in 1945. Our encounter enacting unconscious memory of human origins in Africa, and historical migrations out of Africa. Meeting at a dance in Kansas City, we bonded instantaneously. We pledged our troth, married a few weeks later, and lived together in magic for sixty-six years. After Wally passed away high noon on September 4, 2012, I have constantly felt his presence … feeling/seeing him in our kids, grandkids, great grandkids, and extended family of kin/kindred spirits.

Finding our story difficult to parse, I remember that ancient historians were poets.

Whirling unconscious ~ preconscious ~ conscious knowing
into bodily resonating ~ envisioning in spirals of birthing ~
blossoming ~ dying ~ harvesting seeds ~ rebirthing whose
signifyers, for me, are light coming out of darkness ~
black falcon sending/returning messages ~
black owls whose eyes pivot to the past ~
look sidewise in the present as they soar and swoop
signifyers of African Isis ~ Asian Cybele ~ pre-Judaic Inanna ~
Jewish woman star Astarte ~
African Berbers coupling with Semites of Africa & Asia
sharing Jewish Christian Muslim prophets
dark wheat and red poppies—
signifyers of bounty and beauty of the earth,
blooming on flanks of Mt. Pellegino, pilgrim mountain of Palermo
icons of black madonnas stunning me at Tindari, Sicily 1970 …

Trapani, Sicily Easter week 1988 ...
Erice, Sicily 2014 when our kids on this ancient promontory outside
Palermo found the black madonna
I'd been looking for ever since Easter mysteries in Trapani
felt as a fiercely protective dark presence from before time began
underneath abstract ideas of classical Greeks whose empire of raped
goddesses/enslaved conquered peoples topped by elite of free white
males whose power-over enslaved people killed/raped/subaltern
humans became dominant paradigm of the West, whose elites in
2019 threaten nuclear-environmental annihilation of all life ...

Dominant violent paradigm challenged today by dancing, creating
art, telling truthful stories, caring, sharing, healing ... once and
future concert of ancients studying stars ... moderns reading Tarot
cards ... pilgrims walking to sanctuaries of black madonnas ...

Galileo, scientist under church inquisition for heresy
saying under his breath,
the earth does revolve around the sun
Van Gogh in south of France painting flowers reaching for the sun
20th century loyalists ~ partisans ~
anarchists fighting fascists in Spain, France, Italy
... everybody nurturing everybody ...
envisioning/working for just and equal green world
while scientists verify our earth is one of several planets,
our galaxy one of many,
everything so complex, so overwhelming,
some of us fall on our knees in despair
... yet we survive living our deep stories
... sometimes mysteriously

Lydia Ruyle, signifying artist, painted La Befana on one of her spirit banners, depicting the Old Woman as a historically persecuted witch riding a broomstick. She dedicated the banner to me. Some of my kindred spirit students/colleagues who like my challenge to violence of historic/contemporary elites controlling, exercising power over the oppressed of the earth, affectionately call me *strega nonna* (witch grandmother).

Women and others historically resisted subservient status thrust on them by dominant raping and killing elites. In the 1960s and afterward, these women calling themselves feminists, converging with ethnic outsiders and persecuted others, challenged the violent male hierarchies. Shut up for a while!

Awakenings after the unexpected November 2016 election of Donald Trump: the enormous Women's March on the day after Trump's inauguration, with pussy caps; huge airport demonstrations against Trump's ban on immigration from Muslim countries; and Town Halls demanding accountability of National Rifle Association profiting from USA domestic and foreign policies selling guns at home/abroad, inciting never-ending wars abroad and massacres at home via easy accessibility of guns.

The years 2017-2018-2019 were intense and dark with fires, smoke and mirrors, earthquakes, floods, pervasive demoralization … and a macabre dance of USA politics.

Black birds, our primordial ancestors/contemporary signifyers, caw in alarm when human predators approach. Black birds—ravens, falcons, crows, owls—animals closest to humans in intelligence, having perfected intricate tool-making, offer primordial wisdom to over-developed humans in late capitalist societies … feeding not only their own but other hungry baby birds, flying together in unison … reminding us of spirals of life ~ death ~ renewal of life.

Others, notably Natives who originally inhabited the continents and islands later called the Americas, discovered by Europeans in 1492, today recover truthful Native stories: indigenous spiritual beliefs were raped. Native resisters fought off invaders until the late 19th century when USA defeated/incarcerated them on reservations. As found in stories of genocidal murder of Natives, the USA Bureau of Indian Affairs presided over forcible sterilization of Native women.

African Americans, whom West Europeans then Americans kidnapped/shackled into slavery in the Americas after 1619 … followed by founding of USA by slaveholders who protected themselves in the Constitution and in an economy built on profits of slave trade/slavery, and whose USA industrialized version (cotton gin) was the most cruel slavery in human history—including selling children wrested from their mothers (precursors of children today being taken from parents at southern border of USA). Nineteenth century slavery in USA ignited a passionate debate that split the nation ... culminating in the bloody civil war when Lincoln freed the slaves.

In 1876, a postwar nation in a disputed election capped by a political deal: federal troops in the South—protecting civil rights of freed people—were removed, the presidency was given to Republicans, freed people were left to intimidating fiery crosses/lynchings of Ku Klux Klan, and enforcing of social codes stopping African Americans from voting. The raping and systemic subordination/killing persists to 2019 in a corrupt penal system institutionalizing exploitation/murder of black people, in gerrymandering to manipulate results of voting, and in regulations requiring street addresses of Native Americans on reservations.

Mexicans, whose lands were taken as spoils of the 1846 USA war for liberty against Mexico, who having won independence from Spain, had already abolished slavery. That war for liberty expanded the territory of slave-holding USA, taking southwest lands of USA from defeated Mexico. Later, Mexican and Central American farm workers, fleeing poverty induced by USA political and economic exploitation, fled to USA to work in agricultural stoop labor. The farm worker movement of the 1950s-60s, led by Cesar Chavez (supported by many student movements of USA) created resistance via boycotts against fruits and vegetables harvested by exploited stoop labor ...

Trump, in 2018, carrying out his campaign promise of mass deportations of Mexicans, separated children from parents at USA southern border. A caravan of desperate people from Latin America, exploited by United Fruit of USA and its client political rulers, arrived at USA border late October 2018 ... children died.

Latinos, dark others of the Caribbean and Pacific, who were colonists of Spain taken after USA victory in the 1898 war, were subsequently battered by USA client regimes, and then in 2017 by Hurricane Maria, devastating thousands (unreported) of Puerto Ricans. The 2018 election to the USA House of Representatives of Alexandria Ocasio-Cortez, of Puerto Rican inheritance, toppling a liberal stalwart Democrat, is a contemporary signifyer in Congress of outsiders auguring an auspicious future ...

Chinese Americans, called to build USA railroads, but not thanked when their immigration was stopped in the exclusion act of 1887, followed by persecution/subordination. In 2017, the death of the first Chinese mayor of San Francisco, Ed Lee, was followed by the election of London Breed, who, vowing to do something about homeless people leaving their drug needles and human feces on the streets of San Francisco, developed proposals for housing the homeless people who live in the streets …

Japanese Americans, branded "yellow peril" by Hearst media during the USA war of 1898, were interned as enemy aliens in concentration camps at the outset of world war II.[13]

Sicilians and South Italian Americans, branded by progressive reformers as genetically inferior, were hounded as anarchists and their immigration was sharply restricted in 1924 … the year Lucia & Wally were born.[14]

Jewish Americans, whose entry into mainstream USA was earlier curtailed by quotas for colleges, were banned from country clubs, and were victims of discrimination in early world war II when a ship of Jews fleeing Nazis was turned back by USA. During world war II, Nazis—studying USA's popular eugenics movement (considered progressive) to "eliminate" undesirables—murdered six million Jews. In 2018, there was a mass shooting of elderly Jews praying in a synagogue in Philadelphia.

Women, silenced by 2,000 years of rape in the violent history of the West, from imperialist Athenian Greek culture of raped goddesses to 20th century USA, whose paradigm of white superiority normalized culture of rape.[15] As of Fall 2017, many women are coming out of silence and are testifying to the sexual assault of elite men who have been preying on vulnerable women everywhere in USA … converging with other cultural/spiritual/political emergencies, including democratization/universality of rape.

Others, people who are historically and negatively identified by color, gender, sexual preference, or left politics, were scapegoated during the 2016 USA presidential campaign when two major candidates manipulated the rhetoric of "American Exceptionalism"/ "Make America Great Again" … camouflaging the ongoing thrust of USA to world dominance as supported by both major parties. Trump, the winning candidate, unleashed the violent sexual id (as discussed in Sigmund Freud's writings), fanned sparks of banked fires of the collective unconscious (as discussed in Carl Jung's work), and inflamed memories coming to consciousness of the historical violence of Western civilization against vulnerable others.

The imperial myth of Manifest Destiny engendered wars in the 19th, 20th, and 21st centuries, expanding the territory of slavery and fixing the dominant paradigm: Violent White Male Supremacy at home and Unending Wars Against Dark Others of the world.

✦✦✦✦✦

In 2018, a USA topped by a president with unprecedented, unchecked power—given to the presidency since the Iraq war of 2003—initiated global wars girded by USA holding the monopoly on nuclear bombs. Support for an authoritarian president in the USA was sustained by a toxic demography of people with long memories of old defeats (civil war, Voting Rights Act, affirmative action), people feeling personally defeated and numbed by opiates, and people who reach for a suicidal Kool-Aid in a climate of hatreds ... updating Sinclair Lewis, *It Can't Happen Here*[16] ... George Orwell's, *1984*.[17] These lethal ingredients were stirred in a soup of environmental pollution, loss of jobs, and economic inequality within the USA/world economy—where a bloated 1% elite are at the top, starving people are at the bottom, and in the middle is a demoralized middle class. All the while, mindless bureaucracies manipulated by geopolitical elites continue to exploit, rape, and kill dark others at home and across the world ... while burning up the planet ... while unleashing a president who daily creates domestic and world crises from which elites profit ... while the planet seems headed for extinction ...

✦✦✦✦✦

The year 2019 brings the United Nations report on looming environmental annihilation—lightning flashes, storms, fires, floods—and unprecedented alliances of defying oligarchic plutocrats staffing their white nationalist governments and operating outside constitutional, legal, historical, and moral boundaries ... recalling Nazis of Germany killing millions of Jews ... Mussolini's fascists of Italy pouring castor oil down the throats of dissenters ... oligarchs of contemporary Russia.

Ordinary Italians, during Italy's government of fascism from 1921 to world war II, purposefully bungled bureaucracy thereby saving many Jews from being murdered in Nazi concentration camps. Italian resistance against Hitler in Germany was swiftly stopped by killing its leaders. The West, in a world war II alliance with Soviet Russia, French Partisans, and Italian Partigiani, defeated Nazi Germany. This was followed by the Nuremburg trials for bringing Nazi criminals to justice, but with many Nazis fleeing, changing their names, and escaping to South America and elsewhere ...

Victory of Western Allies in world war II ended with Italians impaling Mussolini on a meat hook in a public square of North Italy. This was followed by a postwar season of high creativity in arts and ascendant egalitarian politics, with a notably signifying Italian feminist movement aligned with Italian male communists—called Italian communism with *ragù* ...

⚜

Hitherto suppressed questions have hit the fan. *Who am I? What color are your politics?* The writings of William Barber, head of the North Carolina National Association for the Advancement of Colored People (NAACP), remind everybody that Martin Luther King's 1967 talk at Riverside Church connected his opposition to racism and poverty in USA to the imperialist war in Vietnam. Replacing mainstream's benign image of the black leader, Barber reminded everyone of MLK's statement before he was murdered on April 6, 1967: "USA is the greatest purveyor of violence in the world today."

Contemporary violence simmers in a pressure cooker of veterans returning from wars in which USA tortures Muslims, creating more terrorists daily, and in which USA-made weapons kill USA soldiers. An institutionalized denial of the atrocities of Western history exists, yet contemporary unprecedented books on USA's "dirty wars" are today crazing ordinary people whose multiple stresses are ready to snap —and do—killing others/themselves in mass massacres.

CHAPTER 6

Historical context: **USA Spiral downward to most dangerous
purveyor of lethal power in human history**
Personal context: **Women, peacemakers, dogs**

·»)«·

The cold war between USA and Soviet Russia after world war II hid
a mutual aim to extend areas of world hegemony, notably control of
third world oil and minerals needed for cybernet instruments. Trump
policies have turned a searchlight on suppressed information of previous
Republican/Democrat administrations ... while a gathering constitutional
crisis in USA in Spring 2019 throws everything into unprecedented emergencies whose outcomes are unpredictable.[18]

The only nation to have used the nuclear bomb, USA today adds "small
nuclear bombs" to an already terrifying nuclear arsenal of "small" bombs
much more powerful than the bombs USA dropped on the Japanese people
in 1945. Nuclear reactors of USA, Russia, Israel, North Korea, and other of
the nine nuclear powers portend cataclysm (interesting "cat" word) when the
earth trembles, another tsunami floods, or provoked/panicked authoritarian
fingers can kill all life on earth.[19]

The dominant paradigm warns that we need to remember history lest
we repeat its tragedies. This historian adds a corollary: history is marked by
unexpected outcomes. Russian tampering with USA 2016 election throws
world glare on USA manipulating elections of other countries—at least 80
known cases since 1945. An egregious example from 1973: USA replaced a
democratic socialist government in Chile with a murderous repressive government.[20] Spring 2019 brings USA sanctions of Venezuela and escalation of
tensions with Iran.

Unexpected breaks in history:
* Women, in a break from historical silence, courageously speak out
  against rape/sexual harassment in USA; write dissertations on the
  culture of rape from Classical Greece to the present.

- Peoples of the world sign Paris agreement for World Climate Justice. Natives of USA put their bodies against the Dakota pipeline polluting rivers and all life. Black Lives Matter movement in USA is in implicit alignment with the world of dark others. Black women take leadership, organizing the vote in 2018 critical elections, in Republican strongholds in Virginia, Alabama, Texas, and other unlikely places … stopped from winning by dirty tricks of the Republican GOP (see story of Stacy Abrams in the many articles in *The Nation*).

- Young, old, independents, and left-outs respond to a call for equality~justice~peace found in the contemporary "Our Revolution" offered by a prophetic Semitic disheveled seventy-four-year-old senator, in third parties led by women, in unlikely coalitions, and in enormously popular demonstrations demanding a stop to the USA policy of perpetual wars everywhere, a stop to continuing inequality/violence embodied in sexual violence, a stop to gun violence in schools, a stop to nuclear/anti-environmental policies accelerating planetary catastrophe (another interesting "cat" word), and a stop to historic Republicans preventing African Americans from voting. In May 2019, we have an extraordinary galaxy of democratic presidential candidates, led by Joe Biden in a coalition against Trump.

- Sicily, an island signifier of colonized third world peoples, whose midwives have been helping women birth babies since before time began, today leads movements against USA surveillance/militarization/poisoning of all life on the planet.[21] Resistance banners "No al MUOS!" (military installations for USA surveillance) fly in southeastern triangle of Sicily—the paleolithic African/then Sicilian region where Lucia & Wally's historical ancestors may have met.

  Niscemi, a Sicilian interior town in the province of Caltanissetta, where Muslims historically fled Christian persecution … where I spent Easter Sunday 1988 … offers a chilling preview of "automated global wars of the 21st century" as a site of USA automated missiles gathering information in Africa, Europe, and Asia for war use.[22]

- Midwives in USA in Dakota resistance camps, joined by Native tribes from across the Americas, point to contemporary intersection of historic imperialism/rape of women/Mother Earth. "We can Decolonize,

Respect Women, and Respect Mother Earth" by opposing the $3.8 billion Dakota Access pipeline in USA.

In a Dakota camp of indigenous Americans—gathered together in cultural, economic, and political resistance—a baby was born in November 2016. The resistance camp is also a communal place for women's health services, midwifery clinic, and a place of healing for kids lost to drugs and alcohol … a place for justice and healing. Natives in USA … whose lands were stolen, whose women were forcibly sterilized in official USA genocidal policy, whose people were spiritually raped by forcible conversion to Christianity. Genocide is confirmed in the decreasing birth rate of original Natives, whose population—before the white European invasion—covered the continents of North, Central, and South America. Natives are now only 1.8% of USA population, yet are major signifyers of resistance/rebirth of a just and green earth for everybody.

Indigenous peoples across the world may be considered authentic signifyers of contemporary world resistance: they have preserved ancient wisdom, and tap into traumatic memories of others historically raped, persecuted, tortured, and killed, who today signify possibilities. Water protectors of Dakota pipeline say they are resisting "genocide of the river and the water that feeds us all, nourishes us all, just as it did in the womb." Midwives of the Dakota resistance respect Mother Earth, women, and "everyone coming out of colonization."[23]

• Signifying case of resistance in the Pacific region of the earth are Americans of Hawaii, state of USA, treated as a political-economic colony of the USA empire. In 2018-19, Hawaiians are nonviolently resisting their lands being used by USA as storehouses of hazardous biological/chemical explosives, as a dumping ground of depleted uranium and exploded and unexploded ordnance, and as an experimental ground for biological/chemical weapons.[24] This was dramatized in late 2018 by the eruptions of volcanoes in Hawaii.

CHAPTER 7
Linking the personal with other variables
Simultaneity of past~present~future

❧

M y late brother Louie and I had the same birthday, January 3, 1924 (me) and 1929 (him). Stella & Tom, the parents of Nancy (married to our son Marc) and Nancy & Marc's son Matthew (our grandson) were all born on March 20, the Spring Equinox. My late sister Joie and Wally's late brother Norman had the same birthday, March 29, a few years apart.

❧

One October day in 2017, Elsa, Wally & Norman's younger sister, passed away while the home of our kids Naury & Barbara in Napa wine country were within one mile of burning down their home.

One week before the Napa fire, Naury & Barbara attended the wedding of Naury's oldest friend Bence whose mother, a generation earlier, had torn off her yellow star of Judaism and walked with her baby Bence out of a Nazi concentration camp. On the day after attending Bence's wedding to his love, they went to check on their home in the Napa, California region.

Naury looked for items to save from the fire raging close by. His boyhood clarinet—Wally's gift of clarinets to his three sons—is a Semitic riff on African song migrating out of Africa[25] ... Naury & Barbara's original wedding ring. They left these signifiers in their home as a token of Naury's feeling their home would survive ... it did.

Barbara's response to the probability their home would burn down was to pack a bag and travel to New Jersey to represent the West Coast Birnbaums at the memorial for Elsa, Wally's sister. After the service, the family gathered with Elsa's kids, Andy & Maria and Ron & Jill, and their kids, to view Elsa's photos. Wally's high school graduation photo documented a distinctly African countenance. Grandmother Dora's photo as a young woman is that of an Asian beauty. Photos of grandfathers and uncles on both sides of the family—Safir and Birnbaum—verified historic invasions from Asia into their ancestral Ukraine, later a part of Poland, which is remembered in the surname Polansky of Elsa's late husband Irv.

On the Fall Equinox of 2016, shaken by the election of Trump, I reread what I had written. My initial intent to write a memoir connecting my personal and professional lives—while trying to understand my life as a woman, lover, mother, grandmother, great grandmother, visionary activist, and story teller—became my story at one with Wally's ... with our kin, kids, kindred ... with hurting, vulnerable peoples of my country and world ... and by Spring 2019, with everybody.

Like an owl I looked behind me to the past. I saw all sides and how, after Wally passed, I tried not to fall into paralyzing grief. Initially I regarded this manuscript as a synthesis of my life and books, and as a sequel to my 2012 book, *The Future Has an Ancient Heart: Legacy of Caring, Sharing, Healing, and Vision from the Primordial African Mediterranean to Occupy Everywhere*, whose 2013 revised edition I subtitled, *A love story, a vision, and a prophecy*.

Writing this manuscript has become a painful, revelatory, never-ending process of trying to articulate what I bodily know, yet finding very difficult to put into prose. My spiral theory of history leads me into discouraging awareness of this manuscript's redundancies ... I feel un-ease with writing a story simultaneously personal~professional~political~spiritual in a time when all of these seem to be imploding.

During the Purim/Carnival season before Summer Solstice 2019, in the garden of our Berkeley home, black birds soar and swoop in the hollow and visit the western deck of our home that overlooks the Pacific Ocean (peaceful sea). On our deck, long-lived black succulents bloom in golden pubic triangles above our back slope where two Paleolithic Norfolk pine trees I earlier planted flourish.

Spiraling back to October 2017, when Stefan found three perfect pomegranates birthed by our mother-child Demeter-Persephone bush at the entry to our Berkeley home. I explained the Sicilian meaning of this bush to neighbors Sandy & Rob. I kept one pomegranate, gave one to Rob whose mother was named Demeter, and gave one to Sandy who, like me, searches for underneath meanings.

In the Sicilian version of this story, Persephone is Proserpina (First Snake) who every spring sheds her old skin and emerges a new self.

A signifying tree of Sicily is the enduring African palm tree. One stands in front of our 1960s first Berkeley home across from the UCB campus. In November 2017, even though our former home has been replaced by a UCB residence building, the African palm tree remains. Every time I take this route down the hill, I look for it ... feeling reassured when I see the tree.

Olive trees, connoting peace, live in our front garden ... reminding me of migrants out of Africa, notably Etruscans out of Sardinia, who migrated to central Italy—Emilia-Romagna and Tuscany.

Our eldest kids Barbara & Naury planted an orchard of olive trees in their wine country home in Napa, California, and named their black Labrador-Poodle dog a diminutive affectionate for olive: Olly. Joining their once and future family of kids, grandkids, and dogs is a younger Labrador-Poodle whom they named Hamilton in honor of our immigrant founding father of USA from the Caribbean, whose mother was an African quadroon, father a Scot peddler, and was said to have a Jewish ancestor—thereby letting the hot air out of white supremacist rhetoric that founding fathers were white.

I am reminded of Emilio, a frisky doggy who lives with our middle kids Marc & Nancy in Albany, California. Emilio's name reminds me of the Emilia-Romagna region of central Italy where African Etruscans migrated from nearby Sardinia—an island like Sicily and Corsica that separated from Africa when heated waters rose during climate change in 10,000 BCE. Today, the Italian regions called Emilia-Romagna and Tuscany are characterized by black madonnas and red politics.

As an example of our once and future family, Marc & Nancy are parents of Matt & Nicolas and grandparents of Charlotte (Charlie), who is five years old on April 22, 2019 and who brings gifts of East and West. Nurtured by grandparents Marc & Nancy of Jewish Sicilian ancestry, Charlie's maternal great grandfather lived in the northern Italian region bordering Austria, which was a Pleistocene region a million years ago.

Charlie, my numinous luminous great granddaughter of African ~ Asian ~ Italian inheritance, calls doggy Emilio, "Mimi." Oddly/poignantly reminding me of my father weeping while listening to La Traviata, the operatic story of a fallen woman who is dying: "mi chiamano Mimi" (they call me Mimi). At their neighborhood park, Charlie yells at grandfather Poppa Marc to swing her "Higher!" Grandmother Nancy, whom Charlie calls Grega, keeps balls in her purse for Charlie, Emilio, other kids, and other dogs.

Our other kids, Jessica & Rusty, have dogs Odin (named for Norse god) and Fifal (rescued from a shelter) who help them care for their infant Juliet

Lucia Lorraine who arrived December 16, 2016. When Fifal passed away, Jessica, for whom there is no boundary between animals and humans, was bereft ... telling me that caring for Juliet—two years old on Winter Solstice 2018—keeps her going.

CHAPTER 8
Giving and Sharing

⋙⋘

I n the garden of our Mediterranean home—replanted after the Berkeley-Oakland fire of 1991—citrus trees from the African Mediterranean and from Asia are thriving. One tree in the side yard continues giving us lemons after a normal season of fruiting … reminding me that gifts Moors (Muslims) brought from Africa to Sicily are still thriving … as do gifts Saraceni (Muslims) brought from Asia to Sicily.

Christian Crusaders conquered Muslims more than a millennium ago, yet Muslim gifts of fruits, sweets, and ice cream continue to sweeten the lives of everyone across the world … while USA conducts endless bloody wars to kill Muslims, who they call "terrorists."

Muslim gifts remind me of when Wally and I, looking for our ancestors in Sicily, on our daily *passagiatta* (stroll) before dinner, would stop for ice cream. Wally would choose hazelnut; I would choose *stracciatella*—meaning soup of rags of old clothes, consisting of beaten eggs in a healing chicken soup.

My ophthalmologist tells me I have one hazel and one blue eye. My hazel eye evokes Wally's love for hazelnut ice cream, perhaps connected to close encounters of brown-eyed Africans with blue-eyed people migrating from colder places. My blue eye may refer to Scandinavian-French Normans and Scandinavian-German Lombards from northern Italy who came, on papal errand, to Christianize Pagan Sicily. The surname of my maternal grandmother, Lombardo, is a reminder of her ancestors in northern Italy—initially African, then German tribes (Vandals and Ostrogoths) who raided North Africa and Rome in early CE and left descendants.

Wally, with deep brown eyes, loved hazelnut ice cream. Lucia, with one hazel and one blue eye, loved *stracciatella* ice cream—which evoked for me deliciously dipping dark brown chocolate into vanilla ice cream.

In 1969, in Portofino on the Ligurian coast of northern Italy, where there was an intersection of migrants from Africa~Asia~Europe, a necklace of nuts beckoned. Wally said hazelnut, I said acorn. We stormed off in opposite directions … spiraling back to where we had started, where our nine-year-old son Stefan impatiently waited for us.

Disagreement … one of whose meanings may have been who loved the other more … over the names of nuts of the same species … may confirm May Elawar's hypothesis: humans, sharing the same primordial story of migrating out of Africa, with different riffs of the same melody, lived peacefully together until a historical age when ruling elites incited wars over names.[26]

Our Berkeley garden died in the great urban fire of 1991. Afterward, with help from Mother Nature, gardeners, and rising submerged energies, we replanted.

In Spring 2019, our garden is verdant with many signs of regeneration—cherry blossoms, fig tree greening, daisies, calla lily. Icons living together harmoniously: Sekhmet, lioness-headed goddess of Northern Africa … Buddha, wisdom sage of Asia … Francis of Assisi of Italy who considered the earth and all of its creatures holy … Green Man of Rome into whose mouth of truth ("*bocca della verita*") Italians place denunciations of injustice … Einstein beaming on all the garden's diverse signifyers. Black madonnas watch my writings evolve from ultimate dark mother to different riffs of the same song of peoples walking on different migration paths out of Africa while sharing the same seasons: birthing, blossoming, harvesting seeds, renewing life.

Names of our signifyers differ, yet, in my hypothesis, all of us share unconscious feelings … pre-conscious experience … predisposing everybody to live together peacefully, walking/dancing our own paths or intersecting with others, while all of us are on our way toward a green future.

Differing beliefs can inhabit the same body. When I put on my titles—Ph.D. and Professor Emerita—I think we are hellbent toward violent chaos/death of life on our one small planet. In between the dark and the daylight, not yet fully awake—human, lover, mother, daughter, sister, niece, aunt, grandmother, great grandmother, kindred spirit—I wonder, what if the light born of darkness is bringing gifts to everybody … renewing life on earth?

Meditating on the mystery of submerged human wisdom—caring, sharing, healing—rising/colliding today with the dominant Western historical paradigm, whose power over violence seems to be cresting in Spring 2019 …

western power elites promoting perpetual wars, killing, raping, stomping out beliefs of others, while violently ravaging people and the earth.

⚜

Looking at the black bird looking at me, I hoped that writing the story of Lucia & Wally might help get me through the night. Toward dawn, I typed my hypothesis:

> Lucia & Wally's journey, case in point of our one human race, homo sapiens sapiens,
>
> born in Africa, migrating out of Africa
>
> encountering one another peacefully ... in the historical epoch violently ...
>
> Yet everybody shares the same spirals of nature
>
> birthing ~ blossoming ~ harvesting ~ dying ~ seeding ~ renewing life
>
> over and over and over
>
> otherwise (thinking tautologically) we could not have survived to the present.

Previous research gathered in my books presented evidence of genetics, archeology, history, and everyday rituals. Wally and I, traveling the world together, learned on-site of our ancestral ways of being ... while this story keeps welling up from my unconscious and preconscious. From what remains of my ripped rationality, the human story seems to me grounded on self-evident, as well as empirical, truth confirmed in our bodies (*in utero*), on-site, and in our lives and the lives of kin, kids, grandkids, great grandkids, kindred spirits.

Our one human race, born in the African Mediterranean Sea, has survived to our perilous now ... predisposed in nurturing uterus, migrating out of the mother's body (continent) on journeys where everybody learned to care, share, and heal each other.

Dominant elites in historic epoch, exercising power over conquered people, killed, enslaved, and raped them into submission/obedience to elites' paradigm of violence ...

51

Yet our primordial/migration gifts have survived … renewing life with wisdom gift-wrapped in different names, different tribal particulars, different geographies, different cultures, different traumas, different liminalities, different seasons of life, different stories … illumined by messages from Mother Nature.

⁕⁕⁕⁕⁕⁕

On March 1, 2017, Mt. Etna of Sicily, the largest active volcano of Europe, erupted into a dark winter night with embers of red—traditional color connoting life—gifting black lava rock to Sicilians to rebuild their homes and replant their gardens/orchards in the rich volcanic soil.

We were gifted by great grandkids:

Charlie (Charlotte) Kimura Birnbaum, our great granddaughter born to Nickie & Nicolas on April 22, 2014, brings gifts of East as well as West, North and South.

Andrew Ellis, our great grandson born to Abigail & Jake in September 2016, after Wally's September 4, 2012 *jahrzeit* (year and place of passing), in a season of gratitude/harvesting. Andrew Ellis' initials "A" and "E" remind me of Semitic Abraham, prophet Elijah, and woman Abigail of Jewish~Christian~Islamic scriptures.

Izzy (Isabel) Rose, our great granddaughter born to Courtney & Matt on December 9, 2016, whose name honors a long line of women and men signifyers: Isis, Isabel, Rose, Isidore, Isadora. A merry child—jumping, laughing, loving story time—who coos with her many nurturers: parents, grandparents, aunts, uncles, cousins …

Juliet Lucia Lorraine, our great granddaughter born to Jessica Ann Lucia & Russell on Winter Solstice, December 21, 2016. She reminds us of nine years earlier when her parents were married. With a beguiling combination of many traditions in multi-flowered galaxies, her first name evokes an iconic love story of the West, her middle name means light, and her third name points to a sweet woman signifier Lorraine in the historically contested region in between France and Germany.

Adam Murphy, our great grandson born to Sabrina & Peter, whose first name Adam transmutes dominant othering Christian meta-story into inclusive story of Jews~Christians~Muslims while his middle name Murphy honors Celtic ancestors considered Pagan by Romans who conquered them but did not kill their legacy. Gifted by his German maternal grandfather Fred with passion for a job well-done and by his Semitic paternal great grandfather Wally with superb dancing and math genius, Adam gives his paintings to his maternal Latin great grandmother Lucia. One painting is a mandala connoting holism, and his latest is a painting of an inclusive galaxy forming a many-pointed star/garden in multi-colored bloom.

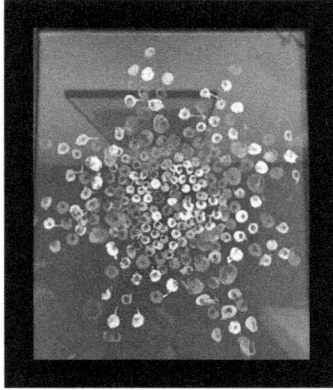

Josie (Josephine) Ann Lucia, our great granddaughter born to Sabrina & Peter, whose name remembers maternal great grandmother Giuseppina, great aunt Joie, and immediate great grandmothers Ann and Lucia. Her September 9 birth date embraces Poppa Wally's *jahrzeit* on September 4, Poppa Naury's birthday on September 6, and looks forward to the October birthdays of her Uncle Josh and Grandma Barbara. Inheriting a bouquet of gifts, Josie reminds me of me as a child, leaving a trail of books she is reading. In 2016, she was a member of a Hillary Club. In 2017, Josie wanted to be a healer and to explore who she is: dentist and paleontologist. In 2018, she wanted to be a Supreme Court justice. In 2019, like great grandmother Lucia at her age, Josie Ann Lucia studies Latin and, like grandfather Wally, is a card shark.

CHAPTER 9

How this great grandmother is learning how she knows she knows

⋙❈⋘

n the early 1970s, while tracking ancestors in Sicily, I listened to a radio station in Palermo, capitol of Sicily located on Mt. Pellegrino where geneticists, archeologists, and art historians have confirmed—in the similarity of a Sicilian painting found in an Addaura cave outside Palermo and a Native painting found in Australia—that migrations out of Africa reached all continents by 70,000 BCE. Listening to African drumming on the Palermitan radio station spiral into different riffs … resonated in my bodily knowing.

⋘⋘⋙⋙

Wally was religiously brought up as a Jew. Lucia was brought up in a Sicilian American family as nominally Catholic, and whose parents, not themselves churchy, sent their three kids to Catholic church instruction for First Communion and Confirmation.

Each day after attending grade school at Garfield Elementary, which was only a block up the street from our house on Wabash Avenue, I would run to the Holy Rosary Church for religious instruction … as did, a few years later, my three-years-younger sister Joie and five-years-younger brother Louie.

The Holy Rosary Church, which was founded in the 1890s by a monastic order of St. John the Baptist to bring doctrinal Catholicism to Sicilians and south Italians in USA, whose superstitions worried the church, became the signifying church of my family. It was the church where my maternal grandparents were married and buried, and where my mother and father were married. The church was located in the North End of Kansas City, Missouri. It was first the church of Sicilians and Southern Italians, then of other Latinos (Mexicans and Cubans), then after the 1960s, of refugee Vietnamese migrants to USA … all considered dark others by dominant WASP (White Anglo-Saxon Protestant) political/cultural elites.

The priests and nuns who instructed me and my siblings were predominantly Irish American and German American. In the 1830s, fleeing famine in the old country, Irish American Catholics were met with signs in Protestant USA: "No Irish need apply." During the second decade of the 20th century, Irish American Catholics were just becoming accepted as marginal members in the dominant paradigm of White Anglo-Saxon Protestants. German American Protestants, political refugees of 1848 revolutions in Europe, were accepted at first, yet during world war I they were tarred and feathered as enemy aliens in the world war against Germany. Contemporary USA president Donald Trump, of German ethnic origin (Stumpf), may carry this trauma in suppressed memory.[27] In the 1920s, most outsiders, in a continuing pattern since the beginning of Western civilization, joined dominant WASPs in considering themselves white Americans, regarding in fear/fright "new immigrants" as dark others from south/southeastern Europe ... lumping Jews, Slavs, and Sicilians with older Black/Brown/Asian scapegoats.

During world war II, Wally, while studying at City College of New York (CCNY) in 1940-43, would walk past cafeteria stalls identified with different sects of Marxism. His world view was older. Every day, wearing a tallit (prayer shawl), he studied Old Testament scriptures, today called Jewish Christian scriptures by today's Vatican II Catholic pope, Francis I, in remembrance of the history of Semites: Jews/Christians/Muslims.

In 1943, Wally learned that Nazis had murdered his Jewish maternal great grandmother who lived in Poland's Ukraine. He changed his major from statistics to physics, graduated at age eighteen from CCNY and, omitting his birth name Isaiah, went into the USA Army.

Lucia, escaping arguing parents and a noisy Sicilian American neighborhood, fled to school and constant reading. As a child, on Saturdays, she would walk to the downtown library and bring home as many books as she could carry; reading them in addition to school homework, and on subsequent Saturdays adding more cultural classics.

As an honor student in high school in 1940, she was awarded a work/study scholarship to the new (three years old) University of Kansas City where she studied with stellar professors ... until 1943, with the world aflame with war, she dropped out of college and went to work in a company that polished crystals for wartime military radios.

I thought about our life journey together after Wally and I met. We migrated to California where we brought up three sons while studying/graduating from UCB with doctorates: Wally in Physics, 1954 / Lucia in History, 1964

... simultaneously parents/scholars/Berkeley radicals in liberation struggle of oppressed/colonized of USA and world.

Serving as the backdrop to our deep story were the migrations to USA of our immediate kin. Wally's family: African origins, European pogroms inciting violence against Jews in Poland's Ukraine, migrations out of Africa and Ukraine. Lucia's family: African origins, Canaanite Jews from nearby West Asia, northern Italian government quashing 1890s Sicilian religious/socialist uprisings.

Wally's mother, Dora, named Deborah in Judeo Christian scriptures, whose surname Safir, the Semitic word for holy book, worked as a bar maid in the family tavern in Ukraine. She thereafter hated the smell of beer. In 1912, she migrated with her brothers to USA and went to work sewing in the New York textile industry.

Wally's father, Harry, whose first name Heschel in Yiddish means "deer," was named following an African tradition of naming people for animals and other natural phenomena. His surname, Birnbaum, refers to the European custom of identifying Jews with local markers on the migration paths out of Africa. Jews migrating out of Africa traveled to Levant of West Asia, stayed for a while in Sicily, then stayed for a while in Frankfurt, Germany—whose neighborhood named Birnbaum was marked by a pear tree (which we visited many years later)—before migrating to Ukraine in Poland, the immediate homeland of Harry and Dora before migrating to USA. Jewish folk culture of Ukraine has been brilliantly evoked in paintings of Marc Chagall, and in the stories of Sholem Maleichem—represented in the musical play, *Fiddler on the Roof*.

⚘

Coincidences have marked our journeys of exploring our ancestries. In the first years of the 1960s, Lucia, at the time a doctoral student in History, was given a fellowship in Social Science at UCB: teaching a class on the Frankfurt School of scholars, "Marx, Weber, Freud." In 2016, her youngest son, Stefan, while appraising the Berkeley home of a UCB professor researching his own family story, was shown a photo of the Frankfurt neighborhood named Birnbaum.

Studying at the University of Kansas City in 1940-43, several of Lucia's professors were Jewish scholars who escaped Nazi Germany and later became Frankfurt school scholars ... deepening Lucia's insights of Marx on dynamic economic trends of history, Freud's analyses of power of sexuality in the unconscious, and Weber's study of cultural conditioning of religions, whose Protestant Ethic and Spirit of Capitalism stimulated me to think about the cultural conditioning of all religions.

◆◆◆◆◆◆

Wally's immediate family story: his parents migrated from Trembovla in Ukraine to USA where Harry & Dora met one day on the Lower East Side of New York City. Harry was sick, and Dora brought him a healing chicken soup. Immediately drawn to each other, they married, brought up their kids as religious Jews: keeping kosher food rituals, observing high holy days (Rosh Hoshonah, Yom Kippur, Passover), identifying with Ashkenazi Jews of northern Europe and Conservative Judaism. While sharing ultimate beliefs with Orthodox Judaism, Harry & Dora did not share the Orthodox Jewish subordination of women.

In the Ukraine, with horse and buggy, Harry sold ribbons, in keeping with the trading tradition of Jewish Canaanites. In between pogroms, Jewish traders exchanged gifts with Christian peasants during the Winter Solstice. In USA, Harry left home at dawn to work with his brothers in a window-washing business with an office that was located in New York's Harlem, the neighborhood of African Americans.

In 1929, Harry & Dora returned to the Ukraine with their kids— Norman (nine) and Wally (five)—bringing back Dora's mother to live with them in their Bronx apartment in New York City. Baba, Wally's maternal grandmother, whose mother was later killed by Nazis, was named Miriam Rebecca, a signifying woman in Jewish/Christian/Islamic scriptures. Genetically gifting her grand and great grandkids with her mathematical talent (verging on genius), Baba conveyed primordial human values while sitting on a stool in the kitchen.

Living in California during our summers in graduate school, Wally and I would take our kids to visit both sets of grandparents. Their great grandmother Baba, in New York, while watching toddler Naury, who loved (still does) to dance, would clap her hands, chanting in Yiddish "dance, dance, live a long life." All of Baba's grandkids—Wally, his siblings Norman and Elsa, and their kids and grandkids—danced (still dance) superbly in primordial African style close to the rhythms of the earth ... characteristic folk dancing of subaltern peoples, historically, the world over ... how the young of the world dance today.

In 1959, Wally and I left our youngsters, Naury (twelve) and Marc (nine), in New York with their paternal grandparents, traveling, for the first time together, to Europe. For the next half century, we traveled the world exploring our ancestral sites.

❧

My name Lucia remembers the awe of our primordial animal ancestors watching the dark become light. Light became associated with numinous experience and rituals associated with light in major world religions. Later, light was associated with secular mental and moral enlightenment.

In the iconology of doctrinal Catholicism, Santa Lucia is a submissive woman offering her eyes (vision) obediently on a communion plate of the Church.

For subjugated people, folk stories about Lucia in the historic epoch convey sustenance~hope in hard times. Sicilians, my signifier for subaltern or subordinated peoples, kept folklore rituals—nonviolently replacing the official Catholic doctrine of the three Kings of Orient bringing gifts to the Jesus child in Bethlehem as confirmation of the divinity of Jesus with Epiphany, which is celebrated at the end of Winter Solstice season on January 6.

In folk translation, La Befana—Epiphany, personalized as La Vecchia—is an Old Woman who brings gifts not to one child but to all kids … replacing the church doctrine of an omnipotent father and his only son with a subaltern prophetic hope in an egalitarian female form conveyed in a folk story. This popular holiday is followed by Purim in Judaism and *Carnevale* in Christian countries.

❧

Spiraling fast forward to the Puritan Protestants, historical dissenters in England, who became founders of USA and whose first presidents were southern slave holders or northerners benefiting from the African slave trade. During USA civil war, slaves were freed, but freed people were disenfranchised a few years later by the Ku Klux Klan with burning crosses, by enforcing social codes of raping and killing, and by a political deal made in 1876 that gave the presidency to Republicans, who pulled federal troops protecting civil rights of freedmen out of the South.

In USA at the turn of the 20th century, the category of dark others was enlarged by USA expansion into the Pacific and Caribbean. Hawaii was annexed, and Caribbean islands were taken by USA imperial war of 1898. "New immigrants"—differentiated from older immigrants from northern Europe—fell into Progressive racialist enthusiasm for "social control"; notably the progressive reform of eugenics, which targeted "new immigrants" from south and southeastern Europe: Sicilians, Slavs, and Jews, including Lucia & Wally's families.

Subaltern classes often took WASP last names, maintaining their deep beliefs in the first names they gave their kids. For my paternal ancestors of Ragusa Ibla in Sicily, the name Jesus became Salvatore, meaning savior. In the Sicilian dialect, the diminutive affectionate form of Salvatore became "Turiddu." In my paternal Chiavola family, my father Turiddu, was called *u figghiu beddu* (favored beautiful son of his mother).

Sicily is considered by scholars of Antonio Gramsci (the major theorist for understanding peoples of the south of the world) to be a subaltern culture ... and by Eric Hobsbawm to be a heretical subaltern culture whose deep beliefs dominant elites have tried to suppress. Subaltern classes, nonviolently resisting, kept their beliefs in names, dialects, daily and celebratory rituals, and in their behavior. My concept of dark others refers to heretical dark resisters of violent raping/killing dominant cultures ... keeping in mind that it only takes (in favorable conditions) three generations for dark people to fade to human flesh color called white.

On my paternal side: in 1912, my father Turiddu, age sixteen, migrated from Ragusa Ibla, Sicily with his mother Lucia, his brothers Joe and Jim, and his sister Georgia, to Kansas City, Missouri, where they were met by his eldest brother George who had migrated to USA earlier with their elder sister Sarafina in 1907. My uncle George as a youth studied for the Catholic priesthood, and in the 1890s, joined local uprisings of a Sicilian form of Christian socialists—manifested in mutual aid, helping one another, and differentiated from the socialism governed by the elites of the nation state.

Putting his defeated socialist hopes to one side, George was an ethnic success story in USA. He owned a grocery, lived with his family above the store, and with his wife Concettina parented five daughters. He became president of the Kansas City retail grocers' association, and transmuted his socialist hopes into founding the ethnic association *Societa' Ragusana Americana* and the Kansas City Lyric Opera.

Uncle George read Dante, and studied archeology and history. After 1959, when Wally and I first traveled together to Europe, our uncle-niece bond became close. Not until 2016 did I learn the spiritual~historical context of this bond. My signifying ancestor, Lucia of Syracuse, and my uncle's signifying ancestor, San Giorgio, of nearby Ragusa Ibla, were both early Jewish Christians killed as Pagan heretics by imperial Romans during the first years of CE.

Today Lucia and George are popular saints. Santa Lucia is celebrated at the time of the Winter Solstice on December 12 (December 21 in the Gregorian calendar). She is honored in the southwest part of Sicily in the region around Syracuse, her ancestral city. Santo Giorgio is celebrated at nearby Ragusa Ibla, my ancestral paternal place, which today has a World Heritage site of the celebrated baroque San Giorgio church, where everybody in my Chiavola family was baptized before migrating to USA in 1912.

My Aunt Sarafina's name evokes Sara, recalling, as earlier discussed, the name Sicilians called the conquered Muslims in Sicily—Saraceni, children of the Semitic matriarch Sara(h)—which may be regarded as unarticulated resistance underneath the dominant paradigm of privileged whites of the West. After the 1693 earthquake in Sicily, this resistance erupted into baroque art and architecture. Classical Greek buildings were rebuilt with symbols of the island's suppressed peoples: Jews, Jewish Christians, and Muslims.

After migrating to USA with her elder brother, George, my Aunt Sarafina married John Panettiere, whose first name honors John the Baptist, the prophetic Jewish contemporary who baptized Jesus. Uncle John's French surname, Panettiere, means bread maker. In USA, he crushed rock for cement for the highways of Kansas City. John and Sarafina brought up three children—Andrew, Lucy, Concetta—saved money, and sent their son to medical school. A vivid memory of my childhood is the wonderful sesame brittle (Muslim sweet) that Aunt Sarafina baked for us when we visited.

The first family tragedy of the Chiavola family happened in early world war II. We gathered in shock to mourn the death of Captain Andrew Panettiere, doctor in USA Army, killed in the South Pacific. Thereafter, Aunt Sarafina and her daughters Lucy and Concetta wore black.

Nanna Lucia, my paternal grandmother, a major signifying woman in the Chiavola family, and for whom I am named, transmitted both dominant and suppressed meanings of our shared name. Nanna, the Italian word for grandmother in the Sicilian pronunciation, conveyed a memory of a pre-Judaic signifying Semitic woman: Inanna of Sumer. The name Lucia remembered the healing visionary who lived in Syracuse, the capitol of the Greek colony of Sicily, and who was killed by Romans as a Pagan healer.

Lucia, first called Pagan heretic of Syracuse, then called Christian martyr … along with Barbara and Maria (Mary), the Jewish mother of Jesus, were left out of the Christian doctrinal trinity (father, son, holy ghost). After the Christian church aligned with the Roman empire in the 4th century CE, Lucia, Barbara, and Mary were beatified Christian saints. Popular artists, story tellers, and people enacting everyday rituals remember Lucia … not as Santa Lucia giving up her eyes for the church … but as the woman whom Caravaggio painted—not ascending into heaven but buried in the earth by workmen.

In USA, my Nanna Lucia lived with my Aunt Georgia, her husband with the French name Cheve', their child Anna, and a parrot that perched on Nanna's shoulder. On the Sundays of my childhood, my father would ritually take his kids to visit his mother. Since I was named for her, she intrigued me.

Nanna Lucia, a seemingly strong matriarch, I later realized, was a subordinated woman suppressing a great deal of rage. Her husband Luigi was born and lived closely/familiarly with the lords and ladies in the Norman castle of Ragusa Ibla, as a falconer and game warden. After the 1970s, when Wally and I started our regular visits to Sicily, we visited the Chiavola home in a cave dug into the Iblean mountains where Nanna Lucia brought up their kids, in effect, a single mother. In the *miseria* after the socialist uprisings were defeated, she breast-fed infants of the ladies of the castle whom her husband knew in close encounters.

In Sicily, the name of Ragusa Ibla honors signifying woman Cybele of West Asia with its diminutive affectionate suffix: -ibla. First the town was called Ragusa Nera (black), then Ragusa Hera (subordinated wife of Roman god Jupiter). In the Iblean mountains of my paternal ancestral town, Ragusa Ibla was finally named for West Asian Cybele whose memory is kept in ritual to this day: every spring, white doves are released from Iblean mountains to fly home to ancestral Africa.

Later, researching the deep story of women's resistance to domination by males, I recalled the parrot on Nanna Lucia's shoulder who, in Sicilian dialect, proclaimed very bawdy messages (unprintable). Later, after migration to USA, Nanna had choice epithets in Sicilian dialect (also unprintable) for the country to which she and her kids, fleeing poverty and sexual humiliation, migrated in 1912.

Nanna Lucia turned her rage on her daughters-in-law. My mother, Kate, returned the animosity. My father brought his paychecks to his mother every Sunday; reserving money to buy an annual new suit, a new car, or pocket money for himself … and $5.00 a week for his wife to buy food for the household.

Concettina, Uncle George's bride, was also harassed by Nanna Lucia. Concettina's name simultaneously transmitted the religious Catholic doctrine—the immaculate conception of Jesus—and the subaltern political hope for socialism. The diminutive affectionate form of her name meant "beloved concept."

Following Sicilian tradition, George and his brothers Joe, Turiddu, and Jim, and his elder sister Sarafina, all named their first daughters Lucia, consciously honoring their mother Lucia, while unconsciously, perhaps, remembering the primordial light emerging from darkness.

The church icon of Santa Lucia, submissive and obedient, offering her eyes on a Catholic communion plate, sacrificing her vision to the church, inculcated a religious model for Sicilian women: blind obedience to patriarchal family, church, state, and society.

For subaltern cultures, Lucia is a signifying woman celebrated to this day at the time of the Winter Solstice—remembering unconscious primordial origins in the sea which initially covered the planet. On Santa Lucia day, Sicilians eat cuccia (couscous), African wheat blackened with octopus ink, celebrating the emergence of Africa from the sea and the dark of the longest night bringing the dawn of a new day. They also eat dark African wheat with twice-cooked ricotta cheese made with goat milk and mixed with honey.

The beliefs of first- and second-generation Sicilian immigrants to USA are suggested in the names that my Uncle George & Aunt Concettina gave their daughters. First daughter, Lucia. Second daughter, Tina, a diminutive affectionate for Santina, the beloved mother of Jesus left out of the Trinity who became Saint Mary. Third daughter, Edea, for the ideal of mutual aid socialism. Fourth daughter, Wanda, in an expression of the love George and his brothers held for Italian opera, as well as for a celebrated Polish opera singer. Fifth daughter, Louisa, honored our paternal grandfather with the American female version of Nannu Luigi's name. The suffix -isa, a diminutive affectionate of popular speech, melds names of African mother Isis and Semitic prophet of peace Isaiah.

Uncle Jim, marrying out of his Sicilian ethnic group, wed Lillian, an Irish Catholic whose name remembered the Gauls (Celts) who were vanquished by Caesar, and pre-Judaic woman Lilith who would not lie beneath her mate and instead fled.[28] Jim & Lillian named their first daughter Lucia, Americanized to Lucy, and their second daughter Mary, for the mother of Jesus. Both Lucy and Mary were nurturing women. Mary, a casualty, committed suicide when her husband left her for another woman. Lucy, a family survivor, led an unconventional life, choosing whom she loved and nurturing everyone who crossed her path.[29]

Uncle Joe, my father's next older brother, migrated from Kansas City to Chicago and married, but after naming his first daughter Lucia, he left the marriage. Thereafter, he was an anticlerical wanderer whom the respectable side of the Chiavola family considered a black sheep, and whose story his granddaughter Kathy Chiavola is rescuing today (see below). Kathy is for me and my sister Joie, a kindred spirit. Her Irish American mother suggests the family's Celtic connection … vanquished by Caesar, yet whose legacy in folklore (Wicca) persists to the present.

This Celt ancestry is deepened by our family's connection with French Cathars (heretical prophetic women of 13th century France) in names like Catarina, Kate, Katie, and Kathy … names that keep popping up in family stories of our kin, kindred spirits … and most recently in Kate (whose immediate heritage is eastern European), the bride of our grandson Matthew (whose immediate heritage is Japanese American).

Nurturance, in Celtic, Cathar, and Sicilian cultures, is visible in my kindred spirit cousin Kathy Chiavola, granddaughter of my father's older brother, my Uncle Joe. A generation younger than me, Kathy was trained in the Conservatory of Music of my alma mater University of Kansas City to sing classical Italian opera. Today, suggesting the curious spiraling of cultural change, Kathy Chiavola is an internationally celebrated Bluegrass singer.

Kathy, in my view, is a catalytic (another interesting "cat" word) combination of Celtic ancestors killed by Caesar, and Cathar women of France who so challenged the Pope that he declared a domestic crusade against them.[30] Celtic wisdom has lived to this day in the Pagan feminism called Wicca, the lore of wise women.[31] Kathy Chiavola's deep story transmits love for the Italian grand opera that gloriously expresses the dramas of human life. Today, Kathy lives in Nashville, Tennessee, in the heart of Bluegrass culture.

In July 2016, Kathy telephoned from Nashville to tell me she was leaving in a few days to go to our mutual ancestral town Ragusa Ibla on the Sicilian southeastern coastal triangle fronting Africa and Asia. She had been invited to sing Bluegrass in an international music festival on Kathy's and my primordial beach Marina di Ragusa.

Memories of Marina di Ragusa floated to my consciousness. My research when we visited Marina di Ragusa hypothetically confirmed it as a place of Wally's and my ancestors. In the 1970s, I asked my great uncle Carmelo—living in upper town Ragusa, married to my Aunt Concettina's sister Carmela—to show us the small ancient Pagan shrine on the beach.

Serendipity hit me. My cousin Kathy was going to be singing Bluegrass music on the Marina di Ragusa where a ruin of an early Jewish/early Christian sanctuary remains today on the beach of our mutual ancestral town Ragusa Ibla.

Associations raced to my consciousness. I thought about Kathy's name, her Celtic mother's name, my mother's birth name Catarina, and the earliest Jewish Christian sanctuary on Mt. St. Catherine still standing today in the Sinai Peninsula ... where 13th century CE Cathar women of France were living uncodified Jewish Christian beliefs opposed to killing, were making their own decisions about whom to take to bed, and were challenging patriarchal Christian religious and social codes that imposed political/sexual subservience on women.

Kathy also evokes the controversial roots of Bluegrass music. For people who begin USA history with the dominant story, Bluegrass music came out of the pre-revolutionary culture of white people living in the Appalachian Mountains. Yet these people share African origins with Jews, Christians, and Muslims living in a poor subordinated culture they share with oppressed black people. Dominant white culture calls them "poor white trash."[32]

For organic scholars, including me, Bluegrass music originated in everybody's music in primordial Africa. A contemporary Nashville colleague told me: Kathy is an internationally acclaimed Bluegrass singer who is also the "heart of Bluegrass" ... she is the first one anybody in the Bluegrass community of Nashville calls when they need help.

Kathy's story reminds me of other self-determining women who, today, call themselves "pagan feminists."[33]

In the continuing cultural revolution since the 1960s, the word "pagan" is a positive term for suppressed beliefs that everybody needs to bring to consciousness for the whole deep story of humans ... acknowledging dominant history and finding promising possibilities emerging from subordinated women and men.[34]

The suppressed stories associated with my name Lucia are cases in point. All my Chiavola uncles and my Aunt Serafina named their first daughters Lucia, or the Americanized Lucy. The eldest of my Uncle George and Aunt Concettina, Lucy was a faithful daughter who kept the family grocery store when the rest of the family traveled to Italy. She married Nino, whose name is a diminutive affectionate for Saint Anthony, an early Jewish Christian who was killed by imperial Romans about the same time as the killing of our son's namesake Stefan Anthony, a Jewish dissenter who is called the "first Christian Martyr."

A few years ago, in Kansas City when this eldest Lucy was passing, she couldn't speak, but looked piercingly at me.

Lucy & Nino's one child, Suzanne, is today a Vatican II Catholic nun who, does good works in the world. Sister Suzanne read my book, The Future Has an

Ancient Heart, and sent me a note saying she also shares my values of equality, justice, compassion, and transformation. Her nuns' order, the Community of Saint Joseph, was founded in 1636, at the height of the Inquisition. It is in Le Puy in France, and is today a departure point for European pilgrimages to the sanctuaries of black madonnas.

Saint Joseph, venerated as a human (not heavenly) father of Jesus, is depicted on popular prayer cards in USA Sicilian American culture as a nurturant father holding a child. He is celebrated by Sicilian Americans in a popular ritual of St. Joseph tables on March 19, preceding the Spring Equinox, when tables of food cooked by women of the community honor the human holy family—Joseph, Mary, Jesus—who equally bless the food that is, after the ritual, given to the poor.

Thinking about this today, I find it revealing that Joseph—a popular prophet shared by Jews~Christians~Muslims—blesses the food on St. Joseph tables equally with mother Mary and their child Jesus, thereby democratizing the holy trinity.

This brings to mind the religious icons my mother placed on the hearth in the parlor of my childhood home in Kansas City: two standing adult figures, of equal height—Mary and Jesus—mother and child. No patriarchal trinity for my inwardly (and outwardly) raging mother who felt betrayed by a philandering husband.

For older Italian Americans, the celebration of Columbus Day on October 12 used to be their signifying cultural holiday. A cultural change since the 1960s is suggested in the May 2017 edition of The Italian Voice, which discusses the choice of a Grand Marshal for a Columbus Day parade on October 12, 2017. (The Italian Voice is an Italian American newspaper published in New Jersey where many Italian Americans today live.) Rapid cultural change was evident in the 2017 article. There was not one reference to the contemporary controversy over the change of the iconic day for Italian Americans from Columbus Day to Native Americans Day … just a discussion of the choice of a woman to be Grand Marshal for the upcoming October holiday that formerly celebrated Columbus' "discovery" of America. The woman chosen to be Grand Marshal of the October 12, 2017 parade of Italian Americans, was being honored, not as the traditional women suppressed under patriarchy, but as a woman respected for her education and civic activities.

Columbus Day was celebrated in 2017, 2018, and 2019 in a variety of ways by Italian Americans … most of the time avoiding honoring the explorer who is today associated with white supremacy in USA. In the dominant male violent culture in USA stoked by Trump, many Italian Americans, coming from several sources of resentment, voted for Trump in 2016 while some Italian males attempt to rescue the image of Columbus … calling him a great mariner—whom a rising culture of dark others calls a white supremacist.

Spirals bent by popular cultural change are suggested in a March 19, 2017 invitation to a St. Joseph table in my city that in the 1960s called itself "Peoples Republic of Berkeley." Kindred spirit Barbara W, whose name evokes peoples whom Romans called barbarians of Africa, and West Asia whom religious agents of the Holy Roman Empire sought to Christianize, invited me to her St. Joseph table celebration.

This Sicilian American Barbara, who shares my passion for finding our ancestral roots, creates sought-after necklaces of ancient beads. She tracked her ancestors via her maiden name to Anatolians (West Asia) who migrated to Lipari, an island off the coast of north Sicily. Anatolia is named for the goddess of the harvest, Ana, whose name harks back to the African tribe, Anu.

For her St. Joseph table, Barbara made a typical Sicilian American dinner of pasta, greens, and cannoli for a small group of expatriates returning home after living, since the 1970s, on a Greek island now over-run by world tourists taught by the dominant paradigm that Greece is the origin of Western Civilization.

I hoped to find fava beans to bring to this St. Joseph table, but could not find them. In Sicilian folklore, for every fava bean you eat, one sin is absolved. No clerical intermediaries here for the remission of sins; just eat healthy food, like fava beans.

Returning to the women named Lucia in my immediate paternal family in Kansas City, the elder daughter Lucy of my Aunt Sarafina & Uncle John, sister of Andrew, wore black after her brother was killed during world war II. Never married, this Lucia poured her considerable energies into church and family responsibilities; and she went swimming every day.[35]

My kindred spirit cousin Lucy, the elder daughter of my Sicilian Uncle Jim & my Irish Catholic Aunt Lillian (see discussion above), was gifted with both a maternal and fraternal inheritance of cultural rebelliousness. Her father, the youngest son in the Chiavola family, wore his cap backward as a signal of defiance of the dominant culture of USA. Like his brother, my father, Uncle Jim flouted the conventional marital prohibition of adultery … bringing women to bed in the family home—with consequences for his daughters …

My cousin Lucy, in her day, was a stunning intercultural blonde beauty. She seems to me a volatile combination of Celt~Cathar~Sicilian who rebelled against constrictive Catholic schooling in USA. After she was fifteen, this

Lucy led an unconventional life (for dominant Catholicism) skipping over prohibitions of patriarchal social codes while she nurtured everybody in and out of the family.

⁂

I was belatedly baptized/Christened Lucia Teresa on January 1, 1925. Unpacking the connotations of my names, I have tracked a journey from my primordial and historical ancestors to my immediate kin to my contemporary self-identification as nurturing ~ visionary ~ healing writer ~ great grandmother (bisnonna, meaning twice-baked grandmother).

This manuscript may be considered my journey to finding the meaning of this Lucia: nurturant visionary healer depicted on everyday holy cards as woman holding a sheaf of African wheat (also a writing instrument), linking nurturing with food and nurturing by writing truthful stories. The historical Lucia is the patron saint of Syracuse in today's Sicily as well as inclusive signifier for diverse peoples across the world who resonate to Pavarotti singing "Santa Lucia."

Normans, having completed their papal mission to Christianize Sicilians, returned home to Scandinavia—which poses a question. Like other evangelizing invasions … who converted whom? After conquering Sicily in 1060 CE and Britain in 1066, Normans took the story of Lucia with them back to Scandinavia.

Since the 1960s, at the time of Winter Solstice, I have given my multicultural kids and grandkids figurines of Santa Lucia to put on their Christmas trees— originally a Pagan custom when evergreen pubic-shaped pine trees are brought into homes and public houses, where they are decorated and celebrated.

In Syracuse, Sicily, the statue of Lucia is taken out of her niche in the patriarchal Catholic cathedral, paraded through the streets, taken into the sea, and danced back to the streets. This popular celebration of Lucia is similar to the ritual of black madonnas whose icons are also taken into the sea, then celebrated with dancing in the streets.

Recently, I found a Swedish children's book, called *Lucia: Saint of Light*,[36] to give to my grand and great grandkids, some of whom carry my name: Josie Ann Lucia, Jessica Ann Lucia, Juliet Lucia Lorraine, Emma Lia, dog Lucy. Awakening in the long dark night before first light, Lucia and her sisters put on long white gowns trimmed with lace, red sashes, and wreathes of tinsel. "I'm the Lucia bride, so I tie my gown with a wide red ribbon. On my head goes a crown made of lingonberry leaves holding seven candles. When I put it on, I feel like St. Lucia herself, come to bring light and joy to the dark winter land." Nurturing her parents, Lucia puts coffee on a tray with ginger cookies and cross-shaped sweet buns called Lussekatter (Lucia cats).

My mother's birth name, Catarina, was thought to honor her paternal Palermitan grandmother Catarina. My sister Joie's middle name Leona (big cat or lion), lived on in mutual adoration circles of Joie and her cats in a non-conscious (as far as I know) memory of African lioness goddess, Sekhmet. When we were little, I called Joie "kitty face." A Cathar tradition of healing with mud poultices may have persisted in Joie's love as a toddler for making mud pies.

Spiraling values of caring and sharing, intermingled with the ritual of the Lucia bride, is evident in the Swedish story of Santa Lucia day. Kids bring coffee and "Lucy cat" sweet buns—first to their parents still in bed, then to sick and lonely Jewish neighbors and the elderly. In the story, Mrs. Sundstrom said, "When I vass a young girl in Sveden, I vass da Lucia bride."

Asking their mother, who in her youth in Sweden before coming to USA was a Lucia bride, to tell them about her. "Saint Lucia isn't actually a Swedish saint. She was born in Sicily, an island off the coast of Italy" when it was against the law to be a Christian, so they had to hide their faith or risk "being arrested, tortured, and put to death."

Across the world, a common feature of Lucia stories is that Lucia's mother was very ill. Lucia convinced her mother to go with her on a healing pilgrimage to an indigenous Sicilian woman healer, Agata of Catania, who lived on the eastern coast of the island, facing Asia. Roman authorities learn of this and have Lucia arrested as a Pagan. When she is to be carried away to be tortured, Lucia could not be moved, even when pulled by several yoke of oxen. Ordered to be burned, the fire did not singe her. Lucia was finally killed by a Roman soldier ordered to thrust his sword down her throat.

The Swedish story about Lucia, like most world stories about her, recount a time of terrible cold and famine along with a message of nurturing/hoping. "On the darkest day of the most terrible winter of all, they saw a boat sailing toward them" on whose prow was a beautiful maiden dressed all in white and glowing. The boat came to shore without wind, helmsman, nor oarsmen. When the boat landed, Lucia gave the starving people huge sacks of wheat so they could survive until springtime.

"What about the Lucia cats?" She responded: Lucia cat cookies symbolize the wheat Lucia brought to the hungry, to the poor, and to prisoners.

The Swedish children's story of Lucia suggests to this Sicilian American story teller that "Lucy cat" sweet buns—like cuccia (couscous) blackened with octopus ink eaten on Lucia day in Sicily—are food signifyers transmitting the truthful story of everybody's origins in the sea ... then in stories of Santa Lucia, the woman who comes from the sea bringing wheat to famished people so they can survive until spring.

All of this is relevant to my methodology as a truthful story teller, wherein I respect everybody's signifying stories, including those of the dominant culture—church, state, society, academia—while valorizing folklore of popular culture ... and also respecting the findings of scientific investigators. Knowing that beliefs of the dominant culture often sustain beliefs of self-serving hegemonic elites, this means to me that everyone needs to look inward for the courage to express what you believe to be true ... all the while knowing that all human beliefs are partial carriers of the truth ... people may differ in their beliefs as to what is true.

All this means that I need to work for equal playing fields in education, society, and politics; respecting freedom to express true beliefs ... having faith in yourself while being self-critical ... and checked and balanced by institutions of a free society. In my case, this is nonviolently expressed by giving reparations in some form to those who have been historically subordinated—a first step in creating a just and peaceful green world.

In my hypothesis of the ubiquity of African ancestors—almost everybody has dark relatives, or dark others persecuted for their beliefs—I pose the problem: to whom are reparations owed? A solution the Italian feminists settled on in the 20th century is: universal free education/universal free medical care—equalizing possibilities for everybody.

Other signifying political issues for me are the abolition of nuclear bombs and an end to all wars. If we don't abolish nuclear bombs—right now—all life may be destroyed. If we know the true stories of people who were killed in wars that benefited dominant elites, you may find they are your sisters and brothers whose music carries the same bass melody of primordial origins, with different riffs in our intersecting journeys with others who are migrating on different paths to a just and equal green world.

CHAPTER 10

Lucia and feminist precursors ... other problematic categories

꘏꘏꘏

Searching for my feminist precursors has been a spiral journey because the major premises of dominant feminist spirituality have been upturned by the males in my family who do not fit the dominant feminist beliefs into the universality of oppressive males. Wally, the love of my life, was/is my prophetic signifier of a new paradigm of egalitarian/nurturing males. The theme of our life together may be described as dancing together with other dark others to riffs of the new paradigm ... of everybody caring, sharing, healing.

My parents' third child, my brother Louie, born on my fifth birthday on January 3, 1929, seems to me a prophetic male whose greeting "Make a good day!" implies the arc of justice is not bent by waiting for extra-terrestrial help, but by humans on earth bending spirals toward justice.

Louie is named for Nannu Luigi who, before migrating to USA, lived in the Norman-Angevin castle in Ragusa Ibla, Sicily. In our immediate family we used the French pronunciation of his name, "Lou-EE"; identifying him with French saints and kings, while locating him in the vernacular, or everyday culture, of Sicilian Americans in Kansas City, Missouri.

In the historic patriarchal culture of the West (Western Europe and USA), with Sicily as case in point, upper class males bought and sold their daughters in dynastic marriages while looking to women of the lower classes for their pleasure.[37] The lord of the castle in Sicily considered peasant women sexually available, as did slave masters in USA.[38]

Normans—in England and in Sicily—after invading on errand of the Roman Pope to Christianize Pagans, enacted into law, Droit du Seigneur, the right of the lord of the castle to sleep with the prospective bride of a tenant on their nuptial night ... this was an intense sexual assault on both bride and groom.

For outsider novelists and sociologists, Sicilian women were historically kept housebound in strict chastity/obedience to male hierarchies of religion, culture, society, and family. Yet, as I uncovered in my book, *Liberazione della donna*, subservience was not the case for the women who worked in the fields, notably northern women rice workers singing Bella Ciao ... women in cities working as artisans ... fishwives hawking the seafood their men caught ... midwives anywhere helping to birth new life ...

One of these urban women was my paternal great grandmother Catarina of Palermo, Sicily, mother of my grandfather Nannu Joe, who organized neighborhood women to make pasta, which she then sold. A feminist capitalist who rose in the world, she would, my mother recalled, extend her hand, in the manner of upper-class ladies, to be kissed.

My on-site research in Sicily revealed an alternative to my previous findings that peasant women seemed to be enclosed mothers/wives whose outside excursions were to the town well and to church. What I discovered while being there, is they were self-determining women who believed, as did women who later called themselves feminists, *"L'utero e mio e lo gestico io"* ("It is my uterus and I govern it"). Historically, they tightly governed their families. In the 20th century, they formed a formidable Italian feminist movement that secured a long list of improvements in women's lives.[39] Today in Italy, women are elected to posts in their towns and provinces, and work prominently in national governing institutions ... recovering ancient values of caring and sharing ... transmuting violence into enhancing life initiatives.

Historically, fetching water at the town well every day, Sicilian women exchanged significant information, and planned nurturing communal activities ... for a woman expecting a child ... for a woman whose husband was brought home with malaria ... in whose courtyard to shell peas together ... whom to choose to enact Joseph, Maria, and Jesus for the neighborhood St. Joseph tables in celebration of the human holy family.

Thinking about the St. Joseph tables of my Sicilian American childhood, I was never considered to enact Mary; I was Kate's odd bookish daughter. Neither was my sister Joie, who changed her birth name Josephine to the French word for joy, *"joie,"* and who played with the boys. Our younger brother Louie, who lived the nonviolent Jewish beliefs later called Christian, notably the beliefs of St. Francis, was often chosen to enact Joseph in the neighborhood ritual of St. Joseph table at the time of the Spring Equinox.

My Nanna Lucia, signifying woman of my Chiavola family, strengthens my hypothesis that popular beliefs, which under the Roman empire were called Pagan, continued to be considered subversive to official Catholic doctrine, yet continued to be practiced by Sicilian peasants. Nanna was born Lucia Poidomani, a surname conveying hope "and then tomorrow," in Vittoria,

Sicily, a few kilometers from the town of Ragusa Ibla where my historical Chiavola ancestors lived.

In Vittoria, up until the late 19th century when Nanna Lucia was born, women would press their bare bosoms to the nurturing earth in a Pagan reciprocal nurturing ritual. This ritual, I am told, is similar to that of African American women, a generation ago, who liked to sit bare-bottomed on the regenerative black earth. My *comare* Chickie Farella remembers a Sicilian grandmother who pressed her bare bosom to the black earth.[40] Women's reciprocal nurturing rituals with the earth remind me of Wilhelm Reich's orgone box, for which he was prosecuted by the USA government in the 20th century.[41]

My mother, who changed her birth name Catarina to Kate, conveyed mixed patriarchal/subversive messages to me. She stayed with a philandering husband because of her kids whom she considered one with her, yet her behavior was always defiant, dramatically so after my father died and as she aged. Kate broke taboos of gender, culture, and age: tarring the roof of her ancestral home in Kansas City in her seventies, and dancing to "I Wish I Could Shimmy Like My Sister Kate" in a San Francisco bar in her eighties. Simultaneously, she was a very nurturant mother, grandmother, and great grandmother, and a fiercely independent liberated woman who could cuss like a sailor.

Kate's father, my grandfather Nannu Joe, physically resembled the dark Semites, notably the Canaanite Jews. Kate's mother, my Nanna Giuseppina (whom her grandkids called Nanna Jay Jay), of Lombard (northern Italian/German heritage), was fair and blue-eyed. Born to Nannu Joe & Nanna Giuseppina, in Kansas City, Missouri on July 5, 1900 was Catarina, my mother. Her name Catarina transmits the story of Mt. Saint Catherine, the earliest Jewish Christian sanctuary in the Sinai Peninsula. After this area was Christianized, her name carries the story of Santa Catarina of Alessandria, Africa. In the 13th century, Cathars of the south of France transmitted the heritage of women making their own decisions. Later comes the story of my paternal great grandmother Catarina, who was a woman entrepreneur of Palermo. Today Kate's great grandkids creatively design their names, recovering many traditions ... from lioness goddess of Africa ... to a joyful future.[42]

Cipolla, my mother's maiden name, in Italian folklore has been carried into contemporary subversive USA folklore, such as the "seditious" newspaper, *The Onion,* by honoring the onion, a popular vegetable signifier of a woman's womb. In today's highly violent masculinist dominant culture of the West, the most hurtful word a contemporary male chauvinist can hurl at a woman is "cunt," vernacular for a woman's womb.

Whatever the church promulgates in the doctrine of immaculate conception, any woman who looks at her body knows the birthing place is the womb—vagina. They must have known this in Classical Greece among whose imposed patriarchal notions—the goddess Athena was born of Zeus' forehead—took away woman's control of her body, giving power-over women's bodies to men.

Historically, subordinated peoples adopted a code language—dialect—that subordinated people understood, but cultural and political *prominenti* (elites) did not. In Sicilian folklore, the white folds of an onion are signifers of the labia of the vagina. My Uncle Jim teased my mother by pronouncing her maiden name Cipolla in dialect, La Cipudda ... Lady Onion.

Names transmitted signifying particulars of subaltern/suppressed peoples. Kate's father's birthplace, Palermo, signified the dominant social custom of naming Jews for the town (or town marker) where they were born. The names that Nanna Giuseppina & Nanna Joe gave their kids—seven girls and a boy—were Jewish/Christian/Muslim names conveying our deep family story: primordial historical migrations out of Africa to Levant in Asia to Sicily before migrating to Kansas City, Missouri in USA.

In USA in the early 20th century, when my mother Catarina changed her name to Kate, she tapped into unarticulated memory of early Celts in Sicily, whom Caesar called Gauls and conquered. While exploring in France in the 1970s and 1980s, Wally and I were startled by palpably felt memories of Gauls when we visited Les Baux in the south of France ... bodily confirming what German historians and educated Westerners of the last century called spirit of place, or zeitgeist. In this case, we felt a palpable memory of the Gauls being defeated by Caesar—whose legacy remains alive to this day in 2019.

Mary, Kate's next sister, was the midwife who delivered me and was also my Christian godmother who baptized me. Historically, Mary was the Jewish mother of Jesus. Patriarchs, while "purifying" Jewish writings, left her out of Hebrew Scriptures; Christian patriarchs demoted her to a Virgin Martyr, and left her out of the official Christian trinity (father, son, holy ghost), then beatified her Saint Mary when the church, in 4th century CE, aligned itself with the Roman Empire.

Trying to find my deep story, I learned that logic doesn't help me understand my mother and her sisters. Both my mother and her sister Mary had philandering Sicilian American husbands. My mother Kate stayed (because of the kids) with a husband who betrayed her, and took her revenge by humiliating and tormenting him. Kate's sister Mary defied patriarchal social tradition by not staying with her husband after he betrayed her. When she was old and living with her eldest daughter Tina and her husband, her suppressed rage was expressed by constantly criticizing her son-in-law.

Yet there was another side of my godmother Aunt Mary, suggesting the many selves of women. My Aunt Mary seriously embraced the nurturing responsibilities of aunt/godmother, seeing to my spiritual development as her niece/godchild. For my thirteenth birthday she gave me a typewriter … she was the first person to encourage me to be a writer. When Nanna Jay Jay died, Aunt Mary sent me Nanna's Bible—as a signifyer of my Catholic grandmother with Lombard/German roots who studied the Bible long before Vatican II allowed Catholics to do so.

In the Cipolla sisterhood, my mother Kate and godmother Mary were lifelong rivals for supremacy in a tribe of self-determining sisters whose Jewish/ Christian/Muslim names transmitted the deep history of Sicily … open ended with different outcomes.

My mother's next sister, Annie, whose name spiraled back to the Anu tribe of Africa, then to Anatolia, West Asian "land of the mothers" in whose folklore Anne is the goddess of the harvest when seeds are gathered for new life in the spring. My Aunt Annie, whom Nanna Jay Jay threw out of the house for free spiriting, went to live in the Bottoms of Kansas City along the Missouri River where brothels and black jazz enlivened the dominantly ascetic Protestant Midwestern city. In overheard wisps of this story, I learned my father went to the Bottoms to rescue his wife's sister. Later, Annie married a man named Palermo, whose name remembers Neolithic Africans in Sicily and is ubiquitous in the Sicilian North End of Kansas City, Missouri. With Palermo she gave birth to my cousin Carl who later married Chata (Margherita) of Mexican inheritance. Later, Aunt Annie wed an Irish cop named Casey, then a kindly man named Connole, whom I remember as somewhat brow-beaten.

My mother's sister Jennie was named for the female version of John, the Jewish colleague who baptized Jesus. My cousin Carl later described Jennie as the family workhorse, taking over Nannu Joe's stall in the City Market when he passed. My mother contested Jennie's appropriation … although Kate similarly took over the Cipolla family home in the North End. Unforgiving sisters, they both died of cancer.

Rose, the middle sister, whose name remembered the medieval symbol of the Christian madonna, was sensuous, loving, and baked the best chocolate cake. Her nieces called her Aunt RoRo. She married a Lombardo, a dark one with a close African connection. Speaking in the Sicilian dialect, this uncle would say, *Amoninni* ("Let's go"), replacing the Italian word, *Andiamo*, with the diminutive affectionate vernacular. He died young, leaving Aunt RoRo to mother a very nurturing son, my cousin Jack, who cared for his elderly mother and sick wife for many years. As a postman who pursued an education, Jack shares my passion for knowing the deep story of our family.[43]

Pearl, my mother's sister who looked like Van Gogh's painting of the beautiful woman of Arles, France, was given a Muslim name. Taking on the traditional roles of older sisters/aunts, she mothered her younger sister Lottie and her niece, me. Aunt Pearl took me aside at the time of my first menstruation to convey patriarchal instruction: since I could now become pregnant, I had to be careful around men. Pearl married a WASP man who died young; she lived a martyred mother's life caring for a challenged son.

Lottie, my aunt who is two years older than me, was named for the female version of Lot from Jewish scriptures. We were close in childhood and youth. She married a Cuban air officer … her tumultuous life is described below.

Frank, the only surviving son of Nanna Jay Jay & Nannu Joe, was named for the patron saint of Italy: St. Francis of Assisi. He married a spirited Irish American woman with whom he had one daughter, Teresa Jo, who has lived her life with the outlying/nurturant values of Teresa the Jewish conversa who became a heretical Catholic nun. Jo is the female vernacular version of the Jewish Christian Muslim prophet Joseph. Later, my Uncle Frank, who cared for Nanna Jay Jay in her old age, gave me the card of his Protestant evangelical church, Black Nazarene. His daughter, Teresa Jo, a self-determining woman, has become the archivist of the Cipolla clan.

My mother Kate, was called Queen of the North End—the neighborhood of Sicilian immigrants in Kansas City whose center was the Holy Rosary Church where Kate played the organ on Sundays. On weekdays, she presided, as the elegantly dressed queen, over her father's "Radio Joe" fruit and vegetable stall in the Kansas City market. Purveyor of fruits and vegetables to the city's upscale restaurants, Nannu Joe sang the market call on a greengrocer radio program, in celebration of the bounty of the earth: "Tomatoes, tomatoes, cabbages, beans, and potatoes." He would sign off the radio program with messages for my sister Joie whose birth name, Giuseppina, was the female version of Nannu's name, Giuseppe (Joe).

My mother, the beautiful brunette Queen of the North End in Kansas City, was asked for her hand in marriage by one of the dons of the Mafia (then called "the Black Hand"). This early 20th century version of the Mafia, to whom Nannu Joe would not pay bribes, burglarized his family home, traumatizing my mother. Kate turned down the mafia don's marriage proposals, as well as those of "big shots," wealthy bootleggers of illegal whisky during the era of Prohibition from the 1920s to 1933.

At age twenty-two, Kate made a romantic but disastrous decision to marry my father, whose family called him Turiddu, a diminutive affectionate for Salvatore (savior in Christianity). Kate's family, genealogical descendants of Semitic Canaanites, called him Sam, remembering the Jewish/Christian/Muslim figure Samuel in their common Jewish/Christian/Muslim scriptures.

Turiddu and his brothers identified with romantic French troubadours. Passionate about music, in their case, Italian opera, they considered it their right to love women ... in addition to the one to whom they were married.

Kate and Sam met as bridesmaid and groomsman at the wedding of mutual friends. Their wedding photo suggests the power of the continuing myths of classical Greeks who colonized Sicily: a bower of goddesses and gods (bridesmaids/groomsmen), flower girls, and a ring boy. Yet Kate's sequined wedding dress suggests her resistance to the dominant patriarchal culture's view of women as covered and chaste ... her dress featured daring see-through sleeves. Today the fair, good-looking groom (my father) in the wedding photo looks to me vaguely Asian, reminding me of the constant historic incursions into Sicily from West Asia.

Kate & Sam danced romantically at their wedding. "It's three o'clock in the morning. We've danced the whole night through."

Aside from a truce when I arrived, Kate and Turiddu's marriage was ill-fated. My father loved me, saying his baby meant more to him than his beloved automobile. My parents' marriage was a collision of his romantic patriarchal belief that he could be married to an obedient, chaste wife while he bedded beautiful fallen women (*puttane*) ... and Kate's resistance to this. On the piano she would play "Bye Bye Black Bird," seeming to me now to be defiance to her philandering husband, whose name Chiavola, means black bird. In my childhood, I never heard anyone make the connection between Chiavola and black bird. Kate's playing of "Bye Bye Black Bird" on the piano could not have been conscious. Later, when Kate went out to work after Sam fell ill, she retaliated for his many dalliances by not kicking him out of the house, but out of her bed ... and by constantly putting him down.

This simmering drama overflowed into violence when I was about twelve years old ... when I screamed at my father who was running after my mother with a butcher knife. He thought she was having an affair with another man because she did not come home immediately after work. After sewing all day on a power machine in the textile industry, Kate had stopped for a beer with her women friends.

I must have suppressed the violent incident because my adult memory of my father was his listening/weeping to Italian opera, empathizing with the bohemian life of artists (*La Boheme*), intercultural love (*Aida*), fallen women (*La Traviata*), troubadours of France (*Il Trovatore*), and the force of destiny (*La Forza del Destino*).

Early on I became very good at repressing trauma. When I was about ten years of age, my mother asked Lena, who lived in our neighborhood, to be my godmother for the Catholic ritual of first communion/confirmation in the church. Lena had confided in my mother that her father sexually abused her (I knew nothing of this story at the time). My mother's heart went out to her. For my confirmation gift, Lena, out of her hard-earned money at a menial job, gave me, her godchild, a rose quartz wristwatch. Afterward, Lena's father forbade her to marry the man she loved. Lena, my godmother, committed suicide.

Exhibiting unconscious resistance very early, as an infant I flipped off the cement ledge of the front porch of the Cipolla family dwelling where we lived, onto the sidewalk six feet below. My broken bones delayed my Christening for almost a year. As a toddler, my younger cousin Tina, daughter of my Aunt Mary/godmother who lived across the hall in the Cipolla family duplex, pushed over my highchair. As a curious child, I drove my paddy car down the steps of our 2nd floor apartment.

Our younger selves may nurture us when we are grown. I've been told that when I was a youngster, I sang a song that today, in my life without Wally, brings tears: "What'll I do when you are far away and I am blue. What'll I do … "

In the invitation to my belated Christening, which took place two days before the first anniversary of my birthdate (January 3, 1924) on New Year's day, January 1, 1925, Mr. & Mrs. Sam Chiavola invited kin and kindred to celebrate my baptism in a hall where wedding parties were held.

Later, after my parents' marriage had deteriorated due to her anorexia, Sam, while working in his brother George's grocery store, fell ill. Kate went out to work, canning soup in a meat packing company. She never ate canned soup afterward. During world war II, she operated a power machine in a textile factory, sewing flies on soldier uniforms. As a labor union steward, she secured better working conditions for her women co-workers. She also contracted the breast cancer (from the lint in the textile factory) that later killed her.

Kate, retaliating for Sam's constant infidelities, threw him out of her bed, but not out of the house—metering money to him for cigarettes and gasoline for his car. Kate's resistance seemed to me—I was studying classical Greek mythology—similar to that of Greek Medea who, in payback for her husband's infidelities, killed their kids.

Not like the Greek Medea, however, my mother was an indomitably fierce Sicilian woman who considered her kids to be one with her. Disparaging her, sister-in-law Georgia called her, in the Sicilian dialect, "the black one." Kate's smoldering rage at a philandering husband was expressed verbally and devastatingly; plotting to get back at anybody who crossed her, deprecated her kids, or violated her territory.

In the alley we held in common with our neighbors, Kate erected an obstacle of scattered broken glass; there was no way these disliked neighbors (their son was the neighborhood bully) could get into their garage without puncturing their car tires. When they continued to back their car into her fence, Kate, from our upstairs bathroom, poured hot water on them … then reported to city health inspectors that their restaurant was full of cockroaches.

CHAPTER 11
Lucia's deep story of her childhood and youth

⊰⧽⧼⊱

While my sister Jo (my name for her) and brother Louie had a glorious childhood of turning on the water hydrant to splash in the street, and playing in the swamp of nearby Cliff Drive, I fled my arguing parents and noisy neighborhood into books and school. During the summers, I stayed with my serene maternal grandmother Nanna Jay Jay and my nearly same age, Aunt Lottie, who had a tent and a pony.

As teen-agers, Lottie and I drank rum and Coca-Cola in solidarity with the Cubans who were resisting exploitation by United Fruit of USA. Today I wonder, how did I acquire this left political consciousness? Lottie and I met Cuban air officers stationed in Kansas City. Lottie dreamed we would marry handsome officers and go to live happily in Cuba, a plan I did not share.

Lottie married Tito, and they lived happily in Cuba until the Castro socialist revolution when Tito—a British airline executive—was jailed for ten years by the Fidel Castro regime.

With her husband in prison, Lottie made an incognito journey to Tito's family in Spain for money to support their child. After ten years of incarceration, separation, and sorrow (their child died in a swimming pool accident), Lottie & Tito were reunited in Kansas City when he was released. Nearly blind from the years of incarceration, Tito told me, remarkably, that Castro's revolution that overthrew the oppressive Batista regime was justified.

My early support (like that of Italian feminists) of Che Guevara and Fidel's socialist revolution was later dampened when its notable achievements—sending Cuba's many doctors to heal in the global health crises, universal education, and universal medical care—were accompanied by Castro's curtailing of human rights, segregating homosexuals, and encouraging dissidents to go to Florida, USA, where they joined the right wing of the USA Republican party.

During the summers I stayed with my Nanna Jay Jay and Lottie in the beautiful home Nannu's earnings built on Benton Boulevard. During the rest of the year, I ran away from my parents' arguments to my life in books and school. I won a scholarship to the newly founded University of Kansas City, today the University of Missouri (Mizzou), whose home campus at Columbia, Missouri—in Mark Twain country—is the energy center of the transformative movement, Black Lives Matter. Many demonstrations against racism at Mizzou have brought much controversy/prophetic significance.

At the University of Kansas City, I met Gene of a Scandinavian (Danish) American farm family who lived in North Kansas City and who studied physics. Both the studious kids of our families, we bonded, went to the movies, went ice skating, and planned to marry. Before he entered the army early in world war II and was to be deployed to the China-Burma-India theater of war, Gene sealed our intention to marry by giving me fine dishes, silverware, a cedar chest, and a diamond engagement ring. We wrote to each other every day.

In 1943, I dropped out of college and went to work in a war company—then and later called a "defense" industry—Quartz Laboratories. Later, after years of opposing war and the military-industrial complex (the revolving door of war industrialists and posts in the national government), I made the belated connection that Quartz Laboratories was a subsidiary of Hallicrafters of Chicago, which was a corporation connected with Dick Cheney, the iconic figure of the military-industrial complex in the Nixon administration.

In 1943, the President of Quartz Laboratories was a sociology professor who had left the campus of Washburn University to head the wartime company. A Scandinavian American, he capriciously appointed me, a Sicilian immigrant daughter, as secretary-treasurer of the corporation. A Sicilian ethnic outsider, I was the youngest (at eighteen) and (I later learned) the first woman in the history of the state of Missouri to hold the corporate post.

Quartz Labs was a curious war operation. A government official sat and watched in the front office. After work hours, we danced at wild parties, read poetry together, and fervently discussed the world we wanted after the war.

In Fall 1945, at the end of world war II, I received a letter from Gene, the soldier to whom I was engaged. He had married an army nurse.

Jilted, I was jolted yet not overcome by great grief. At the war's end, my overwhelming physical reaction was nausea at seeing newspaper photos of starved emaciated Jews being liberated from Nazi concentration camps. My father, ever the romantic, brought sandwiches from the elegant restaurant where he polished their silver to my office at Quartz Laboratories, that was then converting from war industry to the peace time manufacture of toy gyroscopes.

I gave Gene's gifts to my mother ... feeling an uncanny sense of expectancy ...

Writing this I am struck by what we do not know. Before Wally and I met that night after Thanksgiving November 1945, neither of us imagined we would suddenly be swept into a genetic/experiential encounter that became an incredibly joyous and transforming journey.

CHAPTER 12
Deep story of Lucia & Wally

꧁꩜꧂

We met on a November night after Thanksgiving 1945 in Kansas City, Missouri at a jazz concert at the Pla-Mor Ballroom where my adventurous cousin Tina had taken me. A tall soldier with no insignia on his uniform asked me to dance ... and something happened.[44]

Dancing to "Stardust," the good night song of our world war II generation, he asked me to meet him the next night at a club where Catholic girls were encouraged to welcome returning soldiers. Three days later, I received a letter from an unknown Wallace Birnbaum ... when we met, he had given me the surname Gerrie of his maternal grandmother killed by Nazis.

On the next weekend, we met in downtown Kansas City at Katz Drug Store whose name, plural of vernacular cat goddess of Africa, was a signifier not to come to consciousness for decades. At that third meeting, Wally asked me to marry him. I reached for his hand and said, "Yes."

In December 1945, we walked together in the Winter Solstice lights of Kansas City's Plaza, an architectural reconstruction of Seville, a Moorish (African Muslim) city we later explored on-site in Spain. Trying to measure the ineffable, we danced to "How deep is the ocean? ... How high is the sky? ... " We tried to separate in the face of disapproval of both sets of parents ... but could not.

On January 1, 1946, we danced in the new year at the Municipal Auditorium of Kansas City. I wore a long red dress. That January, on the weekends, we traveled in Missouri to Columbia and St. Louis, where the signifying movement Black Lives Matter later began.

On February 3, 1946, Wally came for me and left my mother a two-pound box of Russell Stover chocolates. We took a Greyhound bus to Lawrence, Kansas, where there was no required waiting period to marry.

Wally telephoned a judge who was eating his Sunday dinner, who came to the county courthouse to marry us, and wish us well. After one night together, Wally shipped out the next morning to army camp at New Rochelle, a few minutes from Wally's family apartment in the Bronx, New York City.

On February 5, upon his arrival to army camp, Wally told his parents he was married. They said the Hebrew prayer for the dead. When I told my parents we were married, my father turned to my mother and said, "Your daughter." My mother went to the medicine chest to swallow iodine ... but she didn't. After preparing dinner, my parents called me down to eat.

Thinking today (Spring 2019) about both sets of parents' initial hostility to our marrying, I realize the power of traumatic memories and inculcated historical prejudice. Wally's Jewish parents worried about persecuting Gentiles; I was, in Jewish dialect, a *shiksa*, a *goy* woman. My Sicilian parents were conditioned in Christian lands to historical bigotry against Jews ... although their main concern was that marrying Wally meant I would leave Kansas City.

After the initial melodrama, my parents came around, facing a *fait accompli*, and maybe unconscious memories of mutual ancestral migrations out of Africa, preconscious memories of mutual historic persecution of Sicilians and Jews. Wally, who always sided with her in family arguments, became my mother's favored child.

In March 1946, when I joined Wally in New York, his father Harry came with him to the Pennsylvania train station to meet me. He kissed me, saying he knew why his son loved me. Wally's mother Dora taught me to cook, and ironed my blouses for my job adventures in New York City.

On April 2, 1946, Wally and I were married again, this time by a rabbi whose pre-wedding discussion included the signifying datum: Jesus, the central figure of Christianity, was a Jewish rabbi whose mother and father and early disciples were Jews and later called Christians.

Later I realized we were re-enacting close encounters of Semites on their migration paths out of Africa in the years just before/just after the beginning of the Christian epoch ... notably, Jews were later called Christians when patriarchs separated the faith into two religions.

Everyday Jews and Christians, as well as African and Asian Muslims in Sicily—all Semites—share a core of ultimate beliefs including shared prophets: Abraham, Isaiah, Joseph, Jesus, and Muhammad. Until when, in the 10th century CE, dominant Christians in rising European nation states aligned with the Catholic pope/Roman empire declared Jesus the incarnate son of God, spread hateful stories about Jews, incited the Crusades against Muslims, and forcibly converted Pagans~Jews~Christians~Muslims and other suspects in the run-up to the Inquisition that tortured/killed anyone suspected of not having genuinely converted to the Inquisitors' imperial/violent/white/male/heterosexual version of Christianity.

The beliefs of Jews and Christians in historical CE beginning Year One need to be understood, as previously noted, in the context of early Roman imperial persecution of Jews/early Christians whom they branded Pagans ... and later in the context of expanding Islam ... the Christian crusades after the 10th century against "infidel" Muslims ... the 13th century papal crusade against heretical French Cathar women who lived their early uncodified Jewish Christian beliefs.

Some Cathars in France, fleeing killing and persecution, went to Italy. In the 1970s, trying to understand Italian feminists—so familiar yet different from USA feminists—I interviewed a feminist of northern Italy. She asked me if I was a *credente* (believer) in a faith left un-named. I spontaneously (unconsciously) said, "Yes."

꙳꙳꙳

Spiraling back to 1946, we spent the spring and summer living in Wally's parents' apartment in the Bronx. Wally, now mustered out of the army, and I ran away on weekends to explore upstate New York. We won a dance contest in the Borsht Belt. On weekdays, I played with jobs. I wrote ads for a Fifth Avenue advertising agency until told to take off my wedding ring when meeting with clients; I quit. I was executive secretary to the president of a Seventh Avenue swimwear company, then I was asked to model swimsuits. Not liking the way I was touched, I quit.

In Fall 1946, we migrated from New York to the University of California, Berkeley where Wally studied physics, receiving his Ph.D. in 1954. In the fall of 1947, Lucia also enrolled at UCB, completing her B.A. in History, English, Economics in 1948, her M.A. in French and Italian History in 1950, and her Ph.D. in History in 1964 ... while we became parents of Naury, Marc, and Stefan.

Living very happily in Gill Court, both of us cared for our kids, both of us studied, and both of us engaged in radical politics. We communally purchased groceries, and took turns watching our kids in a communal play yard. We met many international students.

We flourished in this benign environment. World war II soldiers were given a G.I. Bill with tuition-free education. UCB charged us $29.00 a month for rent for our apartment in Gill Court. When my initial foray into supporting us while Wally was in graduate school did not work out—I was insulted by male chauvinist bosses, and I would leave without picking up my paycheck—we

---

decided I should also go to graduate school. My university tuition was something like $42 a semester (compare with astronomical UCB tuition today).

Sharing parenting and studying, on weekdays we took a bus called Sequoia Stages to the UCB campus, passing toddler Naury between each other. Wally's seminars in graduate Physics included one with the famed Robert Oppenheimer, who wrote poetry about USA dropping the atomic bomb on Japanese people. Wally considered him arrogant. On weekends, Wally supplemented his G.I. stipend by working in Richmond's intercultural shipyards, Berkeley's bookstores, and hosing down tennis courts and hospital beds.

Lucia, while waiting for infant Naury to arrive in September 1947, sewed orange curtains for our one-bedroom apartment. We painted a frieze celebrating Einsteinian physics—E=MC squared—around our kitchen/living space. I read books on the depth psychology of Freud and Jung, went to history classes, and took my pillow to natural child-birthing classes ... we were living in great joy ... new mother/studying ~ new father/studying ... the present and future were radiant with possibilities.

After our second son Marc came in May 1951, Wally would come home at midnight after experimenting nonviolently (no explosions, measuring the mass of the meson with oil emulsion methodology) at the UCB cyclotron. We would put Naury and Marc in our little car with two Cal Bears stickers on the back window, and go camping in the national parks. When Wally was invited to speak on his research at the University of British Columbia, the boys and I went along, camping on the campus. In the university's physics laboratory, Wally prepared three-month-old Marc's milk formula before giving a lecture to the physics department on his research measuring the mass of the meson with oil emulsions.

In 1954, Wally graduated with a Ph.D. in physics. A few years later, we moved from Gill Court in Albany into a large Victorian house across the way from the UCB campus. We rented out rooms to foreign students. Khalil (later I learned the name means kindred spirit) from Iraq studied graduate botany, baked cumin cookies he shared with us, and played with our sons. He was wed in our home to a woman Iraqi student in an intensely joyous Muslim non-alcoholic celebration in which we participated. Back in Iraq, Khalil sent us three Bedouin teapots, one for each son ... heirlooms of desert Islam ... still in our living room today in 2019. Subsequent politics between our countries—nonviolent turned toxic—have prevented our keeping in touch.

In graduate school, simultaneously parents, scholars, and Berkeley radicals, Wally and I danced at parties at Throckmorton, then a Victorian house on

Telegraph Avenue where UCB history graduate students lived. Wally walked up the Berkeley hill outside our home to the UCB radiation laboratory where he experimented in sub-atomic physics. In a department of famous physicists, at lunch time he played poker with them, invariably winning. For his laboratory research assistants Wally chose a male physicist not enrolled for any graduate degrees, and a female physicist who challenged the conventional notions of universal heterosexuality.

In our home on La Loma street across from the campus, we threw raucous faculty-student parties. One was an "attic romp" spoofing the dominant classical Greek paradigm ... pouring the punch into a peasant chamber pot remembering our mutually historically subordinated Sicilian and Jewish antecedents.

In 1948, we voted for peaceful (later called "communist") Henry Wallace.

In 1952, we climbed a fence on the West Crescent of the UCB campus to hear Adlai Stevenson, a candidate for president.

In 1960, both of us were politically committed to Black Liberation and opposed to the imperial war in Vietnam, yet, swept away by what we later realized was imperialist rhetoric, we voted for John F. Kennedy for president.

In this period, Malcom X was murdered. President John F. Kennedy followed by his brother Robert Kennedy were murdered. Martin Luther King, Jr. was murdered.

In 1964, along with Tom Hayden and others who were opposed to the Vietnam war, we voted "part of the way with LBJ."

In 1968, after my near-death car collision, recovery, and whirlwind trip to the Levant, I returned to teaching at SF State whose campus was in a state of revolution led by black students. I immediately joined the strike and closed down all my classes (I was the only member of the History Department to go on strike).

In 1969, Wally and I were both knee-deep in the cultural-political revolution of our times.

Spiraling back ... our kids arrived while we were beginning to explore our ancestries. Wanting a name that had never been a name, the name of Naury, our first-born, honored the "N" names of Wally's Jewish grandfathers: Nussen (nut tree) and Nissan (month in the Hebrew calendar). Combining the initial N with my childhood admiration for Laurie in Louisa May Alcott's *Little Women*, we named him Naury Kim Birnbaum ... Kim because we liked the non-gender-specific Korean name.

In the 1960s, Barbara was a flower child and Naury wore his hair in an Afro while studying physics and philosophy. In early 1970s, they married, gifted everybody with Josh, then went to Paris to work and live where they gifted everybody with Sabrina. In the 1980s, back in USA, they gifted everybody with Jessica.

Naury & Barbara named their dogs Micah for the prophet of Jewish Christian scriptures, Cassidy for Celtic ancestors, Truffles for the root celebrated in elegant cooking, Krispin for a storybook dog who cared for kids, and Ollie (Oliver) for the olive trees of Tuscany, Italy and Napa wine country in California where Ollie lives with Naury & Barbara in their self-designed Mediterranean home. Joining Olly in 2017 was a new puppy named Hamilton for the signifying blockbuster musical that revised the story of USA founding fathers with an optic of immigrant dark others. When the signifying musical opened, Josh moved mountains to secure tickets for his parents, his grandmother (me), Whitney, his luminous significant other, and himself.

Creating their own traditions, Barbara & Naury follow the Pagan custom later associated with Christianity … finding and bringing into their home, and in public places, the tallest most splendid evergreen tree. They decorate the tree with ornaments transmitting their family story from heretical Jews (later called Christians) to the everyday/celebratory customs of Barbara's peasant German Methodist historical family … to Barbara & Naury's culturally rebellious lives in USA in the 1960s, to their subsequent years living in France, to now … as once and future caring and sharing parents/grandparents.

In December 2016, Barbara & Naury, already blessed with Sabrina & Peter's kids—grandkids Josie Ann Lucia and Adam Murphy—became grandparents again: Juliet Lucia Lorraine was gifted by kids Jessica & Russell.

⁂

Marc, our middle son, honored the initials "M" and "R" of Wally's Jewish maternal grandmother, Miriam Rebecca. Reflecting my study of Jewish Christian scriptures, Miriam became Marc and Rebecca became Marc's middle initial R. My personal middle name for Marc—Turiddu—was for my father in honor of his love for opera, and for telling us stories about Sicily on our front porch of my Kansas City childhood home.

Marc, a later scholar of French culture/Francophile, and Nancy, a second-generation Japanese American whose parents were put into internment camps at the outset of world war II, were married in the 1970s when they lived in Paris, France.

Marc & Nancy named their first son Nicolas, a historic name encompassing Russian czars, a December saint, and a 20th century Italian anarchist killed for his beliefs. They named their second son Matthew, which was the most popular name of the time (we have three grandsons named Matthew). In a custom of the 1960s USA generation (also a Sicilian custom) of giving human names to animals, Marc & Nancy named their beloved dogs Luc (after the early Jewish Christian Luke), Rochambeau (French Revolution), and Zachariah (of Jewish Christian scriptures).

In early 2019, Marc & Nancy were in Italy visiting Matera—primordial grottoes dated to a million years ago where contemporary homeless people live—and back home in March to attend the wedding celebration of their kids, Matt & Kate, in a lively Chinese restaurant without an elevator, where all three of my sons helped me to ascend and descend the stairs.

Marc & Nancy seem to me traditional~prophetic models of grandparents, major caretakers, along with Nic, father of Charlie (Charlotte) Kimura Birnbaum, my luminous blonde great granddaughter who carries the genetic strains and cultural traditions of East and West into the emerging paradigm.

Charlie has Italian American great grandparents with a Germanic last name, Bald, which honors the grandfather who lived in North Italy bordering Austria. She has Japanese American parents on one side, and on other side, Jewish American/Sicilian parents-in-law. Mostly, Charlie is her own self.

❦

Stefan, our third son, arrived nine years after Marc, and thirteen years after Naury. We thought of him (conceived) in 1959 while traveling in Spain, specifically after our visit to the Prado Museum. Tiring of all the masterpieces (Goya, Velasquez, Bosch) we retreated to the bar in the museum basement where we drank (several) ten cent tumblers of gin (pronounced "hin") fizzes before returning to our hotel.

In this 1959 first trip together to Europe, while thinking of our ancestral European countries Poland and Italy, we named our third son Stefan/Stefano. Later, I wondered (see earlier discussion) if the name Stefan Anthony emerged from our unconscious. "S" for Shia (in Yiddish) for Wally's suppressed birth name Isaiah, prophet of peace in Judaism~Christianity~Islam, became the first letter of his name Stefan. His middle name remembers Anthony, the historic saint whose inclusive values—all creatures and everything on earth are holy—are similar to those of St. Francis, patron saint of Italy.

In August 2016, I learned that Stefan's historical name originally referred to a Greek Jew named Stephen who, in 4th century CE, was branded a Pagan and stoned to death by Romans at about the same time as Romans blinded and killed my major woman signifier, Lucia of Syracuse. Subsequently called the "first Christian martyr," Stephen was beatified Santo Stefano.

In 2016, I politically supported Bernie Sanders' Our Revolution, and the Jill Stein-Ajamu Baraka Green Party platform opposing neo-liberals whose democratic rhetoric was accompanied by unspoken hierarchical, unequal assumptions culminating in endless wars. I particularly like Ajamu Baraka's aligning the Black Lives Matter movement with international Human Rights/ Amnesty International.

Stefan, before the 2016 election, supported Trump in hope he would revive the stagnant economy, but did not vote. I voted for Hillary Clinton at the top of the ticket in an effort to ward off a dangerous Trump presidency, marking the rest of the ballot, Peace and Freedom, a third party Wally and I helped create in 1967-68.

Linda Susan Warner & Stefan Anthony Birnbaum have three spectacular kids married to three equally extraordinary spirits. In September 2016, Stefan & Linda became first-time grandparents. Gifted in New York by Abigail & Jake with Andrew Ellis, who may have been named, in preconscious memory, for the initials of prophet Abraham and maybe the woman Abigail in Jewish Christian Islamic scriptures. Ellis may be a preconscious memory of Elijah, the prophet honored in our 1960s Seder celebrations of Passover … for whom a beaker is filled with wine, and the door is left open.

Andrew Ellis rolls with laughter when his father Jake plays with him, and beams at Abi whom he early called Momma—the oldest sound in the world. Abi, a new paradigm woman, taught art to rebellious seventh graders in New York City then rushed home to breast feed Andrew who was cared for during the day by his Sefardic Jewish grandmother Elaine and a warm Jamaican woman whose kids are grown.

In 2019, Abi & Jake are parents of two kids: Andrew & Emma Lia ("L" for mother Linda and great grandmother Lucia) who arrived April 30, 2018.

In December 2016, Linda & Stefan again became grandparents, gifted in California by Courtney & Matt with Isabel Rose, who inherits the valence of previous signifying women of Africa and Asia culminating in the Christian madonna whose signifier is a rose. Isabel Rose, called Izzy, a vernacular for Isidore (the Semitic male form of name Isabel), insists and secures the total devoted love of her father Matt and mother Courtney. The only way Izzy fell asleep as an infant was on her father's shoulder listening to his heart beat. Early on she laughed out loud. By December 2017, she was walking, thereafter walking everywhere. Her second birthday party was at a local museum where she and friends petted a bat, a rabbit, and a guinea pig.

Stefan is overwhelmed by the joy of being a three-time grandfather of Andrew, Emma Lia, and Izzy. Linda, a contemporary woman who works in a real estate office on the weekends, regularly cares for granddaughter Izzy. At the May 2019 wedding of Josh & Whitney, Linda played with grandchildren Andrew and Emma Lia, and looked forward to the renewal wedding of Courtney & Matt in June 2019.

⁂

In the political chaos of late 2016 and early 2017, I became a great grandmother again … doubling three previous great grandkids (Josie Ann Lucia, Adam Murphy, and Charlie) to three more (Andrew Ellis, Isabel Rose, and Juliet Lucia Lorraine). In January 2017, it occurred to me that I have been on emotional overload.

In 2019, I am a *bisnonna* (great grandmother) of Josie Ann Lucia 12, Adam Murphy 9, Charlotte (Charlie) 5, Andrew Ellis 2, Isabel (Izzy) 2, Juliet Lucia Lorraine 2, Emma Lia 7 months, and expecting a baby boy of Whitney & Josh in Summer 2019.

Writing this manuscript may be considered my simultaneous gasp of despair at the world my grand and great grandkids are inheriting and my surprise at watching grandkids steer us out of chaos into an emerging green culture … where great grandkids already play in the new paradigm.

⁂

Barbara, Nancy, and Linda—daughters whom our sons brought home—are living their own stories. Here I'd like to suggest my hypothetical signifying meanings for names of our three daughters who blossomed in the signifying 1960s.

The name Barbara refers to "barbarian"—a name Romans called the people from Africa and Asia … African Berbers and Semites from Asia and Africa with whom they coupled. Patriarchs of the Christian church first called Barbara and Lucia Virgin Martyrs. Jewish patriarchs who were "purifying," left Mary out of Hebrew Scriptures; Christian patriarchs omitted Mary from the Holy Trinity (father, son, holy ghost). After mutilating their stories to conform to Christian doctrine, church fathers beatified Santa Barbara, Santa Maria, and Santa Lucia.

Barbara's ancestors include Jews, Christians, Pagans, and Protestant Christians; Naury's ancestors include Jews and Christians. He was confirmed a Jew (Bar Mitzah) at age thirteen. They named their first child Joshua, aide to Moses, who in Jewish Christianity was called Jeshua (Jesus). They named their second child Sabrina (a diminutive affectionate in several traditions), and their third child Jessica, whose name remembers heretical Gnostics (just before the Christian epoch) meaning "she who knows."

Linda Susan Warner of Celtic Native American Scandinavian Catholic inheritance, whose given name Linda, in Spanish, means beautiful, is a practicing Catholic whose middle name, Susan, remembers Jewish Christian scriptures. Her sister Kathy adds Cathar heresy to the family mix. Linda's intuition is startling. In 2017, her Mother's Day gift to me was lotion and soap named Provincia for Italian folklore beliefs, and the ingredients, Wild Fig and Black Currant, are signifyers of the African black mother's womb birthing everybody.

As life has unrolled for Linda & Stefan, they are nurturing parents to their grown kids—Courtney & Matt, Jake & Abi, and Stefanie & Matt—while simultaneously nurturing their widowed mothers. Linda lives with her mother, Marcia; Stefan lives with his mother, Lucia (me). In this signifying model of past ~ present ~ future families ... everybody nurtures everybody.

Spiraling back to the 1990s and the first decade of the new millennium, while exploring the world, our knowing deepened. After Wally passed away, I participated in Joshua's 2014 gift family trip to Sicily with kids, grandkids, great grandkids (see later chapter).

Wally's and my travels after the 1970s personally confirmed (on-site) research findings of scientists. Supplementing our on-site learning, I studied 40,000 BCE evidence of an African settlement in my ancestral paternal region in southeast Sicily, 25,000 BCE evidence of African settlements in Wally's ancestral region in Levant of West Asia, and expansion after 1200 BCE of "people of the sea" Semitic Canaanites, whom Greeks called Phoenicians, out of West Asia who founded trading settlements all over the known world ... while 5th century BCE dominant Greeks fixed Classical imperial Greece as the dominant paradigm of the West ... up until the 1960s when this paradigm was (is) challenged by subordinated others, notably women, of the world.

Scholarship since the 1960s has taken a critical look at the model of Classical Greece as the dominant paradigm of the West. It is now viewed as an imperial power whose true stories include raping goddesses and killing/ enslaving the people they conquered.[45] The revision of this dominant paradigm of Classical Greece evokes very uncomfortable similarities to the raping and killing culture/empire of contemporary USA.

The sun, a major constant in our journey~story, reaches back to primordial Africans seeing light emerging from darkness ... a belief that persisted to the 20th century when my Sicilian relatives in Kansas City, Missouri sang "O Sole Mio" embodied in *u figghiu beddu* (beautiful son).

In 2019, the sun holds the dual legacy of life-killing climate heating as well as a promise of solar power repairing human degradation of the earth. Hurricanes, tornados, flooding, fires, earthquakes, and other catastrophes kill ... while humans during natural and human crises demonstrate extraordinary heroic caring for and sharing with fellow humans.

Mulling over the gifting spirals of my antecedents, I remembered: in 1946, before leaving Kansas City to join Wally in New York, I visited my Uncle George who welcomed my news that I'd married Wally, a man who was going to study physics in graduate school. I should remind Wally, Uncle George said, that Archimedes, a great physicist, lived in Sicily when the island was a Greek colony.

While visiting my paternal Nanna Lucia, who was also welcoming of Wally, she exclaimed, "Isidoro!" A gift of Isis, recalling Isidore, the Christian bishop of Seville, Spain whose name transmitted memory of African goddess Isis and the Greek word for gift. While visiting my Nanna Jay Jay (Giuseppina) of North Italian-German ancestry, she blessed us, and hoped I would not forget her. I haven't.

Spiraling back to the years just before the Christian epoch (beginning Year One), Romans declared, *Cartago delenda est* (Carthage must be destroyed). African Hannibal sent elephants to defend the African Mediterranean, but imperial Romans, victorious in the Punic wars, extended their empire from Rome to colonies in Africa, Asia, and Europe, reminding me in 2019 of the vast empire of USA.

Suggesting a signifying role of kindred spirits in our extended family, during the last week of July 2016, I received a message from Larry DiStasi, kindred spirit, that our mutual friend-comrade-artist Gian Banchero had passed. I have known Gian since the 1960s when we began exploring our mutual Sicilian roots. Tracking his Italian ancestry from bankers in the north to Sicilian grandmothers in the south, Gian told me his Sicilian grandmothers inspired his paintings.

In 1978, Gian gave us a little painting, that we mounted on Wally's side of our double basins, of fish (Wally's birth sign is Pisces) in the dark blue sea reaching upward toward the radiant sun in a sky where a black bird flies. In the dark sea subterranean green growth pushes upward.

After the 1991 great urban fire burned down our Berkeley dwelling, Gian's gift to our rebuilt home was a painting of a contemporary black madonna: a brunette woman with a crowned black child alongside, on whom a radiant sun shines. In the center of the sun is a black bird. The rays of the sun are French *fleur-de-lys* (lilies). Shoals emerge from the deep sea.

The last painting Gian gave us we put on the third level of our Berkeley home, mounted on the exterior wall of my study: a black madonna at one with her black child holding a lily (signifier of regeneration) on a seascape where the sun nurtures all life, and humans navigate a ship without helmsman among shoals, signifying life emerging from the subterranean sea. Enigmatically, a woman's head on the beach, looks at the viewer. On a date I've forgotten, Gian sent another message: a postcard painting of a Sicilian seascape, titled "Even the sun comes to warm its self in Sicily."

Gian's name, for me, recalls John, the Jewish contemporary who baptized Jesus, who was sometimes called Precursor ... reminding theologians that, in Jesus' time, many preached a similar message.

The Gian I knew was a nurturing uncle who loved to cook, whose church was St. John the Workman, and who today evokes, for me, the musical play *Godspell.*

In the early 1970s, Wally and I flew to London where we fell under the spell of a play with no separation between the actors on stage and the people in the audience. *Godspell* sends me into the timeless ~ prophetic ~ African ~ Asian ~ European ~ North Central South American ~ Pacific spiral ... the Pagan ~ Jewish ~ Christian ~ Hindu ~ Muslim ~ Buddhist spiral ... still spiraling ...

CHAPTER 13
Outlier feminist cultural historian

꧁꧂

The 2016 conference of Association of the Study of Women and Mythology worded their Demeter award: " … visionary scholar and intellectual leader Lucia Chiavola Birnbaum raises consciousness of our shared ancient ancestral African culture of caring, sharing and giving." Her work is a "door in seeking a different truth about spiritual consciousness and political feminism." The Demeter award of 2016 was also given to Elinor Gadon, founder of the Women's Spirituality program of CIIS.

The award stimulated me to meditate on what I am doing … woman ~ lover ~ mother ~ grandmother ~ great grandmother ~ outlier feminist scholar ~ nonviolent cultural/political revolutionary . . . adapting the story of Wally and me, our kin, kids, grand and great grandkids, and kindred spirits as case in point of the origin story of homo sapiens sapiens in Africa, everybody's different migration stories, yet all of us sharing the same seasons of life … birthing ~ blossoming ~ harvesting-planting seeds ~ dying-renewing life.

The 1960s feminist movements in USA and Italy were aligned with close yet rocky relationships with the male New Left in Italy, and the Black Panthers in USA … causing a fissure for me and most feminists when a splinter of the white New Left went off into violence and Black Panthers in USA separated from whites.

Already an outlier to dominant Western feminism—believing that nurturing cannot be segregated to women as mothers—our on-site research of African origin/migration paths out of Africa uncovered the many ways humans nurture, the many ways dark others are persecuted, and the many ways contemporary pagans, visionaries, witches, and seers live their beliefs, on diverse paths … yet mysteriously forming an emerging paradigm of caring, sharing, healing, renewal …

In 2016, while trying to unknot contemporary political-spiritual dilemmas, I was struck by an illumination … probably indebted to the ten years I spent researching/writing my dissertation on behaviorist psychology while USA empire expanded. In dominant Western cultural perception, the observer considers him/herself white ... wherein dark becomes a projection of the observer's suppressed knowledge/accompanied by fear of dark others. Generalized anxiety of the unconscious coming to awareness ... first in fear/flight ... then in aggression toward dark others ... then in aggression toward self.

At the same time, in another layer of truth, dark refers to everybody's experience in the nurturing embryo ... in our historical experience, learning to survive together in migrations out of Africa ... in caring, sharing, healing.

The illumination became more complex when I realized that opposing dynamics sometimes inhabit the same body. All our journeys are conditioned by where they are located, not only geographically but psychologically, on different exterior or interior migration paths ... all the while cosmos is spinning ~ earth is spinning ~ each of us spins at different velocities (different traumas/epiphanies), whirling us into close encounters, sometimes violent, more often in love.

Thinking about the ten years I spent researching and writing my doctoral dissertation, a delayed insight surfaced. "Enlightened Behaviorism" has become the dominant Western way of seeing, wherein the observer believes he acts, unbiased, out of his consciousness; exempting himself from more "primitive" ways of knowing.

By 1930, John Broadus Watson's behaviorism—in which both observer/observed are both ultimately governed, not by conscious knowing, but by unconscious/preconscious feelings of fear, rage, and sex—was dismissed as "puerile" by "enlightened behaviorists" who implicitly kept consciousness for the observer and implicitly erased consciousness of the observed, with outcomes ultimately leading to killing dark others and suicidally killing the vulnerable dark other within.

Feminists close to the Western paradigm separated themselves from dark others whom they called "racists", "bigots", "rednecks", "ignorant", or "deplorables." Translated into the neo-liberal assumption ... "we" the governing class of the West have noble motives ruling over dark others at home/around the world, while "they" or those being ruled—women and other dark others—are lesser humans tied to their animal instincts ... sometimes called "predators" at home and "terrorists" elsewhere, whose countries, from the perspective of neo-liberals, need to be "stabilized." In a translation by Trumpites who identify with the Alt-Right, countries whose oil or minerals we want, or who challenge our monopoly of nuclear weapons, are given a mafia question they cannot refuse: submit to Western hegemony or be killed.

Neo-liberals in the electoral campaign of 2016 massaged this into the feel-good rhetoric of "American Exceptionalism" while Trump manipulated (using bait and switch tactics) preconscious memories of violence to "Make America Great Again" … culminating in his 2016 electoral victory.

In December 2017, I wrote in an earlier version of this manuscript about how the West lives in an updated version of a dominant paradigm, originating with classical Greek BCE hierarchy of political/cultural/familial social elites whose wealth and power today can destroy the world several times over … topped by an unchecked and unbalanced USA president.

This has accelerated my realization that the control of nuclear buttons should, immediately, be taken out of the hands of the executive presidency of USA—an imperative first step in abolition of all nuclear weapons of mass destruction. USA, the only power to have used nuclear weapons, must take the lead in giving them up.

❧❦❧

In the chaos of 2017-19, I am overwhelmed by the mystery of life. Wally and I, kids of Jewish and Sicilian "new immigrants," were born outside the dominant WASP culture. Yet after our meeting in November 1945, our lives, tossed by postwar USA geopolitics, thrust us into the "best and brightest" generation.

Our journey after 1945 began with personal/political bright hope and passionate activism for equality~justice~peace. In Spring 2017, I wrote about the dance of absurdity and tragedy together in careening chaos wherein silence may be the only honest option for anybody trying to be truthful. Endless wars abroad mirrored in mass murders at home, widening and deepening violence epitomized in looming environmental death of the planet coupled with nuclear holocaust, make me—and a multitudes of others—sleepless, anxious, and despairing.

In Spring 2019, I am a ninety-five-year-old great grandmother who worries that elders are leaving their kids a world rapidly going to hell; while I look, critically, at myself trying to figure out what I mean when I call myself an outlier … a nonviolent cultural/political revolutionary.

Looking at me empathically yet with a scholarly optic, Atiba Rougier—a three-generations-younger Caribbean male—thought about his own inheritance: African origin, slavery, colonial exploitation by Spanish, French, British, Americans … along with nurturing grandmothers whom he remembers weeping at injustice, trying as a child to lift their spirits by painting their toenails. He wondered about one great grandmother ... how did she keep going? In addition to the miseries of all subordinated people ... she was blind.

Intrigued by my cultural research of African origins and the ways of being African migrants took with them out of Africa ... he thought about my personal story. In the Summer of 1968, after a very odd collision with a wall in the desert of a car full of Berkeley radicals given up as dead, I recovered/plunged into intense political activism. Fired from SF State in 1969, my contract subsequently unrenewed at the Stanford women's center, forced to resign at CIIS in 2011, bereft after Wally died in 2012, Atiba concluded: I write to live and live to write.

CHAPTER 14

Suppressed traumatic memories rising to
consciousness and unexpected illuminations

❦

ally and I were both committed to peace, yet violence has scarred our lives. There are memories I have tried to suppress ...

The last decade of Wally's life was marred by a recurring sickness that doctors were unable to diagnose. Only after his passing have I realized that the undiagnosable sickness was probably radiation poisoning ... a subject thrust out of discussion by the dominant paradigm.

Although he was a peaceful experimental nuclear physicist committed to peaceful application of nuclear energy—using oil emulsions (not explosions) to measure the mass of the meson—Wally was exposed, for seven decades, to nuclear physics experiments emitting radiation.

On our way to the 1968 conference at Ann Arbor, Michigan to support the Peace and Freedom Party's nonviolence presidential candidate Dick Gregory, our auto full of Berkeley radicals crashed into a wall in the desert. The driver was unharmed, but the young editor of *Modern Utopian*, in the passenger seat, was killed. I was asleep in the back seat. Newspaper photos of the demolished car conveyed all occupants were dead. My bank, believing I was dead, shut down my account.

I survived. As discussed earlier, after more than two months in a coma, my rantings, from what Wally, at my bedside deathwatch, later told me, tapped the story in my preconscious awareness of Lucia of Syracuse. Lucia, the woman on an African migration path whose uncodified Jewish beliefs (later called Christian) were branded as Pagan by the Holy Roman empire whose soldiers (I later learned) killed her in a violent sexual murder by thrusting a sword down her throat.

In Fall 1968, after my recovery (and rapid whirlwind tour of West Asia), and back to my then teaching post as Assistant Professor of History at SF State, I joined black students leading the campus revolt against oppression at home and the imperialist war in Vietnam. My classes, teaching African origins of humans and everybody's experience migrating out of Africa, gave vital support to the students' demand for a department of African Studies.

Fired on the day after Thanksgiving 1969, the campus newspaper headlined, "May a thousand Birnbaums bloom!" Later, the Black Students Union of SF State gave me an award for helping to found the first African Studies department in the world. Danny Glover, given the same award, traveled with Bernie Sanders' campaign of stopping economic and political inequality, stopping global heating, and stopping the endless wars of profiting billionaires.

In the late 1970s and early 1980s, while working against inequality in USA and the never-ending wars abroad, at home I sewed patchwork quilts with my grandkids. Preschooler Josh and toddler Sabrina helped me select multi-colored patches of cloth with signifying images. Like grandmothers historically, quilt-making with my grandkids helped keep me sane while everything was shattering.

Looking back, I am trying to find shards of light in the shattering …

During a 1964 party in our Berkeley home, held in celebration of the completion of my doctoral studies, I danced naked behind a bed sheet to the music of African drumming.

In 1967-68, Wally and I helped found the Peace and Freedom Party (P&F), whose platform, then and now, calls out violence institutionalized by cultural/political elites. Violence at home and imperialism, its demon sibling abroad, may be considered toxic signifyers perpetuating notions of inequality, power-over, sexism, homophobia, and aggression against disenfranchised/economically oppressed dark others.

Maddened, some of the exploited-disenfranchised turn their rage on their neighbors. Scholars try to understand this paradoxical behavior. Noam Chomsky, linguistics expert and signifying public intellectual of the world, points to the complicity of both USA political parties perpetuating inequality.[46]

In the 1960s, Wally, a peaceful nuclear physicist, founded Physics International with three other scientists: an Iraqi who in childhood had been beaten as a Jew, a WASP with progressive values, and a romantic Irishman. The company's name aligned physics research, not with the hegemonic elites' geo-political interests that were destroying the planet, but with scientists across borders helping to create a peaceful green world.

In 1967-68, Wally and I, and a host of other people, helped put the third political party, Peace and Freedom, on the ballot. Wally, its fundraising chair, arranged for bagels and lox to be sold at rock concerts; while Mike Allen, a black radio announcer/musicologist, with Lucia, nonviolent history professor, were its press secretaries, writing and sending mimeographed news releases to kindred movements around the world from P&F headquarters, which was a little shack across the street from Berkeley High School.

In Summer 1968, Wally and I traveled to my ancestral country where millions of Italian revolutionaries in the streets, including feminists whose banners proclaimed, "There is no revolution without women's liberation. There is no women's liberation without revolution." This resonates in me and in a host of people the world over to this day, with nonviolent revolutionary beliefs and in identification with dark others, notably women.[47] After I recovered from the car crash, Wally took our nine-year-old Stefan and me to the Levant and interior of West Asia, where third world poverty slammed into my remaining illusions about USA geopolitics. Returning to teaching at SF State, I immediately went on strike with students against the imperial USA war in Vietnam and for a department of African Studies. For which, I was fired.

Today, trying to access this period of my life is very painful. Death was present not only in my near-death experience, but in the murders of Malcolm X, President John F. Kennedy, his brother Robert Kennedy, and Martin Luther King, Jr. The police riot at the Democratic Convention of 1968, the election of Richard Nixon, and the continuing carnage unleashed by USA in regime changes throughout the world are painful to recall.

In the summers of the 1970s, I participated in the feminist movement in Italy while Wally was elsewhere in Europe giving workshops on his sub-atomic physics research ... research with a large implication for non-linear thinking. Today, our son Stefan calls his father an ultimate Taoist.

In this chapter, I am suggesting the simultaneity of the past~present~future, a truth glimpsed by musicians, scientists, artists, writers, dark others, and other people (whose fifty shades of black fade to many shades of light flesh tones called white), while transmitting inchoate primordial knowing, historic suppressed knowledge, and the liminal truth known to lovers—of all kinds—for whom falling in love, living in love, generates energies renewing life.

The renewal of life is evident in the uncorrupted wisdom of babies, in the nurturing of mothers, but also in the nurturing of fathers, grandfathers, grandmothers, great grandmothers, sisters, brothers, uncles, aunts, cousins—people of all colors, all ages, all genders, all family roles, all climes—everybody helping to bend the spiral toward life—birthing, blossoming, harvesting, seeding, dying, renewing life.

Earlier I told the story of my signifying island in the African Mediterranean: Sicily. A tale of climate heating in 10,000 BCE separating Sicily from the mother continent Africa … an island of close encounters of humans in diasporas out of Africa: notably Berbers of Africa and Semitic Canaanites (later called Phoenicians) sailing from the Levant in West Asia, who founded trading settlements all around the ancient known world.

Spiraling fast forward to Spring 2011, the African people of Carthage—today's Tunisia in Africa across from Sicily—heralded the "Arab Spring," toppled a dictator, and founded a new nation with a democratic constitution. This indigenous movement was choked by unelected USA neo-liberal elites imposing their ideological notions on other people.[48] Other outside interventions by the West—notably the USA in the Middle East, Africa, Asia, and elsewhere—led to enormous suffering dramatized in migrations fleeing war, famine, persecution, bombings, and political chaos …

In 2017-19, boats of desperate migrants try to reach shores of another country. In the boat, everyone has to stay steady or else the boat will capsize … and often has. Turned away from unwelcoming countries in fiscal austerity crises, refugees live in communal camps where everyone takes responsibility for the survival of everyone. In 2018, a caravan of desperate people from Central America wended its way to the southern border of USA.

Simultaneously, suicidal mass murders everywhere leave devastated communities where people mourn but care for each other. In late August 2017, as floods raged in Texas and Louisiana, I watched people helping each other, with bigotries blown away. Spontaneous caring and sharing was dramatically evident in Las Vegas in the largest massacre in USA history … and in Sutherland Springs, Texas, people were giving their lives to save others.

In 2015, two women of Spain, on sites of African migrations in Spain (Barcelona and Madrid), were elected mayors who are committed to stopping austerity measures that target the vulnerable. Stopping banks and other hegemonic institutions from taking the homes and food from poor people, these women, other dark others, stepped into the new paradigm … where everybody is responsible for survival/thrival of everybody. In 2017, the fight for Catalan independence has thrown all insurgencies into the Spanish political cauldron, stirring memories of the 1930s fight against fascism that has never been forgotten.[49]

❧❧❧❧❧

In 1993, my *Black Madonnas, Feminism, Religion, and Politics in Italy* was published in USA, then in Bari, Italy in 1997, the year *Black Madonnas* won the international Valetutti (name means "everyone has value") award honoring spiritual/political values of justice and equality of the New Left of the world.

In 1995, my talk in Gen Vaughan's Gift Economy delegation in the international women's conference in Beijing, China was accompanied by listening to world delegates … this deepening was reflected in my book, *Dark Mother: African Origins and Godmothers* (2001).

In the late 1990s, Elinor Gadon invited me to teach in the Women's Spirituality program she founded at CIIS.

In 2003, Mara Keller, following Gadon as Director, cited me a founder of the program in Women's Spirituality.

In 2007, I was again a delegate in Gen Vaughan's Gift Economy Panel of World Social Forum in Nairobi, Africa. I was invited to speak in Europe, Africa, Australia, and USA; my beliefs deepened/widened … as evident in my book written when I cared for Wally while he was dying, *The Future Has an Ancient Heart*, 2012 (Revised edition, 2013).

Then and now, the authenticity of all institutions, in my view, including programs in feminist spirituality, may be measured by how genuinely democratic they are, in the sense of how inclusive they are … not only as multicultural teachers, but as ways of teaching~learning~enhancing life, including public stands opposing USA aggrandizing wars, and participating in inclusive projects looking to a better world. Most important, in my view, is removing violence from all institutions of USA … first by aligning programs in women's spirituality with diverse spiritualities of the world.

In 2019, I recognize what a pain in the posterior I must have been. I would quote Lord Acton to program administrators in Women's Spirituality who believed they were simply doing their jobs following historical hierarchical academic precedents: "Power tends to corrupt, and absolute power corrupts absolutely."

As a human being as well as a history teacher, I believe all institutions—church, state, culture, family, the political economy, academia—and all humans need checks and balances. As a cultural/political revolutionary, I hold that women's spirituality programs are not authentic unless they respect, study, and include all spiritualities of the world. All leaders are implicitly teachers who need to be transparent about their beliefs. Teachers, writers, politicians, everyone in a just political economy should be open about the unspoken premises that underlie their research/political policies.

In 2011, as Wally was dying and while world violence was in a deadly downward spiral, I was writing the 2012 edition of *The Future Has an Ancient Heart: Legacy of Caring, Sharing, Healing, and Vision from the Primordial African Mediterranean to Occupy Everywhere*. I beheld a vision: black birds in a "V" flight formation suddenly turning, giving me the sudden hope that the violent story of Western civilization had taken a new direction.

At high noon September 4, 2012, Wally passed away ... coinciding with my glimpsing of transformative possibilities in the nonviolent and radically democratic Occupy movement for justice in Oakland and New York, in which many of our grandkids participated.

CHAPTER 15
Story telling

꙳ꙮ꙳

For fifty years—half a century—Wally and I explored our roots on-site across the world while creating our family pear tree with Semitic ~ Sicilian branches rooted in Africa, whose migrants out of Africa reached everywhere.

In our Berkeley home we planted an ever-changing garden: birthing ~ blossoming ~ harvesting seeds ~ dying ~ new life. Before Wally died, every springtime doves flew from the south to nest in the eaves of our roof. After he died, the birds stopped coming. In Spring-Summer 2017, the doves returned, building nests again in our eaves, this time hiding them. In Spring 2019, birds are trying to build a nest in our mailbox.

Trying to be holistic, simultaneously a mother~grandmother~great grandmother~teacher~writer, I encourage everyone to find their own roots, to tell their own stories expressed in the many ways of creating art ... playing, dancing to music, stringing necklaces, cooking, dreaming, writing. In my case, creating, bringing up, and nurturing kids who are politically opposing violence in all its shapes, writing/living my own story, and being grateful.

꙳ꙮ꙳

Story telling began when ancient poets told stories of the world's origin. Everybody's stories have always been lived, yet scribes of dominant cultures, up until recently, wrote stories focused on dominant elites. Challengers of dominant elites regard this exclusion of stories of the vanquished as one of the ways white supremacy is perpetuated.

Since the 1960s, people of subordinated cultures—women, subaltern ethnic groups, the colonized of the world, all the marginalized and vulnerable ... led by Africans and migrants in the African diaspora whose stories date from before time began—have insisted on telling their own stories in art, handicrafts, cooking, and a myriad of ways.

Transformation, for me, taps everybody's ageless spiritual wisdom while envisioning the future while acknowledging that everybody/everything is perpetually changing while deepest beliefs persist. Keeping our deepest beliefs and acting on them to make the world better is like dancing … performed alone, with a partner, or with many partners.

Established stories of USA and elsewhere in the West, begin, not with primordial origins and diasporas from Africa, but with the story of the European discovery of America in 1492 … obliviating the truthful story: first invaders occupied a land already inhabited by Natives, whom they killed or forcibly converted to Christianity, while kidnapping people from Africa and bringing them to the New World after 1619 to work the land as slaves.

In the established story, the founding fathers of USA, colonists of England, declared their independence and formed a new nation conceived in liberty and "with liberty and justice for all." The story does not mention that liberty and justice were unavailable to those who were subordinated—conquered natives, slaves, indentured servants, women—and does not acknowledge that the political economy of USA was built on stolen land, profits of the slave trade, and by exploiting lashed and sweated labor of slaves stolen from Africa enslaved in New World. That, with the cotton gin (USA industrialized slavery) that has been the cruelest time in the history of the world.

The empire of USA was built on stealing land on American continents already inhabited by Natives, lands then enlarged by purchasing land from other European countries, land they had also stolen from Natives. For example, Jefferson's purchase from France of a large land mass called the Louisiana Purchase. Americans expanded their slave empire by killing/removing Natives from their ancestral lands. Andrew Jackson, father of right-wing populism (whose portrait hangs in the Trump White House), was revered in his time as a great "Indian Killer," forcing Natives to leave their lands.

The first slave ship arrived in the Caribbean in 1619, while the Inquisitors in Europe were torturing/burning humans for their beliefs. In 1846, just as the debate over slavery in USA was heating to a boil, dominant slave-holding patriots declared a war (see previous discussion) for "Liberty" against Mexico (who had already abolished slavery). The war ended with USA taking the southwest part of USA where Mexicans lived, thereby acquiring more land to expand slavery. A few years later civil war came.

In the mysterious ways that history spirals, Lincoln freed the slaves during USA civil war while the empire of USA was enlarged by William H. Seward, a member in Lincoln's cabinet, who purchased Alaska from the Russians. Civil war over slavery put the engine of the industrial revolution (e.g., manufacturing guns) in full throttle, speeding to the present when USA is a major arms manufacturer, a great vendor of weapons for the endless wars of the world.

In the 1880s, USA became a continental empire connected by railroads built by Chinese workers. Not thanked for building the railroads, Chinese immigration was stopped by the Chinese Exclusion Act of 1887.

The industrial revolution in USA was dominated by industrial titans called Robber Barons who founded the elite schools of today (e.g., Stanford University).

In 1898, USA annexed Hawaii and the Spanish-American war expanded the continental empire of USA to the Caribbean and Philippines—whose indigenous peoples fought back but were defeated, becoming colonies of the USA empire.

In 1945, USA ended world war II by dropping atomic bombs on people of Japan … USA became the most dangerous empire in human history.

After 1945, USA founded "intelligence" institutions like the CIA that worked secretly to kill any opposition to the expansion of USA empire, and built hundreds of military bases throughout the world. USA cold war with Soviet Russia, competition with China, USA dominance of NATO in Europe, other regional military and economic pacts, in effect, assured USA world hegemony girded by the history of USA using nuclear bombs in 1945 on Japanese people and subsequent monopoly of nuclear bombs.

After 1945, wars on "terror" have sustained USA leadership of the West in a nuclear arms race that scientists warn is headed to mutual destruction of humans and the earth. The 2019 clock of the Bulletin of Atomic Scientists ticks very close to midnight: annihilation of earth and all life.

❧❧❧❧❧❧

Simultaneously, in counterpoint, people's liberation uprisings and movements against nuclear weapons/environmental destruction of the globe, have been growing—notably the emergence of peoples of the world who in 2016 came together in a climate world pact in Paris to halt the hurtle toward death of the planet.

The rise of subaltern classes of the world include all the historically silenced: women, heretics, prophets, and those who were persecuted/raped/killed for remembering the earth was not always characterized by wholesale raping and killing or by smashing 99% of the world's peoples into fear, starvation, death …

Women have always figured in historical risings against domination. The difference today is that women have taken the leadership ... not by women who are aligned with dominating classes but by women who are, or identify with, the suppressed of the earth.[50] This is concurrent with energies of heretics and prophets of all genders/persuasions heating uprisings from below.[51]

In this contemporary period of accelerating energy from suppressed peoples, all my previous learning seems to be coming together. Primordial peoples of the Bantu tribe in eastern Africa have always lived peacefully. Marijah Gimbutas' research that Old Europe (south and southeast Europe) venerated women deities. Genevieve Vaughan's research that gifting in history has been associated with mothers. Subordinated ethnic feminist writers pointing out that peaceful life-enhancing movements of the past have, indeed, made a healing transformative difference.

In 2015, people in the World Social Forum in Tunisia, Africa—originally connected with Sicily, which is today separated from the African continent by only a few kilometers—reminded the world that life and death decisions cannot continue to be left to a small world oligarchy led by a few men.

A fraction of 1% of USA population and 62 billionaires of the world manipulate the world economy, making decisions affecting everybody on earth, as well as torturing and killing in genocidal wars against dark others widening into the hell of drone bombers killing anybody ... hastening looming nuclear, environmental, political, and economic catastrophes.[52]

⚜⚜⚜

I fell out of logic into poetry.

> Riddles, or paradoxes, hover over logic-defying
> ways that humans evolve

> We live today in massive drought, torrential rains,
> shattering earthquakes, breath-taking pollution
> huge snowstorms, rising waters
> destroying humans and all life

> Robot drones whose buttons are pushed by technocrats in
> California, kill anyone across world

> ... yet glimpses of human nurturing/resisting and a flood of
> truthful stories erode fraudulent official reports/deceptive histories

> while caring, sharing, healing bloom in likely

and unlikely places across the world …

Podemus in Spain … Occupy in Hong Kong and Paris …

People rising against client governments of USA

in Central and South America, Asia, Europe, Africa

Black youth in USA creating a signifying movement Black Lives
Matter with world resonance

Harvard students early demanded divestment of the elite
university's endowment from
money generated by fossil fuel mining

Converging with very large world environmental
movement led by indigenous peoples

2017 huge counter movement resisting all elites
in populist surges across the world

While pope from barrios of South America upturns
history of canonical Catholicism,
citing evidence of scientists on global heating, identifying the
church with the poor of the earth, yet beset by mounting evidence
of priests' sexually assaulting kids, nuns

USA president singing Amazing Grace at memorial of
Black survivors of massacre
while forgiving white murderer demonized by drugs

… while on Western slope of our garden
Paleolithic Norfolk Pines thrive
succulent century plants bloom riotously orange

our wolf mail box sticks out tongue for the mail … wolf ears alert/
owl eyes spiraling backward ~ sidewise-swooping

while signifying icons in our garden and courtyard persist—
African Sekhmet, Asian Buddha, European St. Francis, Einstein,
Green Man, Black Madonnas

black birds look at me … I look at them

CHAPTER 16

Living to write and writing to live ~ Heartened by gift givers

※

n 2018, these gift giving signifyers come to mind: Jan Parker, Karen Nelson Villanueva, Remi Omodele, Latonia Dixon, Patti Davis, Gian Banchero, Alice Waters, Molefi Asante, Luisah Teish, Bernadette Muthien, Giuseppe Goffreddo, Simona Mafai, Dacia Maraini, Deborah Santana, In Hui, Vivian Deziak, Shannon Reich, May Elawar, Tricia Grame, Ida Dunson, Carolyn Stokes, Vicki McGee, Mary Beth Moser, Mary Saracino, Sandy Miranda, Rob Robinett, Chickie Farella, Marguerite Rigoglioso, the late Kalli Rose Halvorson, Heaven Walker, Elisabeth Sikie, Marion DuMont, Elizabeth Fisher, Yana Womack, Laura Truxler, Sara Salazar, Sandra Schnabel, Mary Louise Stone, Marilyn Nebolsky, Laura Amazzone, Leslene della Madre, Lisa Christie, Arisika Razak, Mara Keller, Necia Desiree Harkless, Matthew Fox, Mary Pat Ziolkoski, Joyce Brady, Patricia O'Luanaugh, Suzanne Giro, Stacy Boorn, Louisa Calio, Barbara Ardinger, Renate Sadrozinski, Anne Bouie, Barbara Witt, Renate Holub, Larry DiStasi, Clark Blasdell … my contemporary healers: Amy, Susan, Linda …

Women in my feminist study groups, particularly Women & Work, each of whom courageously work as women scholars/sentient humans to transform the world: Ruth, Celeste, Renate S., Rita, Clare, Clair, Maresi, Alison, Joan, Remi, Marge, Bev, Anne, Glenna, Cecile; and W & W sisters who have passed: Pat Cody, Sydney Carson, Estelle Jelinek, Dorothy Bryant.

My late biological sister and brother are part of me. Joie Mellenbruch sang "Bewitched, Bothered, and Bewildered" while she encouraged her three caring and musical sons—Lance, Kevin, and Fred—to find their authentic musical notes. Before she died in January 2015, she e-mailed me, "You've finally found your voice!" In uncanny ways, Joie transmitted ancient and historic insights to kindred spirits (notably Joyce Houston who nurtured Joie when she was passing), to her siblings Louie and me, to her kids, and to her grandkids, Kristian & Katy Jo (who today calls herself Cat Joie).

Joie loved her three sons equally, mothered me her older sister, and with Louie, our beloved younger brother, helped form the woman I am today. My sister's story is expressed in the music of her three sons.

My brother Louis Chiavola, whose birthday is on the same day as mine, five years later, is a continuing presence for his kids and everybody who loved him. He is as close to a saint as we are likely to know. He was a living inspiration to his kids Robert & Patty, Jan, Sharon, Kathy, Steve, Lori, Dena, and Jimmie. At Louie's funeral, balloons were released; some balloons were caught by branches of a tree reluctant to let him go.

He worked the midnight shift, heat treating in a steel mill, so he could be home daytimes for his kids, all of whom transmit his caring, sharing, creativity to their kids and grandkids. The last years of Louie's life were lifted by his love for Lonnie—they were an iconic couple of Kansas City, Kansas. Lonnie brought her kids and Louie's kids into a blended family. Louie's extended family came to grieve when he passed, dark others of Kansas City, Kansas.

Among kindred spirits with whom I have shared transformational in-between space …

Jean Rosenthal Harris, of Semitic Palestinian heritage, born in Iowa, writer of Walnut Creek, Yiddishkeit heretic.

Ruth Rosen, who wrote the signifying book on feminism, *The World Split Open*, sent me an e-mail in 2014: "The future has a Lucia Chiavola Birnbaum heart." Ruth and I, members of Women & Work, the oldest feminist group of Berkeley, support our intellectual/personal sisters while trying to find our particular paths.

Four of us in Women & Work who have passed: Pat Cody, signifying elder for all Berkeley spirits … Estelle Jelinek, pioneer in the African American struggle, who took her own life … Sydney Carson, who left us in August 2017, kept high scholarly standards through her last years of sickness and pain … Dorothy Calvetti Bryant, who passed in January 2018, an Italian American writer who has been a beacon for me.

The remaining members of Women & Work: Joan, who early gave us a model of feminist leadership. Rachel who transmutes remission from a lethal disease into helping everyone. Beverly, whose personal life is incredibly heroic, stays in academia taking on controversial teaching and traveling to Palestine. Renate S. lives her name, reborn. Rita, whose scholarship/activism is grounded working in the United Nations. Alison, our youngest, has just edited a monumental book on midwives. Marge, my long-ago student at SF State, has taught me a great deal as we whirl in similar~different generational spirals toward the future. Remi, who focuses on gifts from Africa. Claire K, writer/political activist may be our most mysterious member; she reminds me that we may be on the cusp. Maresi, who now lives elsewhere but her model as teacher/scholar continues to inspire us. Marcia, who transmutes scriptures into poetry, gifts us with seeing something very familiar, differently.

Other kindred spirits: Mary Beth, Annette, In Hui, Marguerite, Sandy, Chickie, Karen, Jan, Tricia, May, Vivian, Marilyn, Shannon, Randy C, and David. All live in transformative spaces, illuminating the underneath meaning of the words of this book.

All my kin are part of me, especially those recently passed: three others named Lucia, and Tina, a signifying cousin who was a principal in our deep story.

Wanda, the remaining matriarch of the Chiavola clan. Teresa Jo, archivist of the Cipolla clan. Kathy Chiavola, is my Celt~Cathar~Sicilian signifying cousin who today sings Bluegrass.

A gift bouquet of nieces and nephews include my sister Joie's kids, Freddie Lee & Linda, Kevin, and Lance and his kids; my brother Louis' kids, mentioned above, particularly Robert & Patty who lost their home in the Paradise fire; Stella & Norman's kids, Nancy & Phil and dog Lucy; Neal & Linda's kids, Jennifer, Lauren & Jay & Lily Harper (my bonus gift grandniece); Wally's sister Elsa and her kids, Maria & Andy and their kids, and Jill & Ron and their kids … in our expanding extended family, including my sister grandmother Marcia and her kids and grandkids, in addition to ones she and I share: Jake & Abi & Andrew & Emma Lia, Courtney & Matt & Izzy.

My life signifyers include democratic leftists across the world who gave me the international Valetutti prize in 1997 for *Black Madonnas* … and spiritual progressives of religious and ethnic groups who may also be heretics/prophets: the Berrigan brothers, Michael Fox of Creation Spirituality, and Michael Lerner of Spiritual Progressives.

Bill Barlow, who led the student revolution at SF State in the 1960s … Barbara Davidson, there at the beginning of our journey who reminds me today that the point has always been what is fair … Peter Shapiro, student revolutionary, then postman, who walks his principles … Clarence Walker, retired dean of Humanities, who lives his beliefs.

Gifts of my kin and kindred are especially dear to me in 2017-19 as crises multiply along with the nagging painful undertow of knowing that nobody can avoid the very painful awareness that all of us are living on icebergs rapidly melting and on earthquake faults already imploding, waiting for the big one. We are in an endgame of blind desperate wars in the Middle East and Africa. The oppression in USA and elsewhere is instigated by elites, some of whom may have begun their careers as left-outs but who now, sensing they are in peril, desperately use their power to stay in power by starting wars, inciting retaliation, and furthering demoralization at home. Desperate people commit mass murders, exposing themselves to their own death, while radiation and polluted air and water carry death everywhere.

In an irony conveying death pang humor, publicists finding themselves in a crumbling patriarchy are at a loss how to market my books; they choose headline, "Feminist dedicates book to her husband!" Elites of the dominant violent culture, hanging onto their jobs, purvey conscious or unconscious moral disarray while they drain words of meaning. A professional male reviewer for a library journal was reduced to calling me a "reactionary progressive," and my book, *The Future Has an Ancient Heart*, a "strange brew," evoking a witch riding broomstick.

Lydia Ruyle's spirit banner dedicated to me honors all the women persecuted as witches who have been murdered or who have killed themselves in despair.

CHAPTER 17

Science and religion are both myths,
but myths are far from signifying nothing ...
George Santayana, Scepticism and Animal Faith

※

George Santayana, my signifying philosopher, whose name remembers an ancient woman called Anna of Africa and Middle East, lived in USA at beginning of the 20th century, but died in Italy. His message: skepticism about dominant beliefs in science and religion while respecting what he called animal faith and what I call the unconscious, preconscious, liminal glimpses in consciousness.

※

Humans are more than logical beings. For me, being human means everybody is responsible for life ... along with knowing that, however persuasive your truth is to you, all truths are conditioned by genes and by experience. Each of us works out—unconsciously, preconsciously, consciously—how we find our truth. In healthy societies, constantly evolving institutions provide checks and balances ... every human figures out their own evolving mixture of feelings, beliefs, and myths—signifyers of their truth.

※

Responsible scholars, like Jan Parker in her 2016 CIIS doctoral dissertation[53], recognize the imperative of speaking openly about pervasive bodily rape in the dominant myths and reality of the world. For organic scholars of the West, bodily rape was accompanied by spiritual rape of the poor, humiliated, and vulnerable, whose stories are silenced—or smothered in statistics—by agents of dominant politic and cultural institutions.

I thought about the historical context of my deep story. In the transformative 1960s, trying to uncover submerged knowledge, the younger generation and hitherto silenced cultural minorities asked themselves and others, "Where are you coming from?"

Lucia Chiavola Birnbaum

Trained as a historian in the decades when history in the West was considered a social science whose positivist first stages left out anything uncountable or unmeasurable, I analyzed and tried to fix times and places. From Wally and Einstein, I learned that the observer/observed are both constantly changing in constantly changing time and space. In graduate school, a colleague described our study of history as a "jelly sandwich nailed to the wall."

For my evolving epistemological perspectives, I am indebted to more than a decade of researching and writing a doctoral dissertation on the intellectual, cultural, and social history of the social sciences, and adapting Behaviorism as a particular case in the history of psychology.[54] Trying to be objective, not subjective, I tried to keep myself out of the story I was writing about a Southern Baptist trained for the Protestant ministry who became a psychologist.

Today, aware of the significance of submerged beliefs, I see Watson's behaviorist psychology as an outsider trained for the Baptist ministry who aimed to destroy the major spiritual belief of Liberal Protestants: idea of God in consciousness. This is a long story going back to classical imperial Greeks in 5th century BCE, and perpetuated in subsequent decades in different guises up to the agents of contemporary neo-liberalism.

The former southern Baptist disrupted the established secular discipline of Psychology which, before modernity, was called study of the soul. In 1913, John Broadus Watson upturned the main premise— consciousness—of dominant WASPs declaring: there is no consciousness—in the scientific laboratory, all that is observable are fear, rage, and sex.

The backdrop for Watson's manifesto was a cresting of the Progressive reform movement whose leaders, after a string of social and economic reforms, looked for a way to connect science with "social control" of the 1912 tide of "new immigrants"—Jews, Sicilians, Slavs, other dark others. This desire updated the history of USA kidnapping Africans into slavery … enclosing defeated Natives from whom land was stolen … disenfranchising black people legally freed during the USA civil war whose civil rights were denied afterward … plus peoples annexed by USA in Hawaii, in the Philippines, and in Central America, after the 1898 Spanish-American war.

In 1913, others in USA included "imbeciles" in the highly regarded eugenics movement wherein dominant whites blithely discussed "extermination" of unintelligent imbeciles, while considering themselves a superior intelligent caste of white people with conscious intelligence motivated by religion and idealism.

For these Progressives, who inspired subsequent reformers of the New Deal up to contemporary neo-liberals, unconscious fear of dark others may have accompanied earlier laudable attempts to better the lives of those Progressives considered less fortunate.

With my contemporary optic, Progressives (1900-1914) unconsciously melded color with race in their unarticulated anxieties about dark others … creating a category including anarchists whose belief in self-government threatens autocratic elites in any society. During world war I, this anxiety came to the surface after the Bolshevik Revolution of 1917. Hysterical fear swept dominant elites who jailed the socialist presidential candidate Eugene Debs, destroyed the offices of the political left and labor unions, and deported anarchists. In the 1920s, fear of dark others was made palpable by a resurgence of the Ku Klux Klan. In 1924, the year Lucia & Wally were born, fear of dark others was institutionalized in immigration restriction laws targeting people from south and southeast Europe.

Spiraling back to 1913, dominant WASP elites concerned about new immigrants saw great possibilities in Behaviorism for what they called social control: conditioning fear, rage, and sex to whatever beliefs the dominant white elite wanted dark others—Blacks, Browns, Sicilians, poor Jews, Slavs, anybody suspicious—to believe.

In the late 1920s, after Watson made it clear that behaviorist psychology referred to everybody, elite psychologists distanced themselves from Watson's "puerile" psychology. Calling themselves "enlightened behaviorists," they implicitly retained consciousness for themselves while considering stimulus-response psychology handy for conditioning the masses. In a historical pattern dating from the beginning of the Common Epoch, upwardly rising others sought security by joining the elite establishment.[55]

I spent ten years (1954 to 1964) writing my dissertation on Behaviorism, without considering the personal implications of my study of how elites control the masses. A signifying case of the success of USA education, I did not realize, while writing my dissertation, that my study of elite manipulation of beliefs of those assumed to be inferior masses was about me, a Sicilian immigrant daughter, and about Wally, a Jewish immigrant son.

Later, I considered this historical context. The conditioning beliefs of the masses, earlier a progressive notion in USA to manipulate beliefs of inferior classes, but after 1945 was taken up by dominant political elites—against a backdrop of the cold war with Soviet Russia—to condition everybody in USA against socialism and communism. Imposing the myth that USA was a case of exceptionalism in world history. Americans, unlike everybody else, upheld democracy at home and abroad. As a logical inference of this established paradigm, USA was to democratize the world, first by ridding the world of terrorists who destabilized the status quo, then by installing democratic regimes, defined as regimes friendly to USA capitalist elites' economic and political interests.

This established myth of USA exceptionalism hid the thrust of USA for world dominance, including manipulating regime changes across the globe, controlling domestic and international media, installing uncounted nuclear bases and black op sites for enhanced interrogation (torture) ... for those who threaten the hegemonic rule of USA.

I am trying to track when I consciously started to realize that I had spent ten years researching and writing a dissertation whose historical backdrop was populated by eugenicists who considered my Sicilian grandparents, parents, and me (Sicilian granddaughter), a subordinated imbecile class to be exterminated ... as were Wally's Jewish grandparents, parents, and himself. During world war II, Nazis in Germany admired and studied USA eugenicists before they murdered six million Jews.

While trying to reconstruct why Wally and I became flaming political activists for equality and justice by the early 1960s, in addition to the rapid surge of events in the Black Liberation struggle and world uprisings, I think now our bonding must have tapped dynamic energies from our unconscious inchoate knowing: we were African in origin, whose ancestors migrated out of Africa leaving memories in our preconscious, embers in consciousness that flamed our political activism.

From 2017-2019, I've been trying to understand our instantaneous bonding ~ simultaneous identification with dark others. I found this cannot be logically articulated. What I do know is we fell in love, and created three sons who brought home three daughters who gave us grandchildren and great grandchildren, a family extended by kindred spirits. This grounded/enabled us to see more clearly, giving us the courage to act more boldly because we gave each other unquestioned support while we nurtured our kids ... we supported all of the vulnerable of the human family.

Wally's and my shared deep beliefs in everybody's African origins led to exploring our roots on-site across the world, giving us personal experiential confirmation of scientific evidence that we, like everybody else, were ultimately black and African, whose historic migrations spiraled out of Africa into Asia, Europe, Africa, and USA.

By the 1970s, our world explorations were accompanied by my trying to figure out what motivated Italian feminists … to whom I immediately gravitated when visiting their home sites. I consciously wondered why their grandmothers were so passionate about black madonnas.

Simultaneously, I studied the writings of Antonio Gramsci who lived in Sardinia, an island adjacent to Sicily. Gramsci, 20th century founder of the Italian Communist Party, helps me understand why Italian communists differed from Stalinist communists. The dwarfed and hunch-backed Sardinian transformed positivist Marxism into everyday beliefs of ordinary people, which are evident in daily and celebratory folklore rituals enacting justice and equality.

A subversive outlier, Gramsci in his writings, in guarded language under the eyes of censors, implied that religious and secular elites historically have tried to inculcate their beliefs into subaltern others … yet subordinated people, despite the elite's efforts to control their beliefs, persisted in keeping deep beliefs in justice and equality in everyday and celebratory rituals in many ways.

Subaltern beliefs in justice and equality, Gramsci suggested, are uncovered by organic scholars who know themselves, and who know the historical context of their beliefs. In my case, studying Gramsci on subaltern beliefs converged with my continuing study of depth psychology, notably the insights of Freud and Jung on the power of the unconscious … fitting very well with my study of Marx on dynamic long economic trends in history. This convergence of beliefs, against a backdrop of USA imperial activities abroad and discriminatory practices at home, had something to do with energizing my political activities—as well as that of many others—in the 1960s continuing to the present in 2019.

Wally and I lived our deep beliefs, trying to stop the massive murder of war and everyday violence of injustice and inequality. As a physicist, Wally tried to keep violent uses of nuclear research out of the hands of USA militarists and imperialists. As a history professor, Lucia challenged the dominant false history of white-washing USA by teaching the true history of killing and aggression against dark others: Natives, African slaves and later freed people who were kept from voting, Asians, Latinos, political dissenters … anybody suspected of beliefs that unsettled the dominant paradigm. This is white supremacy.

We became passionate political activists. Aware that all beliefs are conditioned by genes, family, and education, we tried to be transparent about our own beliefs; nonviolently trying to bend the arc of justice toward a peaceful and thriving planet.

Knowing our own deepest beliefs, as well as taking into account the beliefs of others, may keep everybody from killing other people over their beliefs. Feeling our way toward our shared inclusive beliefs, Wally and I were grounded in knowing our African origin, and our shared African/Asian/Semitic Canaanite/European American deep beliefs.

Wally's world view (I glimpsed it by living in caring, sharing with him for sixty-six years) was formed by largely unconscious inchoate African beliefs from his early study of Hebrew scriptures, Ashkenazi Jewish rituals of his childhood and youth, and his rebelliousness after 1943 when he learned his maternal grandmother had been killed by Nazis.

My world view was formed by a Sicilian childhood grounded on largely unconscious African beliefs, Sicilian folk beliefs, Sefardic Jewish rituals, beliefs of South Europe/Asia, and my outlier view emerging from rebelling against top-down authoritarian instruction in Catholic doctrine.[56] Falling in love, creating three sons, our deepest beliefs resonated in and strengthened each other. After Wally passed, our shared deep beliefs continue to ground and sustain me, strengthened in seeing glimpses of ourselves in our kids, grandkids, great grandkids, and kindred spirits.

Our deepest beliefs were transmitted to us, unconsciously for the most part, in the genetic heritage of our immediate families, and in Wally's case by religious study followed by an excellent college education at the City College of New York in its golden age: the 1930s and early 1940s when refugee Jewish intellectuals from Germany taught there.

My education was capped with a work study scholarship at the University of Kansas City, 1940-1943, a private innovative college also gifted by Jewish professors fleeing Nazi Germany. The University of Kansas City, just three years old when I enrolled in 1940, not only attracted Jews of the brilliant Frankfurt school but other scholars questioning conventional truths. The great Italian American poet and Dante scholar, John Ciardi, stimulated me to ask large questions. Engaged professors of French, Spanish, and later my teachers of the Italian language, gave me a life-long love for languages and cultures enhanced by traveling to Italy every year ...

Participating in Italy's feminist movement after 1969, I learned to understand my ancestral culture not only by studying its history and by learning the language, but by immersing myself in cultural as well as political feminist activities.[57]

Heretics throughout the ages have been beaten and tortured, yet their beliefs have persisted in unconscious as well as preconscious memories, in daily
and celebratory rituals, and glimpsed in visions. Deep beliefs are felt when
playing, listening to, and dancing to music. These deeply felt beliefs, Wally told
me, are the initial "hunches" in scientific hypotheses. For story tellers (and
poets), these deeply felt beliefs lead us to follow wisps and murmurs, seeking
to understand what pulls us. I studied the beliefs of my ancestors expressed
in their art and handicrafts, and widened the boundaries of art and literature
to include every day and celebratory rituals. Researching suppressed cultures,
I learned to be imaginative about what constitutes a "primary source." In the
historic epoch, suppressed truth/wisdom is transmitted in popular dialect,
aphorisms of common sense, blasphemy, stories, and different patterns of
nurturing or giving; helping us understand their nuances and many ways of
knowing—particularly in liminal moments, when visions of possibilities give
us the energy to try to transform our lives and our societies.

I am redundant here as well as elsewhere perhaps because my
primary way of knowing is a spiral constantly curling forward and
back, forward and back,
whose meaning in folklore and history is
taking two steps backward to gather the strength to spring forward.
Historically, for dark others, this has meant many steps backward
sometimes too beaten, for a while, to step forward.
Yet for dark others, including women, seeking to know who we are,
knowing/telling our deep stories can be reservoirs of liminal
knowing and courage.

Our Paleolithic origin in Africa and migration to Asia and Sicily were confirmed when we saw a 70,000 BCE Addaura cave drawing in Palermo in the region of my maternal ancestors, and while visiting an on-site 40,000 BCE African
settlement in the region of my paternal ancestors in southeastern Sicily. Wally's
and my mutual Semitic inheritance was confirmed in West Asian Semitic
Canaanite city states of the Levant, whose mariners explored the known world,
at some point after 1200 BCE, creating peaceful trading posts/settlements in
our mutual ancestral triangular region of southeast Sicily—including the city
of Lucia at Syracuse … my paternal ancestral Ragusa Ibla.

Place names helped us uncover suppressed history. Confirming my African origin, my ancestral paternal site Ragusa was first named Ragusa Nera (Black Ragusa). Dominant elites of colonizing Greeks, then Romans, replaced the African name Ragusa Nera with Ragusa Hera, after the subordinated wife of Zeus-Jupiter, a dominant male deity of hegemonic classes of Greece and Rome.

Subaltern resistance to dominant violent classical male Greek civilization headed by an omnipotent male god is suggested in the current suffix of the name of my ancestral paternal town—Ragusa Ibla—transmitting a diminutive affectionate form of West Asian woman divinity, Cybele, and contracting the first syllable of Isis and the last syllable of *bella*.

Cybele, a signifying black woman, gifted both sides of my lineage. On my father's side in the suffix of my paternal town, Ragusa Ibla. On my mother's side, her maiden name Cipolla is a variant of name Cybele whose folklore meaning is onion, or womb.

Violent salients in Greece (then Rome) of dominant male paradigm were expressed in continual wars that imposed slavery on the conquered. In early Christian epoch, this violent paradigm of the West was adopted by Christian patriarchs aligned with Roman emperors, who subordinated women and slaves in the dominant violent hierarchy of doctrinal Christianity which simply left out subordinated peoples.

Pagan tradition challenged the dominant paradigm of Greece and Rome.[58] Subversive energy in the genetic unconscious and preconscious of every human being gifts everybody, in my hypothesis, with possibilities for a better world.

The dominant violent paradigm of the West, aligned with Christianity, divided people into the saved and the damned. This belief was later used to justify the Western European slave trade of kidnapping Africans and enslaving them in the New World ... later justified the cruel industrialized slavery of the USA ... later justified domestic and foreign aggression against dark others and women ... and later justified hierarchical violence of unchecked and unbalanced capitalism to the present, wherein the bottom line of profit justifies the destruction of the world environment and all living creatures, and the exploitative capitalist way of life takes the world to the brink of extinction of all life.

Four decades ago in 1968, after I recovered from the near-death collision in the desert, Wally and I and nine-year-old Stefan traveled together to West Asia, in today's Yugoslavia. Wally led Stefan and me on a rigorous hike at high noon on the ramparts of Dubrovnik. On this trip into West Asia we traveled to Pec, where third world poverty crashed into Western elites' idealization of classical Greek culture, the high culture that included the cruel wars subordinating peoples of the Peloponnesus, Troy, elsewhere.

The legacy of the violent paradigm of Classical Greece—dividing humans into a dominant class of free people living on the sweated labor of unpaid and raped slaves—was a system of power-over characterized by myths of gamboling goddesses (raped goddesses) and rape of actual women. Slaves in Classical Greece—and those considered "terrorists" by the West today in 2019—were/are tortured to extract the truth.

The consequence of the classical Greek paradigm of power-over, based on slave labor and other humiliated labor, became a legacy of cultural rape of dark others from whom their true stories have been violently wrested.

All this is visible today in the aggression epitomized in the almost ritual killings of black men and women on the streets of USA, by police trained in institutionalized violence on the black underclass, sustaining the dominant institutions of violent white male political, cultural, and economic supremacy.

Yet another legacy has come down to us from migrants out of Africa. Personifying beliefs in a universe created and nurtured by the woman African divinity Maat, embodied in the primordial sound, Ma, the name my eldest son Naury calls me. Primordial sounds Ma and Om became Mom, the name my middle and younger sons, Marc and Stefan, call me.

Belief in a nurturing universe, it is my hypothesis, has remained in our suppressed selves in everybody's genetic unconscious, in varying levels of awareness in our preconscious, glimpsed in consciousness when we care, share, and heal.

In Egypt in the African Mediterranean, these values were personified in Isis and Cybele (contracting the name Isis and the word for beautiful, *bella*), and in my paternal hometown of Ragusa Ibla, an adjective contracting the first and last syllables of Cybele in what grammarians call the Italian language form, a diminutive affectionate pronounced "eeblah."

In the Sicilian/south Italian American culture of my childhood in Kansas City, Missouri, a familiar exclamation of my maternal grandmother, aunts, and mother was Bedda Matri! Bedda is the diminutive affectionate, in Sicilian dialect, of *bella* (beautiful). Bella is the name Tony Demartile calls me. Matri is the Latin plural for mother. Both dominant and subaltern cultures of Sicily and south Italy (both part of the African continent until 10,000 BCE) looked to (and continue to look to, often unconsciously) timeless black and beautiful

Mothers, who after the 10th century CE, in lands of the Roman Empire, were identified in subaltern cultures with black madonnas.

In 2015, Sandy M., just back from Crete, said she never saw so many black madonnas. Stefan, my youngest son who lives with me in my old age, rearranges dozens of icons of black madonnas in our home while I exclaim, "Not in a row!" Yet his moving my treasures around uncovers connections I have not noticed. For example, a black deity (whose provenance I cannot remember) is pregnant with lioness goddess of Africa, thereby scrambling unidimensional history, time, and logic; pointing to the spiral of animal~African~Semitic~Jewish Christian Islamic meanings of beautiful black madonnas. On the sill of the large western window in my bedroom overlooking the Pacific Ocean, Stefan rearranges my icons in a changing tableau. He rearranges photos of his kids, grandkids, and my great grandkids (his *nipoti*, an inclusive Italian word that includes all the vulnerable young) on the divider between the front entry corridor and the tall windows of the living room overlooking the Pacific Ocean.

These many meanings of the beautiful mother, in the mysterious ways of stories, became the cover of my book, *The Future Has an Ancient Heart*. Lydia Ruyle, of German and Russian antecedents (beet farmers), who in USA became feminist scholar, artist, mother, wife, mother, grandmother, painted/sewed banners depicting many world images of beautiful mothers, whom Lydia, in reciprocal nurturing, called "my girls."

Falling into a dispute with my publisher over the book cover for *The Future Has an Ancient Heart*, I wanted a painting of a nude pregnant south Italian woman whose African black nipples the publisher wanted to airbrush into invisibility. I raged, Wally mediated, suggesting Lydia's painting of Cybele for the front cover.

In the truthfulness of art, the cover of my book, *The Future Has an Ancient Heart*, is Lydia's banner: a black woman flanked by animals rising from the sea in an embryo of life nourished by rays of the sun and fertile black earth. The frontispiece of the book keeps my favored image of the human story: a nude, nurturing, pregnant African black mother of south Italy and Sicily. The front matter of the book depicts an African grandmother sheltering a child.

Today, Lydia's banner of the dark mother flies on the midlevel pavilion of our Berkeley home. Her banner is flanked by African mud cloth gifted to me by Luisah Teish—an inclusive African American healer whose first name is a variant of my name Lucia—and by a multi-colored scarf gifted to me on my birthday by granddaughter Jessica Ann Lucia. This granddaughter's middle names honor her grandmothers Ann and Lucia. Ann, harvest goddess/signifying woman who gives everybody fruits and seeds of renewal. Lucia, light emerging from darkness gives everybody a new day of possibilities.

Jessica Ann Lucia is a biologist/radical environmentalist. Jessica & Russell, her love, with whom I share a Scandinavian-Norman cultural legacy, gave the world a wondrous baby, luminous Juliet Lucia Lorraine … born December 16, 2016, in between the traditional Winter Solstice holiday December 12 and December 21 (Gegorian calendar). The three hangings on the mezzanine of our Berkeley home—gifts of Luisah Teish, Lydia Ruyle, and Jessica Ann Lucia—are bordered by the staircase going up to my study. On its banister, I entwined a cloth serpent—similar to the one I sewed, that Wally put in a little red wagon for the birthday of Josh, who named him Snaky.

Josh put Snaky and other cherished possessions on the bed Grandpa Fred carpentered, where he slept as a child … where Wally and I slept after our Berkeley house burned down in the fall of 1991.

My Snaky, coiled on the staircase going up to my study where I am writing this in August 2017, may be my half-conscious image of the serpent offering Eve the apple of knowledge. Subaltern Sicilians exclaim, "Santo Diavolo!" (saint devil) …

Hermeneutics of place[59] are suggested in a major historic sanctuary of Cybele located on the African migration path in West Asia at Catal Hoyuk, Anatolia,"land of the mothers" honoring, among others, Ann, goddess of the harvest, who, in the painting of outlier artist Caravaggio, is depicted as the black grandmother of Jesus. This sanctuary at Catal Hoyuk, dated 6500 BCE, was the site in Turkey of an international women's conference in which I participated, and Wally photographed.[60]

On a 2014 gift journey with my family to Sicily, we uncovered a more precise point of our ancestral Semitic Canaanite encounter: a promontory near Palermo at Erice where I found, with the help of our kids (particularly grandson Peter), the black madonna I'd been looking for since Easter 1988 in Trapani, Sicily.

After my deeply emotional Easter experience 1988 in Trapani, Sicily,[61] I returned to the American Academy in Rome where three nights later I was awakened by an apparition of a black madonna—whose face was that of my own mother. Later I associated the apparition with Hindu, Buddhist, and Byzantine black mothers. Three days after I saw the apparition, Wally telephoned to tell me my mother was dying.

Wally always consciously knew his African roots with Asian bloom. We discussed this with our kindred spirit Ida Dunson who shares a similar spiral—African American father / orphaned Chinese American mother—conveyed by Ida in a life marked by resistance to unjust top-down rule and imposed beliefs. (see Ida's poetry in the last chapters of this book).

In the 1970s and 1980s, Wally became a constant traveler in the Nixon-Kissinger initiative to thaw the cold war, as a scientist/entrepreneur in the USA Technology Transfer effort, particularly to China, where Wally felt very much at home. In China, healers were sent to soothe his aching back, and magicians played havoc with his scientific way of knowing. He was impressed by the women chief operating officers in factories, who folded baby diapers while discussing Technology Transfer initiatives between USA and China ... including wheelchairs for the disabled and elderly.

In 1989, Wally went to Tiananmen Square where he heartened Chinese dissidents for democracy. When the Chinese government sent in tanks, some of the demonstrators followed Wally to his hotel room; he counselled them to come back another day. The Chinese government imprisoned the demonstrators. Yet the memory of Tiananmen has persisted in China in dissent against unjust rule to this day.

In the 1970s and 1980s in Italy, I felt a bodily recognition of my African origins, and glimpsed my Asian connection, but did not consciously understand the identification with Asia of our two sons, Marc (Buddhist) and Stefan (Taoist) until the wedding of grandkids Abi & Jake in November 2014, preceded by a signifying art exhibit in New York.

Suggesting how I have learned from our kids and grandkids, Stefan, our youngest son and father of Jacob (our grandson, whom we call Jake), found a notice of the show at the Metropolitan Museum of Art, "Assyria to Iberia at the Dawn of the Classical Age." Joshua, our eldest grandson who identifies as a Jew, is a Wall Street trader living his Semitic Canaanite-Phoenician trader inheritance. A gift giver, he took us to the art exhibit at the Met on the day before Jake & Abi's Sunday wedding.

Seeing the splendid artifacts in the Met's display of historically denied cultures of the Middle East gave our family an unexpected shaft of knowing on the eve of Jake & Abi's wedding. We viewed artifacts of Semitic Canaanite origins of Wally's paternal Birnbaums/maternal Safirs in Levant of West Asia ... artifacts of Jewish life in Ukraine in Poland ... artifacts of Abi's Jewish Sefardic ancestors in the Mediterranean countries.

The museum exhibit, followed by the family wedding, gave all of us a glimpse of the rich cultural complexity of contemporary Judaism. Abi is Sefardic (her mother) and Ashkenazi (her father), Jake is Sefardic (his grandmother Lucia) and Ashkenazi (his grandfather Wally). Abi is simultaneously respectful of religious tradition and an open-minded artist and teacher. Jake blends identification as a Jew with his many selves: mystic, internet wizard, documentary film maker, political activist. Both Jake and Abi were political and cultural activists in the West/East Coast Occupy movement.

Abi's ancestors, after originating in Africa, fled the Inquisition in Spain, migrating to Lebanon, Greece, then to USA, settling in New Jersey. In addition to Jake's Sefardic and Ashkenazi Jewish paternal family inheritance, he is enriched by an ethno-spiritual legacy on his mother Linda's side of Celtic and Catholic beliefs—Irish forebears—as well as learning in a recent DNA report that his mother Linda has Native American, Asian, and Jewish ancestors.

Abi & Jake's acute sense of justice, perhaps tapping religious and spiritual traditions, may have had something to do with their participation in the 2011 Occupy movement on the East and West Coasts of USA. For Jake this was deepened by the mysticism of Burning Man rituals in the desert in which he has participated the last several years. In July 2016, Jake & Abi showed me their photo of them shaking hands with Bernie Sanders, whose prophetic denunciations of injustice and inequality may tap preconscious historical memories in his supporters.

In the late 1960s, Italians stimulated contemporary appreciation of Phoenicians (Semitic Canaanites), excavating underneath the omission or misinformation about subordinated cultures purveyed by dominant Western cultural elites.[62]

All the foregoing may be considered personal and cultural context for my envisioning an emerging paradigm: an inclusive peaceful green world where everybody thrives. For me, this includes a recognition of African origins and diaspora ~ equality of all world cultures including cultures erased earlier by Western white hierarchical/violent male paradigm of 5th century BCE Classical Greece.

The Classical Western hierarchical and violent paradigm based on 5th century Athens, Greece was re-enforced by subsequent religious/cultural elites of Judaism, Catholicism, and Protestantism, then by agents of modern secular hegemonies. In my hypothesis, this Western classical paradigm has sustained Western historical appropriation of lands and peoples, from the 1492 discovery of an already inhabited America to today's Western aggression against contemporary peoples of the African Mediterranean, including USA military devastation in Africa and West Asia accompanied by demoralization at home in USA.

USA invasions in West Asia and Africa since 2003, and subsequent destabilization with threats of using nuclear bombs, seem to many scientists,[63] and me, to be leading to the mutually assured nuclear destruction of everybody. This becomes mute horror when coupled with undismissable scientific evidence that we are also approaching—unless we stop it—looming environmental catastrophes signaled in massive fires, floods, earthquakes.[64] All of this is made more toxic in USA by the manipulation of truthful information. How the hegemonic West earlier did this by suppressing African origin of humans is discussed in the early chapters of my book, *Dark Mother: African Origins and Godmothers* (2001).

Writing has helped me understand the scientific genetic evidence of everyone's origins in Africa— persisting in the unconscious and in historical experience of migrations out of Africa ... transmitted in the folklore and art of the world, notably in popular icons of black madonnas and other black women divinities. On the liminal edge of religions and cultures, black madonnas, despite the hostility of church officials, convey a dark woman's presence preceding and persisting underneath and beyond the dominant western object of ultimate belief in the West: the omnipotent white judgmental father.

This awareness has motivated me to meditate on the Western distortion of stories of subordinated peoples, distortion that has led to genocide. The Holocaust of Jews by Nazis is the horrific example of this in our time. So is the Turkish genocide of Armenians. Spiraling back, so is killing Natives on already occupied continents, later called Americas, and so is the Western European kidnapping and enslaving of Africans in the New World. So are the distorted myths of the world's women leading to the Christian Inquisition killing witches ... and to the political and sexual subordination (epitomized in rape) of women throughout the Common Epoch to the present.

Killing Native Americans is documented in the writings of Barbara Mann and others. Western enslavement of Africans, followed by the murderous subordination of African Americans, and the attempt to relegate African beliefs to "superstition" are described in the writings of Cheikh Anta Diop, Molefi Asante, Cornel West, Luisah Teish, and others. The suppression of the ubiquity of signifying women and their erasure from history has stimulated contemporary feminist research, notably studies on the significance of a Gift Economy and Matriarchal Studies emphasizing nurturing mothers.[65]

Bernadette Muthien—the contemporary African woman whom I personally know—and I participated in Gen Vaughan's Gift Economy delegation to the 2007 world conference held in Africa. While looking for her ancestors, she came across a very old woman in the south of Africa who remembered a woman divinity.[66]

Styles of telling truthful stories change. In earlier books I toppled capital letters. Today this has given way to my realization that the arrival of the emerging paradigm will not be hastened by feminists lopping capitals off icons of elites. My intermediate way is to default to capitals, equalizing upward, or equalizing the playing field, so that everybody, in all cultures, may work in their own ways for a just and green earth. Today I cannot be consistent about capitalization—everything is moving too fast.

❦

My particular contribution as an outlier to contemporary feminism dates from the 1970s, when I realized I did not share an unspoken premise of mainstream Western feminism: the othering of all men. My books are grounded on Wally's and my journey together toward an equal, just, green earth. This book records a continuing legacy, visible in our case of a multicultural nurturing family whose kids, grandkids, great grandkids, and kindred spirits care, share, and heal; a very human family with lots of family dramas, differences, pouts, and idiosyncrasies, including my beliefs as an outlier. I am a Sicilian American woman who traces her Sicilian roots to African beliefs with a Semitic Canaanite (Phoenician) overlay, with historical experience as a Sicilian and Sicilian American woman, and a contemporary feminist cultural historian who combines academic research and political activism for abolition of nuclear weapons, deflecting accelerating climate disaster, and working for a green and just USA and world.

I encourage everyone, including my kids and kindred spirits to find their own stories, respect the integrity of spiritual traditions of the world while following their own hearts and visions ... while this mother~grandmother~great grandmother needs to follow her own heart and vision, to make her own spiritual and political decisions.

My own journey has been a spiral path full of brambles. Drawn to Sardinian Antonio Gramsci's writings on subaltern cultures of the world, I have come to realize that Gramsci's insights are truthful, now part of the mainstream, particularly Gramsci's theory of a Civil Society which I interpret to include outliers and prophets outside dominant beliefs, clergy inside churches, religious and secular leaders of institutions, as well as prophetic trouble-makers—indeed, everybody on different points of the spiral toward a better world.

Gramsci's continuing gift to all of us who struggle for a just society is the significance of folklore or the culture of subaltern classes. Students look for their own signifying cases of subaltern wisdom taking into account complex back and forth migrations from Africa. We also need to deepen Gramsci's insights with psychological variables: personal, often traumatic, experiences influence how suppressed memories may, or may not, emerge in consciousness ... traumatic experiences can suppress or distort deep beliefs. We need to cherish liminal moments which hearten us by giving us lightning flashes of possibilities.

For me, knowing our stories from the beginning of the human family, sensing our inchoate genetic beliefs formed originally in Africa, and migrations out of Africa have created a multicultural ever-changing world in which all of our world religions and multicultural stories are indispensable for knowing who we are, for shedding light on critical issues. How historically suppressed people and cultures, when exercising unchecked and unbalanced power, can become oppressors themselves. At the same time, people long suppressed can become lighthouses in the choppy dark seas of world transformation.

Spirals suggest that history may repeat itself, but history does not repeat itself in the same way. Spirals do not return to the same point, but to a further place along the spiral. Different listeners hear stories differently. Any story teller knows that everything is not necessarily what it seems to be.[67]

As economic and political injustice becomes more acute in the world today, dominant as well as suppressed classes of people who think they are white hold onto false notion of races, some desperately holding onto the one thing they think they still have—white racial superiority over dark others—while the dominant paradigm of the West, white supremacy, crumbles with corrosive questions. Who is white? Who is black?

Dominant classes tend to react to inconvenient truths with denial. People of good will often assume the beginning of their stories dates from the Common Epoch (Year One) or the modern era (1492), misleading by shortening a very long story. Youngers sometimes seem, to elders, to want only to live in the burning now.

For the truthful story, everybody has to go further back in time, to the primordial beginnings of homo sapiens sapiens, our one human race, in Africa, while keeping our eyes open to possibilities in the historic epoch, valuing liminal glimpses of the future in the burning now, and learning from subaltern uprisings and experiments.[68]

From my stance, cultural and political elites of the West, in their adherence to the dominant classical Greek model of violent male hierarchy, not only have denigrated non-Western cultures but also disregarded non-Athenian (considered lower) defeated cultures of Greece, including oracular women.[69]

Today, millennia after the classical age of Greece, left-out Greeks won a national election in January 2015, inspiring other suppressed groups of the world, notably colonized nations who have suffered humiliation-exploitation historically and today suffer fiscal austerities enforced by dominant Western elites … realizing they do not have to continue to suffer dangerous oppressive secret decisions made by reigning elites of the world … right now as extinction of life has become palpable …

In 2015, it seemed to me we were at a critical point. Dominant Western male elites (including their token female agents) try—as they have tried in the modern era, notably ever since the French Revolution—to keep suppressed cultures of the world from shaking off the chains of the dominant violent paradigm of the West. Yet the world seethes with injustice today sharpened by endless wars and endless regimes installed by USA to stabilize or keep the world order that benefits world elites.

In June 2017, when I wrote the first draft of this chapter, I expressed my hope that subaltern or dark others may nonviolently symbolically occupy wherever they are … with everyone participating in life decisions, recognizing that the vital place of energizing transformation is the space in-between humans. In our case, the in-between place beyond words that Wally and I shared for sixty-six years.[70]

The enchantment of the November 2014 wedding of our kids Jake & Abi, and other cross-cultural plighting of troths in our family, deepened this knowing while I am reaching for words to describe what all lovers (any kind) instantaneously know: when all of a sudden, the world seems brightly new and everything is possible.

CHAPTER 18

Our case: Semitic Canaanites (Phoenicians) ~ Semitic Jewish Christians ~ Semitic Moors (Muslims) ~ other dark others

~❧❦~

I n 2015, I noted that remotely controlled drones of the West kill un-counted scores of dark people, including children, in Iran, Iraq, Syria, Palestine, Yemen, Libya, Sudan, and elsewhere, while a Mutually Assured Destruction nuclear poker game is played by nine nuclear states, while the CIA of USA installs unpublicized black ops holes in the world where en-hanced torture is practiced on detainees, daily producing more terrorists, more retaliatory murdering.

Ads in USA, using stimulus-response psychology, successfully deflect attention away from what the elites are doing. Everything is fine, just buy powerful automobiles. Big Pharma sedates everybody with drugs.

The desperation felt in USA is enacted in regular suicide/mass murders with easily available assault weapons ... dramatically, on October 3, 2017, with the largest massacre in USA history at Las Vegas by an aging wealthy white USA citizen who liked to gamble, who adjusted his guns to become automat-ic—and killed fifty-nine people, wounded hundreds, and traumatized swaths of others ... including Emily in my extended family.

While USA, sitting on a huge stockpile of nuclear weapons, chokes on its self-interested Western attempt to curb nuclear proliferation of others. In 2017, unstable leaders of North Korea and USA taunt each other with public postures of defiance/cooperation ... embracing the suicidal reactions of a little state trying to prevent a big state dropping its nuclear bombs.

For me, this is crazy-making. All of us, in unconscious predispositions, shafts of knowing in our preconscious, flashes in consciousness ... have mo-ments—particularly in crises—when we know we are brothers and sisters of one human family. This is evident in the immediate outpouring of nurturing during and after mass murders.[71]

Seen through a surreal lens, USA policies are a shadow play of murderers killing without feeling,[72] soldiers of the West mouthing "savages" learned from official propaganda and/or learned from history books written with the arrogance of western cultural elites ... supported by a society of complicit others, with many numbing the pain with loveless sex and opiates. Economic elites purchase USA's political system, distributing *panem et circenses* (bread and circuses), the Roman empire's way of holding off the gathering rage of oppressed dark others. Circuses in 2017-18 include watching (officially edited) film of wars on television and listening to the world elites' threats of war while the world leaders finger nearby nuclear buttons that can wipe out all life on earth.

My selection of signifyers in our personal story was related to my desire to find my own ancestors, my belief that if everybody in the world knew their truthful stories, this would deflate the ballooned stories of dominant political and cultural elites. I knew this would require a preponderance of scholars with integrity writing truthful stories about Western hegemony whose code words—discovery, exploration, development, exceptionalism, indispensability of USA in controlling and policing the world—would pierce the lies covering USA's real murder, real rape, real torture, real starvation, death of real babies.

What I did not, initially, realize was the personal price that accompanies telling the truth ... this was realized as I reread drafts of this manuscript.

I started with my own family, my ancestral Italy, specifically Sicily. On my paternal (Chiavola) side, my great uncle and aunt in Ragusa, Sicily as case in point. After world war I, Carmelo, the returning veteran was spat upon by Italian pacifists. He became a fascist marching on Rome with Mussolini. Afterward, Carmelo became a schoolteacher and married my Aunt Concettina's sister, Carmela.

When Wally and I visited Ragusa in the 1970s, Carmelo generously (we were *famiglia*) treated us to gelato on the daily *passaggiata*, and wrapped food packages for our journeys ... he did not show us the hotel in the center of Ragusa where the revolutionary Red Brigade had met openly. I asked to see the hotel, although he disdained it as "pagan." He did show us an ancient small round stone shrine on the Marina di Ragusa adjoining my ancestral Ragusa Ibla, which I knew to be an early marker of uncodified Jewish/Christian beliefs.

Carmelo's wife Carmela, a Red Cross nurse during world war II and a life-long socialist, built a shrine to the madonna in her yard, considered by the feminist books of Dacia Maraini I gave her in the 1970s to be "strange" ... although her resistance to male dominance/husband's extra-marital affairs, was evident. When her husband's students would telephone asking for the Colonel, Carmela would say, "There is no colonel here."

The long-married Sicilian couple—husband a fascist, wife a socialist—suggests a revealing tension in modern Italian culture ... and shared unarticulated deep memories. The couple insisted on taking Wally and me to their store-front Catholic church in Ragusa where a Franciscan priest, Padre Gregorio, guided the congregation with Vatican II democratizing reforms of Catholicism ... including bestowing a doctorate of the Church on nun Teresa, whose story I carry in my middle name.

Franciscan priest Padre Gregorio, fascinated by our research in African origins and ancestral migrations out of Africa—notably our West Asian Semitic Canaanite inheritance—took us to meet our Chiavola kin, descendants of the historic peaceful trading Jewish Canaanites, living in nearby Palazzola Acreide.

Acreide refers to Acre (Acco) in the Levant of West Asia, historically part of Galilee, the Roman province where Jesus lived. As earlier discussed, under the Roman empire, during the first years of Christian (later Common) epoch, the commonly held faith was split into two religions—Judaism and Christianity—to which Muslims from Africa (Moors) and Muslims from Asia (Saracens) adhered emphasizing prophets, until agents of the Holy Roman Empire in the 9th and 10th centuries incited internecine hatred, and declared crusades against Muslim "infidels."

Spending time with our Chiavola kin in Palazzola Acreide, Wally and I found we had everything in common with this couple, contemporary descendants of mutual ancestors. We shared historic/contemporary stories, mutual nonviolent egalitarian cultural/political beliefs, and activism for a just and equal world. This couple became a signifier for me of the persistence, over millennia, of deeply suppressed beliefs of others in regions of today's Sicily and of Levant of West Asia.

Padre Gregorio also took us to Chiaramonte Gulfi, where we found a black madonna ... sister of the very popular Black Madonna of Clermont in France, whom we had visited a decade earlier. Stories about this black madonna, like stories of Santa Lucia, recount how she came from the sea in a ship without helmsman, taken by oxen without a driver to the site she wanted for her sanctuary. The names of her sanctuaries in France (Clermont) and Italy (Chiaramonte) mean "clear vision from a mountain top."

More than a decade ago, Sandy Miranda, who produces radio programs on the music of the world, came with us on a study tour to Sardinia. Now she lives (with Rob)—in a story that defies rationality but gladdens me—next door. In 2014, she went to Sicily at the same time we traveled there on our family trip. She brought me a gift from the volcano Mt. Etna: a black madonna carved of black volcanic rock with a votive red rose. A symbol of the madonna in Italian culture.[73]

Black madonnas are popularly associated with volcanic eruptions ... also with aroused genitals of women. A 1960s Berkeley bumper sticker announced, "God is black and is she pissed." In Italian dialect, the contemporary earthy adjective for a woman enraged at injustice refers to her aroused genitals—*incazzata.*

Sandy, a kindred spirit, in 2014 also brought me a local pamphlet of the Black Madonna of Milicia outside Palermo, reminding me that many years ago Wally's brother Norman, a dentist then living in East Liverpool, Ohio, sent us a message from his Sicilian American patient to be sure to see this black madonna. We did. Years later, Sandy brought me the prayer card of the Black Madonna of Milicia.[74]

I thought about the persistence of signifyers. Sardinia—an African site whose migrants later crossed from Sardinia into Italy's regions of Emilia-Romagna and Tuscany, land of communism with ragú and black madonnas.

In 2010, earlier acceptance of my research and teaching at CIIS had turned into hostility as the study of women's spirituality was under siege in academic institutions. A professional colleague accused me of having "no boundaries" between professors and students.

I studied the prayer card of the Black Madonna of Milicia in her sanctuary at Altavilla: depicting the black madonna with heretic~prophet~saint Francis of Umbria, who considered all creatures brothers and sisters. Francis, his face radiantly black, is standing and blessing a white boy child; alongside is a seated black madonna, her face bathed in light, embracing a radiant black girl child. There are no boundaries of color or gender in this image of Francis and black madonna.

This mystic Franciscan world view erases the hierarchy of white male humans at the top—all humans are brothers and sisters—and reinstates the un-named mother of everybody whom early Christian patriarchs left out of the trinity (replacing Mary, in canonical doctrine, with the Holy Ghost). The official Catholic image of the madonna is Michelangelo's sculpture of the Pietà housed in the Vatican in Rome—a sorrowful mother holding her dead son on her lap.

Sicilian peasants, bypassing canonical Christian doctrine, considered Mary, Joseph, and Jesus a human family (see earlier discussion of Italian American spring ritual of St. Joseph tables). Subordinated people whose beliefs are not constricted by official fences of religious and political elites, are fond of the name Giuseppe (Joe) for their sons.

For Sicilian Americans, the patriarchal omnipotent god with one son is popularly replaced by a nurturing human father embracing his son. In Lydia's cover of my book, *The Future Has an Ancient Heart*, the dark mother is sustained by two monkeys ~ sustained by two cats ~ internally sustained by black birds and two white women with black hair, bodies in a deep blue sea with black waves, ultimately red earth in a cosmos of red sun bordered in black from whom fire rays emanate becoming purple and blue in a black cosmos ... bordered by title. A love story, a vision, and a prophecy.

At the top of the front cover of my last published book is a quotation from Janice Parker, poet and doctoral scholar of women's spirituality: "This book will add to the new energy of occupy wall street, occupy the world for change, for justice, for fairness ... [giving] this movement the extra force to propel it forward ... into a force of nature, ideas, compassionate action."

CHAPTER 19

In my Sicilian American youth in Kansas City, my father, reaching for the most intense expletive, would shout "Gran figlio di puttana," (great son of a bitch) ... quickly following the blasphemy by saying the mother of the despicable male was a good woman.

⇥⟡⇤

M ulling this over, a memory emerges of a feminist conference a few years ago in Palermo—capitol of Sicily—where I presented a paper on my research of black madonnas. After my talk, a Palermitan woman insisted on taking me to the Basilica of San Francesco di Assisi, located in the Kalsa, the Moorish district.

Moors, as previously discussed, were Semitic black Africans, or Black Muslims, who came to Sicily in the 7th century CE, and who ruled the island until Normans invaded and conquered the Muslims in 1060 CE. Yet the presence of Moors has persisted in Sicily to this day ... in popular resistance after 1060 CE, manifest in the dialect, popular pronunciation, suppressed stories, and art transmitting religious beliefs of subordinated people. I am thinking of the splendid mosaics created by Moorish artisans at Monreale in Palermo. Later, under the dominant Normans, the mural of Jesus in the cathedral at Cefalu depicts a grim/omnipotent/judgmental figure. In a mosaic created by Moorish artisans at Monreale outside Palermo, Jesus is a human pulling a fellow human from drowning in the sea.

The Franciscan Christian church the Palermitan woman took me to see is located in the Moorish district of Palermo, where African Muslim symbols are incised on the entryway. In the oratorio of San Lorenzo, several Giacomo Serpotta statues beguile—seductive icons of the madonna nonviolently changed church doctrine of the passive madonna holding her dead son. Serpotta named two of his sensual madonnas "Obedience" and "Charity."

In 1224, when St. Francis in Umbria, Italy was kissing lepers, speaking to trees, and telling the wolf of Gubbio to stop eating human beings and be a good citizen, a Franciscan church was built in the port of San Giorgio in Palermo. The church was named San Giorgio, remembering the early

Christian martyr whose practice of Jewish Christian beliefs in caring and sharing aroused the worries of agents of the dominant Catholic church and state. A wealthy Chiaramonte family, with clarity of vision, rescued the church.

Stories about black madonnas are convoluted yet their deep inclusive human meaning is immediately recognized internationally.[75]

On our 2001 study tour of Sicily, my prescient sister Joie was very moved at Erice—a promontory in the province of Palermo—finding it unlike any place she had ever been. An African migration stop, a Semitic Canaanite settlement, and a love temple, at Erice in 2014 I found—with the help of our kids (specifically Peter)—the icon of a Black Madonna of Custonaci who had deeply moved me in 1988 during Easter week in west Sicily at Trapani.

A story hovers over Erice, a story I may, earlier, have been unwilling to hear: the mysterious disappearance of physicist, Ettore Majorana, who wanted, like Wally, to turn nuclear power to peaceful purposes. Today, Erice in Sicily has become a favorite place for world conferences of physicists.

The love temple at Erice drew me. Semitic Canaanites, after founding nearby Palermo in 800 BCE, brought with them an icon of Astarte, and dedicated the love temple at Erice to her. Subsequent Phoenicians, then Greek invaders, dedicated the love temple to their love goddess Aphrodite. Sailors brought wine to her, climbing the hill to her sanctuary.

Kindred spirits constantly help me uncover submerged beliefs. The week I returned home from our family trip to Sicily in September 2014, Mary Beth Moser called to tell me about her insights on her reconnaissance trip with Rich, her love, for a proposed trip the next year with her kin: exploring the magic in everyday rituals of the Trentino region in northern Italy.

Spiraling back to 1545, when the Inquisition at the Council of Trent tried to suppress heretical beliefs subversive to church doctrine, pervasive heretical beliefs continued to be transmitted in this region of northern Italy. Mary Beth Moser has collected everyday household beliefs conveying suppressed beliefs as well as rituals surrounding pagan water spirits, remembering earliest life in the sea. A feminist scholar whose CIIS doctoral dissertation I mentored, Mary Beth won the prize of Association for Study of Women and Mythology for her study of everyday rituals conveying ancient pagan spirituality ... on the very day in 2014 that she learned her mother had died.

In 2014, Sandy Miranda came home from her trip to Sicily not only with icons of the black madonna, but with a painting of Santa Lucia. It is a double-sided portrait that changes dynamically when held—Lucia as white maiden/Lucia as black crone—conveying what physicists know, that everything/

everybody are constantly changing. Or, according to the Gramscian wisdom, the difference between what elites want to establish as knowledge (white judgmental father) and what subaltern peoples know (black madonnas and other black women divinities).

On our 2014 family trip to Sicily, I found a prayer card ... simultaneously depicting Lucia dead yet offering her gouged-out eyes to her killer on a Catholic communion plate. Holding the card another way, Lucia is timeless, standing upright, alive ... eyes wide open, healing, envisioning.

My thinking raced to the past. In the beginning all humans were black. Migrations back and forth out of/returning to Africa, whose close encounters with people from colder climes lightened people's skin, mixed brown with blue to create the hazel eye color, lightened/straightened curly hair. Later, controlling dominant elites—when white-washing official stories—whitened dark icons.

Close encounters of migrants out of Africa/returning to the motherland account for signifying datum: it only takes three generations for people originally black to have kids who are one of the many shades of flesh color called white. In a perennial dance of everybody's genes, it is always possible for a black child to be born to parents who think they are white.

Even likelier is the persistence throughout the ages of human values—caring, sharing, healing—by black people on migration paths out of Africa whose skin color is lightened in three generations to what the dominant paradigm calls white.

When I was a girl in Kansas City, Missouri, living in a neighborhood of migrants from Sicily and south Italy, the passports of my immediate relatives identified them as "white" with "dark complexion." During my childhood in my Sicilian neighborhood, a black child was born. His mother, in Sicilian dialect, called him "Beddu," beautiful child; his father would chase him up Wabash Avenue waving a belt to beat him.

My own brunette mother, whose sister-in-law Georgia disparaged her in dialect as the black one, perpetuated the bigotry ... telling her three kids not to dawdle when eating, putting them into competition: "white, pink, black baby." In our case, the bigotry did not transmit.

Adding to this complexity, I remember that my mother Kate's best friends were black women who worked in the dime store in downtown Kansas City, where she would stop after work every day after work to buy sweets. In January 1940, when I graduated from Northeast High School in midyear when there was no graduation ceremony, my mother paraded me around town in cap and gown. Our first stop was her black women friends at the dime store.

Skin color can be a matter of perception, particularly in times of accelerated social change. In the late 1960s, when I was a trouble-making professor in the conservative history department of SF State—where my teaching helped stoke students' demands for department of African Studies—I joined my students on the first day of the strike, the only history professor to do so … and was fired. Encountering a history professor on the stairs, he peered at me and said, "Didn't realize you are black."

CHAPTER 20

"In 1492 your father was a Jew. Your mother was a jumping jack,
and so are you"—a popular jingle in Lucia's Sicilian American
childhood in Kansas City, Missouri

※

People whose origins stories have been erased by dominant rulers need to look to their unconscious or to evidence in prehistory, glimmers in liminal moments in consciousness. This is true for Sicilian Americans as well as other subordinated groups.

Native Americans find it difficult to accept scientific evidence of Paleolithic migrants from Africa crossing Beringia (later the Bering Straits) from Asia to Alaska, migrating down what came to be called the Americas. This is also true for other early migrants out of Africa via Sicily who migrated to Asia via the Atlantic sea on then connected islands to the continent of Australia.

In 5000 BCE, African migrants in West Asia became Semites, later identified as children of Shem. Saracens, Semites in West Asia, were considered children of the Semitic Jewish matriarch Sara.

Semitic Jews were later called Pagans, Christians, Roman Christians, and Black Muslims, whose ancestors came out of Africa, migrated to Asia, spiraled back toward Africa via what later was called Europe.

In early Common (formerly called Christian) Epoch beginning Year One, Semitic Jewish Christians living in Sicily mated with Jews from Asia and Africa. After Romans destroyed the Jewish temple in 57 CE, Jews migrated to Africa and Asia. At the same time, Berbers from Africa, called "barbarians" by Romans, came to Rome.[76]

In my spiral perspective from the beginning to the present to the future, Jews of the Levant in West Asia were later called Christians, Romanized Jews, Romanized Christians, and Muslims of Sicily—all African in origin who historically shared African beliefs with a Semitic historical overlay. Judaism, Christianity, and Islam may be considered in the same African~Semitic continuum, sharing the same monotheist religious beliefs, the same prophets.

Today Jews/Christians/Muslims are called Abrahamic faiths sharing the same ultimate beliefs ... with one major cultural difference. For Christians, the ultimate object of belief is incarnated in Jesus, son of God. For monotheist Jews and Muslims, the emphasis is on prophets. For Jews, the signifying prophets are Abraham and Moses; for Muslims, the signifying prophets are Abraham, Jesus, and Muhammad.

Crusading Christians, after the 9th century CE, required everyone to believe in Jesus Christ as the incarnation of God in the Holy Roman Church: convert to this established Christianity or be killed. During the subsequent Inquisition, dominant Christians, suspecting that forcibly converted Christians (*conversos* and *conversas*) did not truly convert, branded old women healers and seers as witches, torturing and burning them.

Anxiety arising from suppressed knowing of this violent story funneled into killing people whose skin was dark, or perceived as dark.

For this feminist cultural historian, questions rise while studying historical persecutions in the name of religion, persecutions over different shades of skin color, close encounters of migrants out of Africa from the Paleolithic age to the present. Fleeing identification with persecuted people began with Africans ... then their descendants in varying shades of black then white ... then institutionalized obliteration from accepted history of dark others.

Who is black? Who is white? Who is African?

Who is not African in origin?

Who is a Native American?

Who is a Jew? Who is a Christian? Who is a Muslim?

Who is a Jewish Christian?

How do I, or you, know whether you are a believer or non-believer
in which faith or non-faith?

After centuries of religious~political wars, oppression, suppression,
killings, how do you identify anybody's beliefs—
including your own?

And what does all this have to do, anyway,
with being a decent human being?

Adopting Sicily as case in point to explore these questions, African Berbers who early came to my ancestral island held the indigenous African belief in the equality of all religious believers as well as the political corollary: authenticity is confirmed, not in what believers say they believe, but in how truthfully they live their beliefs.[77]

Islam was dominant in Sicily from 8th to 13th centuries CE. Muslims gifted Sicily with irrigation—watering a flourishing agriculture—ice cream, and other sweets. With an easiness that may have been related to holding the same ultimate beliefs, Jews and Christians either converted to Islam or adopted the Sicilian custom of taking Arab and Muslim names for positive tax benefits.

The name of Andalusia in Spain means walk, or go, with Lucia. In the middle ages, Andalusia encompassed nearly all of Spain. Its history begins when the region was part of the African continent before global heating/rising of waters in 10,000 BCE. The history of Spain features African migrants from the Levant in Asia and migrant Semitic Black Muslims from Africa called Moors.

In Andalusia in the middle ages, Jews, Muslims, and Christians lived together harmoniously.[78] In the 10th century CE, agents of the Roman empire incited hatred against Jews, declared crusades against Muslims, and, in 1492, Jews were ousted from Christian lands. Thereafter, Christian rulers sought to explore the world/claim it for Roman Christianity. At the same time, Inquisitors hounded and tortured suspects for not truly converting to Christianity.

France, particularly the South of France, persisting early Jewish Christian, Christian, Celt, and Black Muslim (Moorish) migrants held heresies challenging established Christian institutions. Among these, a Magdalen heresy wherein Jesus did not die on the cross, but instead married Mary Magdalene and came to France.

Related to this subversive underside of French history, is the signifying datum: more icons of black madonnas are venerated in France than anywhere else in the world.[79]

Other signifying datum: the Cathar heresy of the south of France. In the south of France in the 13th century, Cathar women, weavers and healers who lived in accordance with early Jewish Christian beliefs of no killing and making their own decisions whom to take to bed. As healers and sharers, Cathars were considered so heretical the pope declared a domestic crusade against them.

While studying Italian culture after the 1960s, the popular jingle from my Sicilian and south Italian neighborhood in Kansas City, Missouri rose up from the deep layers of my memory: "In 1492 your father was a Jew. Your mother was a jumping jack, and so are you." I thought about *conversos* and *conversas*, men and women forcibly converted to Christianity ... and about the *conversa* Jew who became a Christian nun, Teresa, whose story I carry in my middle name.

In 1492, Christopher Columbus of Genoa (a city state that later became part of contemporary Italy), an adventurer whose religious/ethnic origins are unclear, was subsidized by the king and queen of Aragon and Castile in Spain to go to India. When the ships of Columbus touched the islands and shores of the Americas, he began the forced conversion, exploitation, and killing of Natives that characterizes the history of the Americas. Forced conversions were continued by Catholic priests who established missions in the New World. Diego Columbus, son of the explorer, became a slave master in the New World.[80]

In the 15th and 16th centuries, Spanish lands included the seat of the Inquisition at Palermo, Sicily, where forcibly Christianized *conversos* and women healers who threatened the male Catholic monopoly on healing were swept, with other suspects, into Inquisitors' nets to be branded/tortured/killed.

All of this is personally relevant. Earlier discussed, when I was born on January 3, 1924, I was given the name of my paternal grandmother, Lucia. When Christened on January 1, 1925, I was given the middle name Teresa, honoring my grandmother's sister Za Teresa who, when migrating from Palermo, brought with her my orphaned maternal Nanna Giuseppina to Kansas City ... as well as remembering my mother's little sister Teresa who died in USA at the age of four.

Historic Teresa had a Jewish grandfather who was branded by Christians with a yellow star, and paraded in shame as a Jew through the streets of Spain. Teresa, escaping Inquisition persecution/ killing, became a conversa/Catholic nun. In 1970, after Vatican II reforms of Roman Catholicism included acknowledging shared origins of Jews and Christians, Santa Teresa was named Doctor of the Roman Catholic church.

Contemporary Western feminists are fascinated by Teresa's mysticism, convent reforms with St. John of the Cross, plain-style writing, teaching nuns to express their beliefs dancing, and adopting silent prayer to keep their heretical beliefs away from Inquisitors. Reading her writings closely, I uncovered: Teresa, whose grandparents were Jews, considered the Jewish Rabbi Jesus to be her brother. Many Western feminists consider Teresa a feminist foremother. So do I.

In 2003, the long reach of the Inquisition legacy of torture and killing to eradicate heretical beliefs reached me and women on our study tour in Spain ... coinciding with President George Bush lying about weapons of mass destruction and invading Iraq. At Inquisition sites in Spain that year, some women on our study tour were traumatized, often without consciously know-ing their ancestors had been tortured and killed at these sites.

In 1060 CE, when Normans conquered Sicily for papal Christianity, the mix of peoples in Sicily was dazzling: African Berbers, Semitic Jews of Carthage Africa, Semitic Canaanites and other Jews of West Asia, Semitic Black Muslims of Africa, Semitic Saracens of Asia ... all speaking their own dialects, or creating a new language, Ladino.

After 1060 CE, a great many people adopted protective cover by identi-fying with official Christianity. Thereafter, non-Christian beliefs remained for the most part unconscious or preconscious; persisting in music, dance, art, literature, everyday/celebratory rituals, and vernacular dialect, including profane speech.

In my hypothesis, these largely nonverbalized beliefs have persisted in rit-uals and other ways to the present. Notably in cultural, as well as in political resistance to dominant regimes of the West as manifest in periodic uprisings up to the present (Spring 2019), when suppressed beliefs coming to the surface have boiled over during contemporary Western invasions in West Asia and Africa, in a cauldron of unconscious, preconscious, and dimly conscious knowing.

In the deep unconscious, a spiral of the same beliefs (under different names) may have persisted to the present in people today identified with the West and people identified with the Middle East (Asia)/Africa: African beliefs identifying humans with nature, stateless Canaanite Jewish beliefs, Jewish/early Christian knowing that the mother and father of Jesus were Jews, and Jesus himself was a Jewish rabbi. Wally considered Jesus the most rebellious Jew in history.

After the 5th century CE collapse of the Roman Empire, which was aligned with Roman Christianity, the imperial seat of the empire was transferred to Constantinople. At this time, peoples of Sicily celebrated Christian mass with different liturgies. In 1060 CE, these included a liturgy of Christianity of African Egypt, and a liturgy of Syro-Palestine in West Asia (today called the Middle East), land of Semitic Canaanites. In 2019, these lands are on fire with killing.

✿✿✿✿✿

In our personal riff of this story, in the 1970s, Wally and I explored Semitic Canaanite ruins on the island of Motya, located off the western coast of Sicily. In 1988, while a writer in residence at the American Academy in Rome, I traveled to west Sicily for Easter where I encountered the combustible mixture of Pagan/Jewish/Catholic/Muslim/Sicilian beliefs in rituals of the black madonna.[81]

Easter in Sicily, I learned, harks back to Semitic foremother Astarte, whose name became Esther and whose feminine name in Italian is *Pasqua*, the feminine metaphor for the spring festival of renewal. I just remembered ... my relatives in Ragusa, Sicily, conflating gender and religions, called Wally "Pasquale."

To this day, Easter in western and interior Sicily is celebrated—not in the doctrinal Catholic ritual of Christ crucified and risen—but in a ritual of reconciliation between mother and son, and later as reconciliation between estranged family members.[82] Today this Sicilian Easter ritual evokes, for me, the desperate contemporary need for reconciliation of the human family whose brothers and sisters have been killing one another in wars over names associated with religions ... accompanied by tragic ironies: all contemporary combatants have the same origins in Africa, and all, somewhere in their unconscious ~ preconscious ~ glimpses in consciousness, share same deep animal beliefs in caring, sharing, healing to which they were predisposed in their mother's uterus was re-enforced by surviving in migrations out of Africa to everywhere.

During Easter week in 1988, in Trapani, Sicily, I was thrown into perplexity trying to understand the mysteries of the black madonna. On Thursday and Friday of the holy week before Easter, her icon is carried all over town in a rocking nurturing motion: two steps backward before brisk steps forward. After her son is crucified on Friday, the black madonna is taken to a tent and joined by other women mourning her son. On Saturday, the icon of the dark mother is carried from one Catholic church to another looking for her son. Outside the last church in town, she is made to waver—agonizing over whether or not her son is in the church—before she is swiftly carried inside.

This image returned vividly on the eve of Jake & Abi's wedding of November 9, 2014, at a celebration with ribald singing in a Sicilian pizzeria in Brooklyn, New York. "*C'e la luna mezzo mare. Mamma Mia, mi ha di maritarmi.*" The daughter says to her mother: "The moon is shining on the sea; I need to get married." The mother responds to her sexually aroused daughter in earthy language: "If I give you a cobbler, he will have an aroused penis ... if I give you a fisherman, he will have an aroused penis ... " down a long list of possible husbands identified with their vocations ... always with the chorus, "he will have an aroused penis." The singing ignites my realization that the universal power of sexuality was always known to subaltern others long before

Sigmund Freud, who with the help of hallucinatory drugs, wrote books on the power of sexuality in everybody's unconscious.

In 2017, I listened, on the radio, to another version of this ribald Sicilian peasant song of a daughter asking her mother to find her a husband. The mother answers with the same reprise, but replacing the long list of vocations with a list of Italian regions. The meaning of all this, in my view, is the persistent awareness in subaltern classes of the universality of sexuality ... of everybody ... of all vocations ... of all regions. A bodily knowing that is deeply subversive to the historic reign of dominant classes.

In Sicilian popular culture, this explicit sensuality embraces the madonna and is evident in the blasphemous oath described earlier of older men likening the unmarried mother of Jesus to a *puttana*, or whore. My brother Louie explained to me the connection of the madonna and sensuality in our Sicilian neighborhood in Kansas City, Missouri, existing in the second quarter of the 20th century. Young men looking at a sensual woman would exclaim "Madonn!" linking the madonna to a "hot" woman.

Since the 1960s, stories of the suppressed cultures of Sicily, as well as the rest of the world, are coming to consciousness. In a high school Latin class, which my mother insisted I take, we read about Caesar's Gallic wars. Gauls, later called Celts, were everywhere in the early Christian epoch, notably in Sicily. Celtic history is part of the suppressed history of Europe whose significance I first realized while reading.[83]

Today, while the West kills Muslims, I am concerned about the suppressed story of Muslims in Sicily and elsewhere. Lies, mostly by omission, about the story of the West and Muslims have been useful to hegemonic Western elites ... inciting Christians to humiliate and kill Muslims, and stimulating retaliatory killing by Muslims in an endless cycle of murderous wars sustaining Western economies dependent on perpetual war impoverishing dark others. All this is now roiled by a self-proclaimed Islamic group brandishing the name ISIS, the great mother of Africa, and taking credit for all retaliatory/suicidal murders.

In the West, the right wing has whipped this into a crisis of "civilizations"—God's favorite country battling "savages" and creating an incendiary mixture of unconscious/preconscious emotions.[84] Trump, in his election rhetoric in 2016, incited hatred of Muslims. He used that hatred to extended wars killing Muslims and to exclude Mexicans and other Central Americans from entering USA.

Long simmering Muslim memories of Christian brutalities against them during the Crusades and the Inquisition may hover over the "barbarous" be-headings of Western soldiers by the group calling itself ISIS. I am provoked to wonder at right wing fulminations in USA. Isn't killing Muslim children and others with Western high-tech drone bombers—whose killing missions are guided by USA cybernetic wizards in air-conditioned offices in Palo Alto, California—equally, if not more, "barbarous" than the atrocities of ISIS?

In 1060 CE, the majority of the population in Sicily was Black Muslim. After the Norman conquest, whose bloodiness is suggested in the Bayeux tapestry woven by women, many Christian monks in Sicily moved to Calabria. The monks who remained in Sicily were considered "Arabized Christians."

In Sicily, in the 700 years of Muslim rule before it was conquered by Christian crusaders, Islamic men who married Christian women customarily reared their daughters as Christians and their sons in the Muslim faith of their fathers. Most of these, as Mary Saracino has pointed out, were love marriages.[85]

Older women in Sicily—Jewish/Christian/Muslim—wore, and still wear in non-modernized parts of the island, the shrouded garb of Muslim women … the shrouded garb also worn by Christian nuns. A few years ago, on street posters all over Italy, we saw Sicily's renaissance artist Antonello di Messina's painting of the Christian madonna with an opaque black face dressed in a Muslim blue burka.

On the fateful date of September 11, 2001, Tricia Grame, whose CIIS doctorate in Women' Spirituality I mentored, created a startling painting. A Jewish American woman married to Italian American pharmacist, Tricia gave me the painting which we mounted in the living room of our Berkeley home. The painting is of a third world woman with an opaque black face wearing a Muslim blue burka, and asking in an inscription across the top of the painting, "Can you hear me?" Tricia and her husband founded, support, and regularly bring supplies, with their Asian Indian grandkids, to a Vietnamese orphanage of children whose parents were killed by USA invaders.

In USA, in the early years of the 20th century, Catholic clergy often sent icons of black madonnas to church basements. In Europe, black madonnas are kept inaccessible. Sandy Miranda, recently visiting the sanctuary of Mont Saint Michel in France, insisted on seeing the hidden underground black madonna. A Spanish woman service person arranged for Sandy to see it.[86]

A few years ago, I participated in an international panel on the mysteries of black madonnas, where a male professor teaching Islamic Studies in south Italy clarified the subject. For Islam, the icon of the faceless black madonna conveys the monotheist Muslim (also Jewish, also early Jewish Christian) belief in the human inability to see the ultimate creator … humans and other animals can only have glimpses of her.

The pronoun used by the professor of Islamic studies startled me into thinking about gender, monotheism, and the madonna. In doctrinal Christianity, she has been reduced to the "Holy Ghost." Jewish feminists refer to the *Shekinah*, the feminine face of God. Some religions refer to the "light." Judaism has a festival of lights at Hanukkah, celebrating the time a miracle happened. Christianity identifies light with Jesus, light of the world. Feminists refer to "her."

When I shift from nouns to verbs, I suddenly see: nurturing refers to mothers but also to fathers as well as to brothers and sisters … nurturing not one male child but all vulnerable dark others … all animals, babies, old people, desperate migrants fleeing war/famine, hopeless poor of the earth … everybody in 2019 who are under the threat of environmental/nuclear extinction …

In 1060 CE, Christian churches of Sicily celebrated mass with three different rites: Latin, Greek, and Saracen.[87]

In the 1970s and 80s, I found the story of Sicily written with a Muslim optic in the writings of Leonardo Sciascia who, like Chiarelli, also lived in Ricalmuto. I caught glimpses of the story of Sicily with an optic of contemporary Muslim women when they shared their food with me on trains while traveling in Sicily in the 1970s-80s-90s.

While uncovering the Muslim story of Sicily, I researched other Semites—Jews—who came early to Sicily … especially after 57 CE when Romans destroyed their temple. We found evidence of Jews having settled in my Sicilian maternal ancestral town, Palermo, in the 8th century on the northwest coast of the island … in Agrigento on the south coast fronting Africa where Neolithic stone structures resemble those of Stonehenge in Britain … in the southeast triangle of Sicily, my paternal home region, fronting Africa to the south, and Asia to the east.

On the eastern coast facing Asia, Catania is the home of indigenous healer Agata, a principal in the story of Lucia of Syracuse, Sicily. Catania may have more anarchist drivers than any other city of the world. Particularly exasperating Wally, who did all the driving on our travels in this city, were the autos that were driven on sidewalks.

After the 8th century, Black Muslims—Jews of Africa and West Asia—settled in my primordial maternal place south of Palermo at nearby Erice … as well as on the north coast near my maternal grandmother's birthplace at Termini

Imerese at the top of the island at Patti (Tindari) ... and west to Messina, a portal of migration paths into the Italian peninsula, Europe, and Asia.

In the early years of the Common Epoch, Jews and Muslims lived together harmoniously, notably on the western coast of Sicily where Jewish Canaanite merchants engaged in commercial and religious contacts with Greece, West Asia, and Africa.

Black madonnas constantly intrude in my research of signifying women. In the early 1970s, encountering the Black Madonna of Tindari, located on the north coast of Sicily near the birthplace of my maternal grandmother, inflamed my subsequent intense involvement in the Italian women's movement ... simultaneous with my active engagement in USA in the African American civil rights movement ... capped by the day after Thanksgiving in 1969 when I was fired from SF State.

In the 1980s, while participating in the Italian feminist movement, I was invited by the American Academy in Rome to be Writer in Residence. In Spring 1988, homesick and far from home, I decided to travel to Trapani in Sicily for the Easter mysteries.

On the day after Thanksgiving 1989, my mother died.

In 2001, my publication of *Dark Mother: African Origins and Godmothers* was followed by a highly productive decade of teaching, writing, publishing, and speaking in USA and around the world.

A distinct feeling I held at the time was that the black madonna had burned our home down in late 1991. We rebuilt on the burn site—with a little help from our architect Tim Ward—a radiant white Mediterranean home with a blue tile roof ... signifyer of the primordial sea in the African Mediterranean ... and with red-framed windows ... signifyer of our optic of life.

In 1993 we moved into our new home. *Black Madonnas* was published in Boston by Northeastern University Press, then published in Italian (*La Madre Oscura*) in 1994, then the French and African editions (*La Mere Noire*) were published in 1997, the year the book won the Valetutti international New Left award at Salerno, Italy.

My study of the meanings of black madonnas and other submerged beliefs of Sicily—my signifier of third world countries—converged with my need to understand the woman Lucia for whom I am named; the heretic whose hometown, Syracuse in Sicily, was the capitol of Magna Graecia (Greater Greece).

Spiraling back … Syracuse, before Greek domination, was the site of Semitic Canaanites and their divinity Astarte, whose name remembered primordial light as a star. In the early Common Epoch, Jews who followed Jesus nonviolently resisted the violence of the Roman Empire, which was regarded by Romans as dangerous. The Romans branded Jesus "King of the Jews" and killed him in 33 CE. Lucia, visionary healer, was popularly celebrated with Mary, the Jewish mother of Jesus, with Agata, a Pagan healer, with Barbara, a Pagan African Berber, and with Minerva, a Roman goddess of wisdom to whom a temple was built in Syracuse.

By the 4th century CE, Jewish patriarchs had "purified" Scriptures by leaving the mother of Jesus out of Hebrew texts. In the late 4th century, Christianity was established as the religion of the Roman empire. Christian patriarchs proclaimed Jesus as immaculately conceived and demoted Mary, the mother of Jesus, to the Holy Ghost … naming Mary as the Immaculate Conception of her son. First called "Virgin Martyrs," Mary, Lucia, and Barbara were beatified saints of the Holy Roman empire.

In the 7th and 8th centuries, Black Muslims arrived in Sicily from Africa and turned the Syracuse temple to Lucia into a mosque of Islam. Normans, invading Sicily in 1060 CE, turned the Syracuse temple into a Christian church, which it has remained to this day—a patriarchal Roman Catholic church with a Santa Lucia chapel.

Church patriarchs cut popular saints' stories to fit church doctrine while subordinated people continued honoring beloved saints with subversive meanings in daily and celebratory rituals.

Her official prayer card depicts Lucia offering her gouged out eyes on a Catholic communion plate … an image that repelled me in my Catholic girlhood and continues to unnerve me today.

Her popular contemporary prayer card depicts Lucia standing upright and alive, her intact eyes wide open, envisioning. A nurturing woman, yet she does not hold an infant. Earlier I thought Lucia held a stalk of wheat, nourishing everybody. My son Stefan says what I thought was a nurturant sheaf of wheat looks to him like a writing quill. My granddaughter Stefanie, in a case of the younger generation's reconciling of old/new beliefs, suggests the writing quill is a stalk of wheat.

Lucia is my historical signifying woman inspiring me to write true stories healing everybody, lighting our way to a new/old inclusive world of caring, sharing, healing. The beliefs of popular cultures have sustained and perpetuated this hope.

Popular cultures of the African Mediterranean region—Jewish, Jewish Christian, Christian, Muslim—share a belief in the *mal'occhio* or evil eye. In folklore, Lucia's healing presence protects against the evil eye—repelling the gaze of a jealous/resentful person who wishes you evil.[88]

Healing has been a significant gift of Sicilian women throughout the ages … down to my Sicilian American mother who in the 1920s cut her hair like a flapper, read newspaper articles on nutrition, and spooned cod liver oil into her kids every day. Simultaneously, Kate was a modern healer who replaced traditional herbal unguents with modern equivalents—rubbing her kids' chests with Vicks ointment—to ward off a cold, and an ancient healer who shut our bedroom windows at night to keep out evil spirits.

In the West, healing was associated with others outside the dominant religion whose wisdom was considered dangerous by the dominant culture. Lucia of Syracuse, who looked to Agata, the indigenous healer whom Romans identified with Pagan beliefs, was followed by Jewish, Christian, Moorish, and Saracen women respected for their medical expertise. Sicily and south Italy are regions that, at one time, held more women medical practitioners than any other place in Europe.[89]

The Inquisition took this practice away from women healers, branded them as witches, and gave their practice of medicine to men doctors.[90]

In the Middle Ages, Muslim rule in Sicily became a refuge of Jews from Christian persecution. Jews were considered "People of the Book" and "People of the Covenant." Today in 2019, Pope Francis, a contemporary pope, refers to Jewish~Christian~Muslim scriptures … and Leoluca Orlando, the mayor of Palermo, has a painting of the black saint, San Benedetto il Moro, in his office.

In the Middle Ages, Muslim rule in Sicily required Jews to pay taxes, but they were free to administer their own affairs and free to own property. A revealing prohibition forbade Jews in Christian cultures from owning "Christian slaves."[91]

Beliefs connected with Lucia have persisted to this day. One meaning is suggested by Louisa Calio, whose name is a variant of mine, a contemporary Sicilian American woman who fell in love with a revolutionary Muslim in Eritrea, Africa. Her book, *Journey to the Heart Waters*, resonates in layers of my unconscious, preconscious, consciousness.[92] She quotes Rumi, an inclusive Muslim poet considered the most popular interpreter of spirituality today in the world:

"There's no one more openly irreverent than a lover.

He or she jumps on the scale opposite eternity and claims to balance it.

And there is no one more secretly reverent."

In *Journey to the Heart Waters*, Louisa goes to Khartoum to meet her lover. How much of the old remains today, she realizes, in revolutionary activities … including her own fears and the many layers of her being. "Pagan-Italian, Egyptian, Judeo-Christian-Coptic Nubian-Islamic-Maltese-Sicilian-Greek." She meets her beloved revolutionary … wonders if he and she are their grandfathers' ghost or their mother's prayers to Semitic Miriam who wears all of women's roles: healer, mistress, mothering one, inspired energizer …

CHAPTER 21
Gift family roots trip to Sicily

⟶ꙮ⟵

I n September 2014, our eldest grandson, Joshua Seth Birnbaum, gifted our diverse family with a trip to Sicily. Invited to Sicily were four generations of Birnbaums: Jews (Ashkenazi and Sefardic), Christians (Catholic and Protestant), Buddhists, Taoist, Gnostics, Agnostics, and others curious about their ancestry. We were Americans of diverse ethnic inheritance: Sicilian, Celt, Native American, Scandinavian, French, German, Hungarian, Japanese, Italian, Scot, Scot-Irish, Irish, and English. Each of us transmitting in our unconscious ~ historic preconsciousness ~ glimpses in consciousness, our deep beliefs underneath our names, in our lives, and in our unwritten and written stories.

A varied group with different life concerns, we were parents, grandparents, a great grandmother (me), kids, grandkids, and great grandkids. We were a physicist/world entrepreneur … a world culinary expert/restaurateur … a Francophile linguist … infant boutique owners … a Wall Street trader with Berkeley values … a blindingly beautiful world model … a radical environmentalist biologist (with what she calls "hippie" beliefs) who is an arborist healer of the environment … an administrator of Bay Area cities who copes with urban crises … and an environmental lawyer. Josephine (Josie) Ann Lucia and Adam (Murphy), who are Wally's and my eldest great grandkids, also came on the 2014 trip to Sicily. Charlie, our great granddaughter just born, couldn't come; neither could her parents Nicolas & Nicky.

The trip to Sicily—pervaded by the enduring presence of my late great grandfather—was subsidized by Josh, our very generous grandson, who is a New York trader and named his hedge fund for the park in Berkeley where he hiked as a youth. The trip logistics were arranged by my eldest son Naury. My eldest daughter Barbara researched *la cucina siciliana* (restaurants) and festivals in Sicily. Naury, a philosopher ~ physicist ~ world entrepreneur, wrote daily itineraries based on his research as well as mine.

As a case of a gift economy, the trip became the story of one family of diverse inheritances walking toward the emerging paradigm of caring, sharing, healing ...

Everyone in our immediate family was invited, including Wally's sister Elsa whose health did not permit her to come (Elsa passed in November 2018). New parents Nic & Nicky could not come. Granddaughter Stefanie, an elementary school teacher, could not make it; her lineage includes Celt~Catholic~Scandinavian~Jewish~Native American~Sicilian.

Our middle son Marc, whose lineage—West Asian Jewish/Sicilian/Francophile—came with his love Nancy, a Japanese American, whose parents were incarcerated in Japanese concentration camps at the outset of world war II. Her father Tom volunteered for heroic wartime Allies' ski battalion in Northern Europe while her mother Stella was in the internment camp where their eldest daughter Karen was born. Nancy, youngest of three sisters (Karen, Betty, Nancy), was born after the war.

Marc & Nancy's second son, Matt, came on the trip. Nancy & Marc's sons (Nic and Matt), in my view, are significant cases of the emerging new paradigm. Nic, Japanese American, and Nicky, Euro-American with a northern Italian grandfather, are parents of a luminous Eurasian blonde child, my great grandchild, who in 2016 moved like a mermaid, and in 2019 is a vibrant five-year-old called Charlie (for Charlotte). Showered with love and care in a changing form of family—multi-generational, flowing over contemporary boundaries of mothering and fathering—her father Nic is simultaneously her major caretaker, a highly nurturant father, and an entrepreneur. Charlie's nurturing is helped by grandparents Marc & Nancy as well as by her Uncle Matt.

During the family trip to Sicily in 2014, Matt cared for the kids of his intrepid cousins. Sabrina & Peter's kids, Josie & Adam, swam and jumped in shoals outside primordial Addaura.

This family trip to Sicily included photographers, computer wizards, internet entrepreneurs, mothers and fathers, sons and daughters, grandmothers and grandfathers, uncles and aunts, cousins, grand and great grandkids, and a great grandmother (me). Our family's ethnic places of origin range from Sicily, Ukraine, France, Spain, Germany, Italy, Austria, Scandinavia, Britain, Japan, and Native America. Our family's religious diversity spans established world religions to heresy. Family conversations are lively, "Did you believe in Original Sin?" "No. Neither did I."

Mother, grandmother, great grandmother, and a professor who has written books on world feminist spirituality, adopting Sicily as case in point, I was, by default, the tour guide. This threw me into anxiety, not wanting to lecture to my kids, yet wanting them to know their Sicilian heritage, that of one set of their grandparents, Wally's and my hypothetical ancestral place of encounter. At one point, overcome by nameless panic, I could not put together the daily itineraries, whereupon my eldest son Naury, with superb research skills (physicist/philosopher/entrepreneur), wrote scholarly synopses of our daily schedules, combining his own research with my perspectives.

Just before we left on the trip, Mt. Etna in Sicily erupted and earth tremors were felt in Napa, California. After mopping up the water from a broken water tank, Naury, like his Sicilian ancestors, resumed life ... by preparing for our family tour to Sicily.

On September 4, 2014, Wally's second *jahrzeit,* we stopped, on our way to Sicily, in his native New York. Josh took us to an edgy jazz restaurant owned by an iconic couple of black culture, to a Broadway musical, arranged our stay in a high-tech hotel in the old Butcher district of the first city of the world, and took us to dinner in an Italian restaurant serving chunks of parmesan cheese ... before we flew across the Atlantic Ocean to Sicily.

On September 6, Naury's birthday, we arrived in Palermo, the African Paleolithic site of human origin, the Neolithic site of migrating Semitic Canaanites from Levant of West Asia, and the contemporary site of mafia~feminist~communist politics, including the procession day of the Black Madonna of Tindari.

The rest of our family arrived. During our first week in Sicily, we stayed in a leased villa very near the sanctuary of the Black Madonna of Tindari. Later we learned that the villa, like many businesses of the island, was owned by the mafia.

My memory spiraled back to our 2001 study tour and being in a restaurant outside Palermo adjoining the sanctuary of the Black Madonna of Tindari. The tour women exclaimed in excitement at seeing an etching of naked African women—Amazons on horseback—arrowing invaders. In 2010, the last time Wally and I visited Tindari, the etching was still there. In 2014, I was revisiting, this time without Wally, the Black Madonna of Tindari, who in 1970 may have tapped unconscious/preconscious energies in my subsequent intense spiral of world exploration and learning the deep story of my family.

On this northwest coast of Sicily, we were very near the birthplace of my maternal grandmother, Nanna Giuseppina. We were also near the Vucciria, the city market of Palermo where my Nannu Joe worked as a boy before migrating in the 1890s to work in the city market of Kansas City, Missouri.

Lucia Chiavola Birnbaum

In the Vucciria, famed for market vendors singing their wares, on one of our several study tours to Palermo, Wally slipped and fell in a puddle of ice from a fish stall. Taken to a hospital, he was given a free battery of tests by doctors in the universal medical care system of Italy whose coverage extends to visitors.

Every day on our family group explorations we passed Termini Imerese, the birthplace of my maternal grandmother, Nanna Giuseppina (Josephine), who figures in a roll call of indigenous people/explorers/invaders … paleolithic Africans, Semites from West Asia, Greeks, Semitic black Moors from Africa, Semitic Saracens from Asia, Scandinavian-French Normans, Lombards of northern Italy (my grandmother), Catholic Inquisitors, Spanish Bourbons, Austrians, French, Germans, and Americans.

On our 2014 trip, wherever this Sicilian American migrant daughter had suppressed the Sicilian dialect of my childhood as well as the formal Italian I learned later … both returned. I suppressed the Sicilian dialect when, in graduate school, I learned to read and write in educated Italian. This suppression deepened in the 1970s-80s-90s when Italian feminists would thrust me on stage to speak in public before Italian feminist groups, sending me into crisis trying to thread nouns and verbs in front of an audience of Italian-speaking feminists.

With my *famiglia* in Sicily in 2014, my speaking Italian flowed over dams of repression. From nether depths surfaced the Sicilian dialect I heard as a child in bawdy messages of my Nanna Lucia's parrot … and when my mother and father argued. On this gift roots trip to Sicily, both Sicilian dialect and educated Italian rose to my consciousness.

During the first week of our 2014 tour, I had returned to where Wally and I earlier, with kindred spirits on study tours later, had uncovered signs of my primordial ancestral African legacy, notably the Paleolithic Addaura cave in Palermo and the nearby Black Madonna of Tindari.[93]

Near Palermo, we encountered the suppressed story of Muslims at San Benedetto di Fratello—Saint Blessed Brother called "Il Moro" or Moor, a sainted Black Muslim from Africa in a city called Brother. The popular prayer card of this black saint depicts him holding a white child while white children with black hair play at his feet. San Fratello, geographically close to the Black Madonna of Tindari, suggests how signifyer meanings flow across suppression, transmuting color, gender, and place.

The twin city of San Fratello, sainted black brother, is Palermo, whose August 15 Catholic festival of the Assumption of the Madonna into heaven is celebrated in this capitol of Sicily as a festival to Santa Rosalia … celebrating the madonna as a woman saint whose symbol is a rose. This legacy, discussed earlier, continues to be transmitted by our granddaughter Stefanie in her middle name Rose ... and later, in 2016, by my great granddaughter Isabelle Rose, connecting African beautiful mother Isis with the Catholic Madonna. On August 15 in Palermo, the church celebrates the Assumption of the Virgin Mary into heaven; people celebrate *festa* of Santa Rosalia with dancing in the streets.

On one of our several tours to Sicily, Wally and I joined pilgrims visiting Santa Rosalia's sanctuary above Palermo, where the deep story of the island is kept. At the entry to her sanctuary stands a statue of Spartacus, the leader of a slave uprising against the Roman empire. Inside the sanctuary, in a coffin, one of Santa Rosalia's hands is black; in convolutions of the deep story of Sicily, a black hand became a symbol of the mafia.

Spiraling back to 12th century Palermo, then the seat of the Holy Roman Empire and the center of the Western world, its court gleamed with artists, poets, and heretics. This was followed in 1492 by the Catholic church and state ousting Jews from Christian lands, by nation state imperial enterprises, including kidnapping Africans from Africa and enslaving them in the New World, by Inquisition persecution of killing dark others considered infidels.

Our Palermo tour guide, a woman of Jewish ancestry, gave us a subaltern view of Italian history: "Garibaldi should have stayed home; Sicily was rich before unification in 1870."

This tour guide heartened me because I have a similar way of teaching. As a Sicilian American woman, I think of myself as an outlier, outside the dominant violent paradigm of the West, who considers my task as a teacher to tell the truth ... as I have found it with Wally, my family, grandkids, kindred spirits ... exploring on-site, checked, balanced, enhanced by kin and kith, confirmed in science, religion, heresy, and folklore of everyday and celebratory rituals.

Not wanting to impose my beliefs on kids, students, others, I advise them to study epistemology and the relativity of all human knowledge. As a mother, grandmother, great grandmother, I encourage our kids and kindred spirits to follow their own hearts and vision. Advising them to know the shifting historical parameters of knowing the truth, yet encouraging everybody to explore/tell their own stories because all of our stories may light the way to a better world.

All the above was early accompanied by my hope that telling our stories will help dissolve hatreds that have escalated today into millions of killings.

Telling our stories may help us realize we are all brothers and sisters who need to transform our very dangerous violent world into a green and just planet for everyone.

During the first week of our September 2014 journey on the north and western coasts of primordial African Sicily, we were traveling in the historic place where Canaanite Jews from West Asia settled in 800 BCE and founded Palermo in Sicily/Carthage in Africa. We took a funicular to Erice, promontory town near Palermo where our kids, led by Peter, found the Black Madonna of Custonaci (province of Palermo), whose Easter mysteries in Trapani had blown me away ever since 1988.

Peter found her in the Catholic cathedral of Erice, where I had not thought to look. She is formidable, very black, presiding over a baroque church with many Pagan symbols. Meditating in the baroque cathedral of Erice while my great grandkids climbed the bell tower, I noted defiant human faces sculpted among leaves of Corinthian Greek columns, signifying resistance to the dominant paradigm of Western civilization: violent elites enslaving the conquered in Athenian wars on Peloponnesus and Troy, male racial/gender hierarchy raping goddesses.

Thinking about the persistence of Pagan symbols in Sicily, I recalled the southeastern triangle of my ancestral island, in my paternal town of Ragusa where we had found similar defiant faces sculptured in stucco underneath wrought iron balconies where women every day air the bedding, care for plants, put the laundry out for the sun to dry, from their balcony participating—or not—in religious and civic celebrations in the streets.

During the second week of our 2014 family journey, we drove south to the southeast triangle of Sicily, memorialized in the RAI blockbuster film series, *Il Commissario*, which showcase the adventures of a contemporary Sicilian male detective (who resembles my son Stefan), and was a television film series with local actors and in local dialect, conveying the uncanny persistence of very ancient beliefs in contemporary Sicily.

With 2014 eyes I looked, incredulously, at the seascape of the Ragusa Ibla area from where, in 1912, my father and his family migrated to America fleeing *miseria*—misery conflating poverty/sexual humiliations living in Sicily and the poor south of world.

Historic economic/sexual exploitation/humiliation of Sicilians/other South Italians was codified by Normans in their Droit du Seigneur law: the lord of the castle had the prerogative to sleep with the new bride of a feudal tenant. I wondered what this intense humiliation did to Sicilian women … and to men.[94]

By 2014, the southern and eastern stretch of Sicily fronting Africa had changed dramatically since Wally's and my last trip in 2010. In four years, this strip of land in the African Mediterranean had become an international summer spa of northerners seeking sun and sea, lured, maybe, by primordial submerged memories. Marinas of Ragusa Ibla, Scicli, Modica, and Noto attract sun worshipers against a backdrop of baroque Christian churches and villas for lease to tourists featuring very high technology and contemporary rock music, sending my senses scattering. In fifty-second showers to avoid being scalded, I could listen to perennial Sicilian songs to the beloved sun and saint of light—O Sole Mio and Santa Lucia, 1960s ballads of The Beatles, contemporary heavy metal music … while frantically trying to figure out how to turn the faucet to cool the very hot water.

In 2014, I did not find women in black who, earlier, were all over the island. Today, in Sicily they live in the interior of the island. Internationally, they stand at street intersections of the West, "Women in Black" witnessing silently against the wholesale murder of wars around the globe initiated by global elites aiming to establish a new world order benefiting the elite 1% who own the wealth and power of 99% of people of the world.

On the highly touristed beaches of Sicily we saw women of all size and age in bikinis so minimal a grandson called them "dental floss." How rapidly, I thought, cultural change happens. Yet how persistently do submerged values persevere.

In Wally's favorite restaurant on the Marina di Ragusa Ibla, a light-skinned third-generation African Sicilian suddenly appeared, advised us that *pesci spada* (swordfish, Wally's favorite) was out of season, and helped us choose fish from "the same family." After giving us helpful advice about hotels, restaurants, and beach arrangements, he disappeared.

On the beach, an Asian Sicilian vender from India, who had worked as a migrant peddler on the island for twenty years, from whom I purchased costume jewelry for gifts, looked at our diverse kids enjoying themselves and asked if he could be my honorary grandson.

In the afternoon, my grandkids had me nap in our hotel that was dug into ancestral Iblean mountains where every spring Sicilians release white doves to fly back to Africa … while they went off to find the ancient Chiavola cave home dug into the Iblean mountains named for Asian woman signifier Cybele in the town of Ragusa Ibla.

I have visited my paternal ancestral cave home in the Iblean mountains many times. It is where my Nanna Lucia and kids lived and where my Nannu Luigi visited weekly from the nearby Norman/Angevin *Fortezza* (fortified castle) where he worked. Very close encounters of my Sicilian grandfathers with Norman castle courtiers gifted me and my sister Joie, and other descendants of Nannu Luigi and courtier ladies, with hazel (blue-green-brown) eyes, which Sicilians call witch eyes ...

My case is complex ... my ophthalmologist advises I have one hazel eye and one blue eye. My blue eye may be a gift from my Nanna Giuseppina of Lombard ancestors who came with the Normans in 1060 CE to Christianize Pagan Sicily. My hazel eye may be a gift of close encounters of my grandfathers—falconers/game wardens of Ragusa Ibla—who were born and lived in the castle right up to my Nannu Luigi.

My Nannu Luigi was brought to USA in 1920 by my Uncle George. He spoke French, calling all the women in the family *chérie*. Wearing a romantic long black cloak, he came with other Chiavola elders to ask my maternal grandparents for the hand of my mother Catarina in marriage to their son Salvatore, called Turiddu. Nannu Luigi, whose portrait—gifted to me by Uncle George—looks at me in my study in Berkeley where I am writing this. He died just before Wally and I were born in 1924.

Tracking my Sicilian story, I thought about my legacy of romantic Sicilian men, notably my father who wept while listening to the popular Puccini opera, La Boheme ... and their wives, strong survivor women who nurtured families but also conveyed women's subservience to family values defined by a patriarchal society ... transmitting these values to their kids.

I know this riddle personally. I respected Nanna Lucia's nurturing of her six kids during the *miseria* when she breast-fed infants of the nobility in the castle where her husband worked as game keeper and falconer. In Kansas City, my father took us ritually every Sunday to visit Nanna Lucia along with family reports on his family to his mother. In these visits, Nanna's parrot (whom she carried on her shoulder) proclaimed bawdy messages that I later interpreted as Nanna's resistance to patriarchal subordination.

This mixed legacy of my inherited matriarchal signifyers could have been disastrous for me. I would not have gone to college if my mother and I had heeded Nanna Lucia's pronouncement when I was about to complete high school: I was not to think of college because the *famiglia* needed my earnings. I was to go to Jane Hayes Gates, a vocational school founded in the Progressive era where women immigrants and their daughters were trained to sew on high-powered machines of the textile industry, subservient to male bosses and working in dangerous conditions (women were often locked in and unable to escape fires) ... until progressive reformers and bold immigrant women—including my mother as a labor steward for the union—secured better working environments for women co-workers.

I thought about how historical legacies can have different outcomes. In my case, my cultural predestination as an immigrant daughter was to be a subservient woman in family and industry. In a signifying incident in high school, I almost flunked sewing class, unconsciously trying to avoid my predestined vocation to sew in the textile industry.

Yet after my near-death crisis in 1968, followed by very radical activities at SF State, followed by being fired ... sewing traditional patchwork quilts with my preschool grandkids, Sabrina & Josh, who helped me choose colors and patches, grounded me in the midst of personal and political crises. Today I wonder at granddaughter Sabrina, who keeps cool in incredibly hot crises that come with administering a very volatile East Bay city. Unlike Nanna Lucia, I was blessed/lucky with a husband who was a co-parent; Sabrina is blessed/lucky with her husband Peter, who resigned in 2017 from his job as a lawyer to stay at home. He cares for their kids and supports his wife in the vortex of an iconic city in very fast cultural and political change. I am also thinking of grandson Josh who helped me choose colors and signifying symbols for the patchwork quilts when he was a preschooler ... who today keeps cool in the frantic world of trading.

Outcomes may be determined by the map we follow. Today the site of our family's ancestral cave home in Ragusa Ibla is marked with a sign, "*Chiasso Chiavola,*" on a corner of the piazza of the famed baroque church of San Giorgio where all my Chiavola ancestors/relatives, including my father, were baptized. On our 2014 family tour of Sicily, grand and great grandkids did not find the Chiavola cave home—they followed a misleading map. In 2013 our grandkids, Sabrina & Peter, celebrating their tenth wedding anniversary in Sicily, did find the ancestral Chiavola cave home.

Our family dined in an elegant cave restaurant in Ragusa Ibla where protruding primordial rocks of the Iblean cave were nestled with crystal wine glasses. Driving back to our leased villa at Scicli, we arrived at 3 AM, at which time Josh advised us to be in the van at 8 AM the next morning because we were going to a surprise destination.

Arriving half asleep at the air strip in the corner of the island facing Africa to the south and Asia to the east, I was hoisted up into a helicopter. We flew over Mt. Etna, the active volcano of Europe still fuming from erupting a month before. Mesmerized, I saw golden pools still wet with lava … evoking an image of alchemists/transformation.

Sicily is an island stone garden of volcanic lava rock that inhabitants use to rebuild their homes and churches after regular eruptions of Mt. Etna. The 1693 eruption created today's world heritage site. Sicilians replaced collapsed Greek buildings with baroque churches and city halls, and dwellings with African~Pagan~Jewish~Christian~Islamic signifyers … the contemporary magical baroque backdrop to the Sicilian coast facing south toward Africa/east toward Asia.

Other signifyers, for me, of this African~Asian southeast corner of Sicily, today a part of Europe, are the red-black wine of Avola, the many farm-worker strikes, and the movies in USA cinema, notably the movies with the haunting African-Semitic face of Al Pacino, the actor whose Sicilian ancestors may have come from the town here named Pachino.

This region of my ancestral island gives me to know, bodily, that death is followed by renewal of life. This is signified in the life-celebrating baroque architecture after the devastating earthquake of 1693, today a United Nation World Heritage site.

Baroque passion has persisted in the love of my Chiavola relatives for Italian opera. My father as a youth worked in the fields of Ragusa Ibla, eating an onion for lunch to save up money to go to the opera. On Saturday afternoons in my childhood in Kansas City, I watched my father weeping while he listened, at top decibel, to operas—*La Boheme, Aida, La Forza del Destino*—celebrating fallen women of the lower classes, inter-cultural love of an African and European, the force of destiny, while my mother, hurting from my father's many infidelities, went through the house loudly slamming doors.

On our 2014 family trip, I learned how perception can shape reality. On the steps of a pizzeria adjoining the town square of Noto, the menu for international visitors, in hilarious fractured English, offered one hundred kinds of pizza. I looked up from the menu to see a woman whose legs dangled flirtatiously from the ledge of the baroque church in front of us. Walking up to see her more closely, I realized my perception had transformed a male official in the city square, honoring war, into a woman watching, in amusement, people eating one hundred kinds of pizza. I caught the humor that edges Sicilian relativism[95] … and the wisdom of enjoying the many ways of knowing … in one hundred kinds of pizza.

Thinking on the many ways of human nurturing, I remembered a family photo of my eldest son Naury, then thirteen and holding his infant brother Stefan, with Marc, my middle son, standing alongside. All three of our sons today are hands-on very nurturing grandfathers.

In Sicily in 2014, while driving through the darkness after late Mediterranean dinners, I thought about male nurturance. Josh & Naury, son and father, with the consummate skill of Italian drivers, carrying us through unmarked places in Sicily fronting Africa and Asia, navigated by grandson Jake's computer skills, and helped by grandson Matt getting out of the van to direct the driver on the hairpin turns of the streets of baroque Sicilian towns. Today, Jake & Matt are extraordinarily nurturing fathers of Andrew & Izzy. In October 2018, cousins Andrew & Izzy, while visiting in New York, were photographed at a pumpkin patch where they were celebrating the bounty of the earth.

In May 2019, our eldest grandson Josh at his wedding to Whitney—at whose earlier wedding to Abi, Josh held the one corner of the *hoopa*—gave me their grandfather Wally's *tallis* (prayer shawl) to hold during the wedding ceremony so that Josh could pass it on for the next family wedding, continuing the spiral ...

On our 2014 trip, I learned that when everybody's gifts and interests are appreciated, everybody spontaneously helps and nurtures. For great granddaughter Josie's eighth birthday party, we went to a neighborhood street market to buy salmon, greens, and zucchini. Marc spoke French, I spoke the Sicilian dialect, and Courtney & Matt helped each other to purchase shoes. Later, Aunt Barbara and nephew Jake cooked dinner with help from everyone. Whitney showed us photos of her sister's newborn baby boy. At Summer Solstice 2019, Whitney & Josh are expecting their baby boy.

At the 2014 birthday party for Josie, I told a story to grand and great grandkids about our animal ancestors roaming the earth and evolving into humans ... some of our ancestral grandmothers and grandfathers lived in the very place we were celebrating Josie's birthday. After the party, everybody washed the dishes. The great grandkids, five-year-old Adam Murphy and eight-year-old birthday girl Josie Ann Lucia, danced and danced until after midnight.

One night in a seafood restaurant perched on the sea, Adam, while dancing, fell into the African Mediterranean waters. The proprietor's little girl (also five) gave Adam a dry set of her clothes. Giving, I thought, extends beyond family roles, beyond gender, beyond age.

After a week in Sicily, Adam and Josie had to go back to school. Adam, his African dark eyes sparkling, looked at me, his maternal great grandmother and said, "Sicily is very historic!" Later I learned that Adam insisted, at Erice, on bringing home a painting of a black madonna.

Marc & Nancy left Sicily for France to go on another honeymoon, this time as parents of Matt & Nic and grandparents of a granddaughter born in April 2014. Charlie (Charlotte Kimura Bald Birnbaum) is a multicultural vision: African nose, Asian countenance, honey blonde curly hair, and radiant curiosity.

The 2014 family trip to Sicily was healing for me. Cheering me up the narrow gangplank of our leased yacht, the skipper guided me while the crew chorused in an Italian soccer cheer, "Forza, Nonna!" I could not stop crying. My grandson Jake poured water into my burning eyes to flush out what was thought to be suntan lotion. Later I realized our yacht was docked in the marina of Villa Igeia, named for the Greek goddess of healing, where Wally and I—three years earlier—had stayed.

I thought of the skills of our kids ... everyone chasing their own passions while looking out for everyone. Arriving at a new town I worried when they scattered, yet everyone via cell phones was in constant communication with everyone.

At Noto, Barbara wheeled me down a steep hill to the city square to join the *passaggiatta*, an Italian afternoon walking ritual when people greet one another, eat ice cream, and renew themselves before a late dinner. Abi found a *libreria*, a bookstore where I could find local histories. Naury found *La Repubblica*, an Italian left-wing newspaper, for me.

Abi & Jake made international phone calls while planning their wedding in New York for the upcoming November. Every morning, Jake, from our adjoining room, would awaken me. One of my kids would hold my hand while guiding me over rocky glades to breakfast under the trees.

Ancient~new values of nurturing~giving were evident. Matt Birnbaum, who loves being Charlotte's uncle, cared for Josie & Adam splashing in the shoals while their intrepid parents Sabrina & Peter swam beyond the buoys at Cefalu. Barbara, a grandmother nurturing everybody, saw to it that everyone dined and wined well, arranging a visit to a grape festival in my Nanna Lucia's hometown of Vittoria, where, in the 1970s, Wally had driven us to see the radical political murals ... on our 2014 trip, our kids snipped grapes, then danced on them to make wine.

Nancy asked questions about the mafia. Historically, the original name of men of honor who protected their women from raping marauders on this continually invaded island, was "*Ma figlia*" (my daughter).

My kids' questions about the mafia in Sicily gave me to think of complicity elsewhere. The mafia in Sicily governs, in plain sight, a hideous killing machine. The CIA, a similar hideous killing machine of the USA empire, tortures and kills suspected terrorists at hidden sites … constantly creating more terrorists sustained by the complicity of politicians and citizens in the domestic/international political killing carnival of 2019 …

I thought about Sicily's many invasions/close encounters of different peoples on spiral migrations out of Africa. Sicilians, today considered a "mixed" people, are among the least militaristic and the most tolerant of the world … maybe because they are a dramatic case of genetic origins in Africa and migration experience out of Africa when they learned to survive by caring, sharing, healing.

Contemporary Sicilians' rejection of violence may be connected not only with long historical experience migrating out of Africa throughout the world but with recent political experience. Since the late 1960s and 1970s, Italians have lived through revolutionary hopes, knee-capping corporate industrialists, and the Red Brigade murder of Christian Democrat prime minister Aldo Moro. I just realized Moro's name means Moor—Black Muslims from Africa and Asia who came to Sicily and stayed until conquered by the pope's Christian invaders … yet leaving their descendants with a legacy of nonviolent resistance to imposed rule as well as wisdom from experience that good governing coalitions include everybody on the political spectrum.

I thought about what Italians called, in the 1980s, "repentance" of Italian violent revolutionaries, followed by a national parliamentary stalemate whose unexpected outcome has left people to manage themselves (*arrangiarsi*) … city and provincial governments governing in coalitions that respect everybody/everybody's beliefs … precipitating heated arguments/sometimes unexpected outcomes of the mix of primordial predispositions, pagan, religious, secular signifying rituals. A few years ago in "red" Bologna, the newly elected communist mayor walked, as a barefoot pilgrim, to the sanctuary of the city's Black Madonna of San Luca.

On our 2014 family trip, in contrast to the preceding revolutionary period, Italian criticism of USA bombing and killing in the African Mediterranean, was muted: Graffito advised, "USA, *Stai attenta*." USA, watch what you are doing.

In July 2016, resistance, no longer muted, was dramatically evident in demonstrations against the large NATO nuclear installation at Comiso, outside my ancestral Ragusa Ibla, where many years ago my *comare* Cristina Biaggi, then a young woman, was arrested for protesting the nuclear installation. Now, like me a grandmother she has pictorialized her journey.

In Spring 2017, my contemporary *comare*, Clare Loprinzi, trying to found a natural childbirth center on her family's ancestral home at Trabia on the beach outside Palermo, today advises that the many popular demonstrations against USA military installations in Sicily are often led by midwives whose help bringing infants into the light is part of their concern for all life. Demonstrations against MUOS, the satellite surveillance by USA and NATO, feature midwives' concern for past~present~future. Their contemporary banner of resistance[96] is a three-legged Medusa walking across yellow triangles of dying and red triangles of living ... a woman with regenerative pinecones in her hair.

After the 2014 gift tour to Sicily, I came home ... where everything seemed to be accelerating. More evidence of imminent environmental catastrophe, indiscriminate USA drone killings of innocents in the African Mediterranean, Israeli killing Palestinian children in Gaza, police trained to kill black people in USA ...

... Simultaneous with enormous demonstrations against the extinction of the earth, huge protests against the murder of black men and women, protests against the corrupt rulers from Hong Kong to South America to Saudi Arabia.

On my return to USA, wading through a myriad of e-mail initiatives to change a world whose contemporary condition scares anybody who has not blocked off all human feelings ... and photos and movies from Marc & Nancy of their granddaughter (my great granddaughter), Charlotte Kimura Birnbaum (called Charlie). In a video, her mother Nicky said, "Here's your alligator." The baby reached for it. Mother and father both have enterprises. Charlie lives with her father Nic in a garden cottage adjoining the home of grandparents Marc & Nancy. She is a child who gives me healing balm in a nigh-hopeless time.

On Summer Solstice 2017, I meditated on being a *bisnonna* ... great grandmother meaning twice baked (like biscotti). Every time we are blessed with a child, grandchild, or great grandchild, I think she/he has to be the most beautiful, brightest, most endearing child in the world ... just like every mother~grandmother~great grandmother of the world.

Yet nurturing is not segregated to mothers, grandmothers, great grand-mothers. My own family is evidence … like African villages … like my own childhood in a Sicilian American neighborhood where everybody nurtured their own kids while keeping an eye on neighborhood kids …

Widening of nurturing to include everybody is imperative today in a world on the verge of total extinction of all life.

CHAPTER 22
Gift—Enchanted Wedding of Grandkids

❦

November is a fateful month, for me. Wally and I met on the night after Thanksgiving 1945. On the day after Thanksgiving 1969, SF State fired me. On other days after other Thanksgivings, my mother and brother died. In November 2014, Abi & Jake welcomed many members of the family, scores of kindred spirits, to their wedding on November 9—an enchanted wedding of ancestral traditions ~ living in the burning now ~ walking into a once and future good earth.

Earlier the bridal pair participated in the Oakland and New York Occupy movements. For the last several years Jake, a political activist and documentary film maker, has taken survival gear to desert rituals of Burning Man. Abi is an artist, a political activist, and a teacher. Both are parents of incredibly spirited Andrew who visited me in the summer of 2017. Held by his father, he insisted on dancing on the dining table, jeopardizing the crystal, yet gladdening this great grandmother's heart ... Andrew is going to be a world mover and shaker in a caring and sharing world. Flash! Andrew's sister Emma Lia arrived August 30, 2018.

For three years before going to New York, Jake worked in a San Francisco radio station, choosing to live with us, his paternal grandparents, in Berkeley ... becoming very close to Wally, outlier great grandfather/father/entrepreneur/peaceful physicist ... and to me, outlier great grandmother/teacher/writer/activist for a just and green earth.

One night during Oakland Occupy and while in touch with New York Occupy, Jake knocked on my bedroom door, "We're going to take the Brooklyn Bridge. Now go back to sleep!" After Wally passed, Jake stayed with me until Hanukkah. He then went to New York where he met Abi at a latke party.

Abi, of Sefardic and Ashkenazi Jewish parents, whose historic stories include fleeing the Inquisition in Spain to Lebanon, Cyprus, Greece, a connection with the Lincoln Brigade in the Spanish civil war, and migration to suburban New Jersey where in childhood Abi hid her treasures in trees.

Jake & Abi's wedding in 2014 honored family traditions melded with their own values. The ceremony was officiated by a Jewish rabbi in an Italian restaurant on the East River whose backdrop was a medley of today~past~future ... bridges and skyscrapers of Manhattan, where Jake & Abi work ... adjoining Brooklyn, where orthodox Jews keep seven-thousand-year-old rituals alive alongside artists envisioning the future and contemporary peaceful, creative, and frequent demonstrations are held against injustice.

The wedding rehearsal dinner in a Brooklyn restaurant featured ribald Sicilian singing, "*C'e la luna mezza mare, Mamma Mia, mi ha di maritarmi*" ... and African daisies (Gerbera) in bowls of water with lit candles. Southern Rock music recalled Abi & Jake plighting their troth in New Orleans.

As the eldest grandmother, I read the first blessing. Neal, my eldest nephew and a doctor who, with the passing of his father Norman and his uncle Wally, is now paterfamilias. Looking like Rodin's *Le Penseur*, he held one corner of the *hoopa*. Josh, my eldest grandson, held another corner of the *hoopa*. The other two sides were held by kindred spirits who earlier witnessed the signing of the *ketuba*, the traditional Jewish wedding contract. Kindred spirits from Burning Man and Occupy danced at Jake & Abi's wedding.

Dancing at the wedding featured the *hora*, the center of all Jewish wedding celebrations—two steps backward before dancing forward in concentric circles, joyfully, together. This pattern, a scholar of ethnic dancing tells me, is the characteristic form of folk dancing across the world ... two steps backward before dancing forward ... to a future that humans—along with nature—are recreating as a green earth with human values.

On Winter Solstice 2014, kindred spirit Sandy Miranda, gave me a twinkling icon of Guadalupe, reminding me of the complexity of migrations out of Africa. Veneration of this black madonna began in Spain, then Conquistadors took her to the New World where indigenous Indios integrated her into their Native American stories. Lighting my office in our Berkeley home, this icon of Guadalupe was made in China. Matrona of North and South America, many believe Guadalupe can, with the help of everybody, create miracles. When Rob, Sandy's love and a cybernet genius, comes to untangle my computer, he switches on the iconic light of the Guadalupe lamp and says, "We need all the help we can get."

※※※※※

Atiba, my three-generations-younger kindred spirit of the third world, sent me an e-mail saying, "I think we are on the cusp of something good ... "

CHAPTER 23
Gifting~harvesting seeds of renewal.

꠳꠲꠶

P eter (to whom I give a Mensch award), is a new paradigm father, husband, son, and brother who, in recent years, rose at dawn to cook a hot breakfast and pack a nutritious lunch for his family before going off to his job as a lawyer in an environmentally conscious firm. Peter played in a jazz band with his sister Kerry on weekends. Sabrina, mother, wife, daughter, sister, granddaughter works in a strategic post of a Bay Area city considered a model of dynamic ethnic and political diversity and change. In 2017, Peter resigned his corporate lawyer post to care, full time, for their kids. Supporting Sabrina, a city administrator of a signifying city at the vortex of rushing cross currents of cultural~political transformation, he is a work-at-home father-husband-son-brother-human.

In 2019 as I write this, Peter has just returned from India where he has been recruiting for UCB. His daughter, Josie Ann Lucia, now twelve, is away at a conference of Latinists. Peter's son Adam, along with Adam's grandparents Naury & Barbara, came to visit me ... Adam was rereading a Harry Potter classic.

Sabrina helps her family and city hang in there while a dynamo of fast change hurtles everybody toward the future. She tells her grandmother (me) not to worry, she's "good," and not to worry about the chaotic political landscape. I am awash with incredulity as this granddaughter keeps her cool at the center of crises in the city where she helps keep human values alive in our swerve toward transformation.

My great grandkids are thriving. In 2018, nine-year-old Adam, who plays several sports, may grow up to be a neuroscientist—he will also be dancer ~ mathematics wizard ~ artist ~ gift giver. During the Solstice season of 2016, he gave this great grandmother a crayon design of a mandala connoting holism on which he'd worked for weeks. On Mother's Day 2017, he gave me his prescient painting, in pointillism style, of roses forming a many-pointed star ... signifier of inclusive nurturant world.

Sabrina (holding a younger Josie), who campaigned a few years ago for the Asian woman mayor of her signifying city, said that in her childhood she saw at least one of her four (differently nurturant) grandparents every day. Today I am Sabrina's sole surviving grandparent who remembers her as an infant with eyes wide open in Paris where she was born, and as a preschooler in Berkeley helping me sew patchwork quilts who liked to climb stairs lined with books to play in my study loft.

In her childhood she absorbed Grandpa Wally's math genius; in San Leandro she helped Grandma Ann bake cookies; in Oakland she helped Grandpa Fred build an earthquake-proof doghouse. She went off to college, to Massachusetts Institute of Technology, with guardian angel earrings from me. She learned life skills from her mother and father, Barbara & Naury, who today help out a great deal with their grandkids Josie and Adam. Barbara sewed a sequined tutu for Josie in ballet class; Naury conducted science experiments with both.

Spiraling back to Sabrina's parents … in the 1960s, Naury was a physicist who wore his hair in an Afro, Barbara was a flower child. They wed, began their family in 1972 with son Josh, shortly thereafter taking him to live in Paris. Every day I would mail Josh a book (comfort reading in English, one I remember was on insects) to help him cope with pre-school in suburban Paris where all the kids and teachers spoke French. In Paris, Naury worked as a physicist, Barbara learned French cooking, and Sabrina was born.

In Springtime 2016, Naury and Barbara came with other family members (Linda, Josh & Whitney) to support me in Boston where I gave two keynote addresses for the Association for Study of Women & Mythology, and received the Demeter award. At the end of my first talk, dancer/singer Julie George roused the audience with "Aint Gonna Study War No More!" Barbara invited Julie to visit them in Napa. Naury videotaped all my conference sessions.

In Naury & Barbara's family, their youngest child, Jessica Ann Lucia, is named for her two grandmothers, Ann and Lucia. My granddaughter Jessica Ann Lucia has inherited many gifts, yet she is—in the Celtic tradition—a genuine herself. When she was five, being interviewed for kindergarten in the advanced school where her gifted elder siblings preceded her, tiring of being tested, she swept the interviewer's diagnostic tools onto the floor. When she was nine, Jessica insisted on inviting me to dinner so she could hear about the world women's conference in Beijing in which I had just participated. Later, Jessica (and her dog Truffles) lived with us because she wanted to go to Berkeley High School, a path breaking secondary school producing many celebrated artists, musicians, and political activists found today in all Bay Area demonstrations against injustice.

As a young woman, during ski seasons she lived in our Northstar home at Truckee, where she invited all the ski instructors, and where she met Rusty, her soul mate. Wally and I signed their marriage certificate. Jessica & Rusty now live in their own home near Truckee in Northern California. A biologist, she works as a resident environmentalist in a company. Traveling to sites, she reports on endangered species: animals, birds, and flowers. As a biologist/environmentalist, she can stop construction of a pipe line when she comes across a bird nest. Rusty, an arborist who cares for trees, reminds me of our mutual Scandinavian ancestors who settled in France: the Normans. My Sicilian grandfathers lived in close familiarity in the castle of Ragusa Ibla with Norman-Scandinavian courtiers. Natural caregivers, Jessica & Rusty regularly checked in on Wally when he was very ill, and regularly check in on me today.

In December 2016, Jessica & Rusty gifted everybody with Juliet Lucia Lorraine. whose first name remembers an iconic love story of the West, and whose middle name remembers me and her other grandmother. Her third name remembers a sweet woman in the signifying historically contested liminal region, Lorraine, in between France and Germany.

Rusty beaded me an African necklace, which calms me when I am upset. So does Jessica who once inquired how I am getting along with my new (family selected) computer. I did not tell her I often want to throw the too-erudite mechanism out the window. Sensing this, she said, "How great you're learning by trial and error!" referring to our contemporary monkey ancestors who also learned by trial and error.

Jessica, my youngest granddaughter, for me embodies simultaneity of past~present~future. Her birthday gift to me of a cashmere multi-colored shawl flies on the mezzanine of our Berkeley home … along with Luisah Teish's gift mud cloth from Africa and Lydia Ruyle's painting of the dark mother who comes out of the sea, nurtured by animals, the sun, and the black earth.[97]

Joshua, son of Naury & Barbara, our eldest grandson, lives his spiritual heritage. Everybody remembers his Bar Mitzvah. Reading in Hebrew, he gave an extraordinary exegesis of his Torah passage. When he was fifteen, he wrote a letter to a major financial firm in New York offering to be a summer intern. Rapidly ascending Wall Street ladders, Josh today is a trader who named his hedge fund for the park in Berkeley where he hiked as a youth.

A super active baby, his mother Barbara would come to our house and wordlessly give him to me. I would put him to nap on our western deck where he would watch birds fly in and out of the birdhouse, feeding their chicks. He stayed with us (his parents were traveling) when he fell ill from overworking on Wall Street. He recovered by napping in our courtyard, and discussing life with his grandfather Wally and me. Now he flies in high finance trading ventures while giving his family a roots trip to Sicily in 2014, and trips to Mexico in 2017 and 2019. In April 2016, Josh came with Whitney, a stunningly nurturing and beautiful significant other—with East and West Coast contingents of our family—to my talks and award for feminist leadership in the ASWM conference.

Josh, for me, personifies anomalies/hopes for the future. He combines traditional human wisdom, family values, edgy technology, bold risks ... he is grounded on knowing who he is ... a Canaanite Jew harking back to the period when Judaism and early Christianity were one faith. He is a very generous spirit. Josh, for me, is a signifying male of the emerging inclusive cosmology of the gift economy.

Marc & Nancy offer models, both traditional and very advanced, of grandparenting ... while their sons, Matt & Nic offer new patterns of kin caring in the new paradigm. Marc & Nancy cared for her aging mother Stella for twelve years. Now Marc & Nancy help Nic care for Charlie (Charlotte), their grandchild. Matt is a model uncle who helped care for his cousins' kids Josie and Matt on our 2014 trip to Sicily; he helps out now in Albany with Charlie. Matt & Kate just married in early 2019 ... an intriguing couple of today's generation ...

Charlie, for this great grandmother, is a gift to the new paradigm. She has an African nose (short, like mine), Wally's scientific curiosity, and the good looks of her Buddhist Japanese grandparents. Embodying wondrous multi-legacies, my luminous blonde great granddaughter seems to me an African~Asian~European~American melody. Her favorite outing is going with her father Nic to feed the animals in Tilden Park.

Our youngest kids, Stefan & Linda, offer new shapes of families in the new paradigm, which I see as a Gift Economy grounded on everybody nurturing. After they reared three very nurturing kids (Courtney, Jake, Stefanie) in the complex spirals of life, Stefan came to live with me after Wally died, and Linda lives with her widowed mother Marcia. Stefan works as a real estate appraiser in the rapidly changing demographies that are running beyond his algorithms in the San Francisco-Oakland Bay Area. After a day of appraising ... hearing poignant stories of people having to leave their homes … he comes home exhausted, but I hear "Here's your clean laundry!" and he cooks dinner (he is highly nutrition conscious) for the two of us.

Linda, who worked in a high-end department store, now works on weekends in a real estate office. She also comes home tired, yet sees to her mother, sees to her grown kids, and sees to me one day a week. She arranges family birthdays and holiday gatherings. Linda accompanied me on the airplane and roomed with me at the ASWM award conference in Boston 2016. She gave me a tote bag created by an African woman's co-operative that is embroidered with golden yoni and red poppies, connoting transformation.

Stefan & Linda's kids are examples of this generation's nurturing kids. Courtney & Matt, their eldest couple, have demanding jobs yet, Courtney (her name, in French, means African short nose) earlier found the time to unclutter my office, and untangle my computer. Matt, who works in high technology, is a highly responsible elder brother to five sisters and a fragile mother, but also finds time to help me. Announcing, "Matteo is here!" he fixes (with toothpicks!) my unhinged closet door. In December 2016, Courtney & Matt gifted everybody with Isabel Rose Potter, a magical child described earlier … a gift of a gift-giving family.

Jake & Abi, Linda & Stefan's eldest kids, were active in the West and East Coast Occupy movement before they found each other. In New York, where Abi taught art to rebellious seventh graders, she is now the full-time mother of Andrew Ellis and Emma Lia. Jake produces film documentaries on nutrition. Both gifted everybody with Andrew Ellis in September 2016, our great grandson whose prodigious energies have already taken him into the new paradigm, and his little sister, Emma Lia (named for grandmother Linda and great grandmother Lucia).

Stefanie Rose, youngest daughter of Linda & Stefan, a gifted elementary teacher, carries the female version of her father's name and signifying name (Rose) for the madonna. A special gift to me … she brings computer and other skills to help me format this manuscript … healing my disheveled spirit. Recently she brought another Matt into our family … he came to our 2018 Passover discovering his own story.

CHAPTER 24
Kindred spirits' sampler of the future

❧

"The Peace Girl Is Here to Stay"
by In Hui Lee

A few years back, I wrote a poem, dedicated to The Peace Girl. A young Korean girl leaves home, believing that going to work in a factory in Japan will make money for her family.

Her country colonized by Japan, her family living on tree barks
No toys no schools no food no time to play
She got to survive somehow somewhere someway …
One day after a long and hard journey over many lands and oceans,
in a place she has no idea where, she finds herself in a situation
that she can't speak of. Nobody can speak of. No language can be
spoken by.
Somehow someway she survives
comes back home
is called "comfort woman."
Comfort?
Who?
Comfort?
Whom?
She waits
waits to hear, "I am sorry," for her lost childhood, her youth, her
womanhood, her dreams, and—her life.
She waits,

waits,

and waits …

her back grew bent.

her hair gone white.

she sits and waits rain or shine on the Peace Road, downtown

Seoul.

Princess Bari[98] says,

I know you,

I know your story,

I care for you,

I remember you.

a bird comes and sits on her shoulder

yellow butterflies[99] arising …

n downtown Seoul, South Korea, between the Japanese Embassy and the USA Embassy, there is a short street, named "Peace Road." Here, across from the Japanese Embassy, a life-size bronze statue of a young Korean girl was erected in 2011. Perhaps the girl is in her preteen years at the threshold of entering womanhood. She represents tens and thousands of young girls and women in Korea and many countries in Asia who were forced into sex slavery by Japan during world war II. These girls and women are known today as "comfort women."

Because the usage of the term, "comfort women," is charged with violence and tragedy, and yet the term itself contains a euphemism, it has been fiercely debated by those concerned with issues of "comfort women."

There are crimes that existed for hundreds of years with no name, such as domestic violence and sexual harassment. For the systematic rape of women at the magnitude conducted by the Japanese government during world war II, there simply was no word to adequately describe it.

For many decades, sex slavery survivors could not speak of this horrendous crime against themselves, because in the culture where women's chastity is highly valued, they are seen as prostitutes and therefore are taught to be ashamed of themselves. When I was growing up, there was nothing written about "comfort women" in South Korea; their stories were unheard of. Contemporary right-wing Japanese men don't hesitate to call these victims "whores."

In December 2015, however, South Korea and Japan made a disastrous diplomatic resolution: Japan will pay money for the survivors and in return, the topic of military sex slavery should never be brought up again and the statue of The Peace Girl should be removed. Hearing this, survivors are enraged because this deal completely ignored what they have been fighting for: an official apology and compensation. Youth in South Korea have been sleeping next to The Peace Girl, on the street, in the freezing cold winter weather in Seoul, in order to keep The Peace Girl right there where she is. The Peace Girl is sitting here to stay, with her hands clenched to show her will to get justice done for "comfort women." She is barefoot because most of these young girls were taken by force and she is ready to stand up at any given moment to resist. Now mostly in their nineties, the survivors learned not to fear anything and have become activists themselves. In January 2016, two survivors travelled to Japan and shouted, "Listen, Japan. Listen, Emperor of Japan. Listen, Abe, prime minister. Make an official apology to us. Compensate us legally for our suffering!"

When I saw The Peace Girl for the first time, I offered her a scarf with peace signs that I had bought in San Francisco.

The Peace Girl A bronze statue, in honour and memory of "comfort women," downtown, Seoul, South Korea, across from Japanese Embassy

BIBLIOGRAPHY

꿔》《꿔

This bibliography refers to works cited in this book,
black bird and a pear tree, as well as books I consider indispensable
to lighting our way to the new paradigm.

By Lucia Birnbaum (ordered by date):

Liberazione della donna. Feminism in Italy. Middletown, Ct., Wesleyan University Press, 1986.

Oral Tradition of Italian-Americans. Washington, DC: U.S. Dept. of Education, Office of Educational Research and Improvement, Educational Resources Information Center, 1987.

Black Madonnas: Feminism, Religion, and Politics in Italy. Boston: Northeastern UP, 1993.

Dark Mother: African Origins and Godmothers. Bloomington: iUniverse, 2001.

The Future Has an Ancient Heart: Legacy of Caring, Sharing, Healing, and Vision from the Primordial African Mediterranean to Occupy Everywhere. Bloomington: iUniverse, 2012.

꿔꿔꿔꿔꿔

Adelman, Penina V. *Miriam's Well: Rituals for Jewish Women around the Year.* Fresh Meadows, NY: Biblio, 1986.

Allende, Isabel. *The House of Spirits.* New York: Atria Paperback, 2015.

Anasi, Robert. *The Last Bohemia: Scenes from the Life of Williamsburg, Brooklyn.* New York: Farrar, Straus and Giroux, 2012.

Baum, Frank L. *The Wonderful Wizard of Oz.* N.Y.: of Wonder, 1987.

Belloc, Hilaire. *The Great Heresies.* Milwaukee: Cavalier, 2015.

Bernardini, Paolo, Rubens D'Oriano, and Maria Pamela Toti. *I Fenici Delle Isole.* Firenze: Giunti Gruppo Editoriale, 2000.

Braud, William and Rosemarie Anderson, eds. 1998. Transpersonal Research Methods for the Social Sciences: Honoring Human Experience. Thousand Oaks: Sage.

Calio, Louisa. *Journey to the Heart Waters*. New York: Legas, 2014.

Calvez, Leigh. *The Hidden Lives of Owls: The Science and Spirit of Nature's Most Elusive Birds*. Seattle, WA: Sasquatch, 2016.

Carrico, Eila. *The Other Side of the River*. N.p.: Womanscraft, 2015.

Casano, Filippo. *Erice: Culture Art Science*. Ed. Tiziana Casano. N.p.: Tiziana Casano, n.d.

Caven, Brian. *The Punic Wars*. New York: Barnes & Noble, 1980.

Chiarelli, Leonard C. *A History of Muslim Sicily*. Venera, Malta: Midsea, 2011.

Chomsky, Noam. *Masters of Mankind: Essays and Lectures, 1969-2013*. Chicago: Haymarket, 2014.

Cirnigliaro, Nino. *Sicilia Storia Di Un'Isola Su Cui Continua a Passare L'Umanità*. Ragusa: Genius Loci Editrice, 2013.

Clottes, Jean. *Dolmens Et Menhirs Du Midi*. Portet/Garonne: Editions Loubatières, 1987.

Colby, Jennifer. *California Missions Journey*. N.p.: Blurb, 2013.

Cooper, David A. *God Is a Verb: Kabbalah and the Practice of Mystical Judaism*. New York: Riverhead, 1997.

Da Siena, Caterina. *Lo, Serva E Schiava*. Palermo: Seller Editore via Siracusa, 1991.

Darkwah, Nana Banchie. *The Africans Who Wrote the Bible: Ancient Secrets Africa and Christianity Have Never Told*. Russellville: Aduana Pub., 2003.

Devereux, Paul. 1996. Re-visioning the Earth: A Guide to Opening the Healing Channels Between Mind and Nature. New York: Fireside.

Dumont, Marion Gail. "Reclaiming Women's History in the Region of Marion, Montana through a Hermeneutic of Place and the Stories of Three Individuals: Kau'xuma'nupika, Gail Peters Little and Arlene Wehr Lapierre." PhD diss. California Institute of Integral Studies, 2013.

Dumont, Marion, and Gayatri Devi, eds. *Myths: Shattered and Restored*. New York: Women and Myth Press, 2016.

Euripides, and Gilbert Murray. *The Trojan Women of Euripides*. New York: Oxford UP, American Branch. 1915.

Fisher, Elizabeth, and Robert Fisher. *Guide to Women's Human Rights*. 2015. https://www.riseupandcallhername.com/uncategorized/guide-to-womens-human-rights.html.

Fisher, Elizabeth. A Woman-honoring Journey into Global Earth-based Spiritualities." 2014. https://www.riseupandcallhername.com/.

Fromm, Erich, and Ruth Nanda. Anshen. *The Art of Loving*. New York: Harper & Row, 1956.

Galeano, Eduardo. *Open Veins of Latin America: Five Centuries of the Pillage of a Continent*. New York: Monthly Review, 1997.

Garana, Ottavio. *Santa Lucia*. Siracusa: Egidio Franchino, 1958.

Gilbert, Alan. *Black Patriots and Loyalists: Fighting for Emancipation in the War for Independence*. Chicago: U of Chicago, 2012.

Ginzburg, Carlo, and Raymond Rosenthal. *Ecstasies: Deciphering the Witches' Sabbath*. Chicago: Random House, 1991.

Gnammankou, Dieudonne, and Yao Modzinou. *Les Africains Et Leurs Descendants En Europe Avant Le XXe Siècle*. Toulouse: MAT Editions, 2008.

Goffredo, Giuseppe. *Con I Fiori Dei Mandorli In Faccia*. 2006.

Graves, Robert, and Raphael Patai. *Hebrew Myths: The Book of Genesis*. New York: McGraw-Hill Book, 1964.

Göttner-Abendroth, Heide. *The Way into an Egalitarian Society: Principles and Practice of a Matriarchal Politics*. Winzer: International Academy Hagia, 2007.

Grame, Tricia, Ph.D. " Life into Art; Art into Life: Transformative Effects of the Female Symbol on a Contemporary Woman Artist." PhD diss. California Institute of Integral Studies, n.d.

Guida, George, Stanislao G. Pugliese, Alan J. Gravano, Peter G. Vellon, and Jennifer Kightlinger. *What Is Italian America? Selected Essays from the Italian American Studies Association*. New York: Italian American Studies Association, 2015.

Harper, Prudence. O, Evelyn Klengel-Brandt, Joan Aruz, and Kim Benzel. *Assyrian Origins: Discoveries at Ashur on the Tigris*. New York: Met Publications. 1995.

Harris, Jean R. *Adventures of A Spiritual Dilettante*. Santa Fe: Silver Snail, 2012.

Hedges, Chris, and Joe Sacco. *Days of Destruction, Days of Revolt*. New York: Nation, 2012.

Hedges, Chris. "James Baldwin and the Meaning of Whiteness." Truthdig. N.p., 19 Feb. 2017. https://www.truthdig.com/articles/james-baldwin-and-the-meaning-of-whiteness/

Hedges, Chris. *Wages of Rebellion*. New York: Nation, 2015.

Heinrich, Bernd. *Mind of the Raven: Investigations and Adventures with Wolf-birds*. New York: HarperCollins, 1999.

Iolana, Patricia. "The Controversy of the 'Old Religion': The Necessity of Interfaith Dialogue." MAGO E Magazine. N.p., 28 Jan. 2017. https://www.magoism.net/2017/01/rtm-newsletter-january-2017-4/

Isole Siciliane: Eolie, Egadi, Pelagie, Pantelleria, Ustica: Escursioni Sport Divertimenti Enogastronomia Arte E Cultura. Milano: Touring Club Italiano, 2004.

Italian Americana Cultural and Historical Review. 1st ed. Vol. XXXIII. Providence: U of Rhode Island, 2014.

James, William. *Pragmatism*. Cambridge: Harvard UP, 1975.

Kairos Palestine: A Moment of Truth. Pittsburgh: Israel / Palestine Mission Network of the Presbyterian Church, 2010.

Kaplan, Robert, and Ellen Kaplan. *Hidden Harmonies: The Lives and times of the Pythagorean Theorem*. New York: Bloomsbury, 2011.

Klein, Naomi. *This Changes Everything: Capitalism vs. the Climate*. New York: Simon & Schuster Paperbacks, 2014.

Laszlo, Ervin. *The Akashic Experience: Science and the Cosmic Memory Field*. Rochester: Inner Traditions, 2009.

Lightman, Alan. *Einstein's Dreams*. New York: Warner, 1993.

Macmillan, Josephine and Lucia Chiavola Birnbam. *She Is Everywhere!: An Anthology of Writing in Womanist/feminist Spirituality*. Bloomington: iUniverse, 2005.

Marcuse, Herbert. *One-dimensional Man; Studies in the Ideology of Advanced Industrial Society*. Boston: Beacon, 1991.

Marzluff, John M., and Tony Angell. *Gifts of the Crow: How Perception, Emotion, and Thought Allow Smart Birds to Behave like Humans.* New York: Atria Paperback, 2013.

Marzluff, John M., and Tony Angell. *In the Company of Crows and Ravens.* New Haven: Yale UP, 2005.

M'Bantu, Anu, and Gert Muller. *The Ancient Black Hebrews and Arabs.* London: Pomegranate, 2013.

Meer, Annine E. G. Van Der, and Orla Clancy. *The Language of MA the Primal Mother: The Evolution of the Female Image in 40,000 Years of Global Venus Art.* Netherlands: n.p., 2013.

Moraga, Cherríe, and Gloria Anzaldúa. *This Bridge Called My Back: Writings by Radical Women of Color.* New York: Kitchen Table, Women of Color, 2015.

Morgan, Thomas L., and William Barlow. *From Cakewalks to Concert Halls: An Illustrated History of African American Popular Music from 1895 to 1930.* Washington, D.C.: Elliott & Clark Pub., 1992.

Moser, Mary Beth, Ph.D. "Blood Relics: Menstrual Roots of Miraculous Black Madonnas in Italy." Metaformia A Journal of Menstruation and Culture. N.p., n.d. 2 Sept. 2015. https://www.scribd.com/document/388026697/Mary-Beth-Moser-Blood-Relics-Menstrual-Roots-of-Miraculous-Black-Madonnas-in-Italy.

Márquez, Gabriel García. *Love in the Time of Cholera.* New York: Alfred A. Knopf, 1988.

Muffoletto, Anna. *The Art of Sicilian Cooking.* Garden City, NY: Doubleday, 1971.

Nader, Ralph. *Breaking through Power: It's Easier than We Think.* San Francisco: City Lights, 2016.

Nader, Ralph. *Unstoppable: The Emerging Left-right Alliance to Dismantle the Corporate State.* New York: Nation, 2014.

Oduyoye, Mercy Amba., Isabel Apawo. Phiri, and Sarojini Nadar. *African Women, Religion, and Health: Essays in Honor of Mercy Amba Ewudziwa Oduyoye.* Maryknoll, NY: Orbis, 2006.

Oleszkiewicz-Peralba, Małgorzata. *Fierce Feminine Divinities of Eurasia and Latin America: Baba Yaga, Kālī, Pombagira, and Santa Muerte*. New York: Palgrave Macmilian, 2015.

Oppenheimer, Stephen. *Out of Eden: The Peopling of the World*. London: Constable, 2003.

Orth, Maureen. "How the Virgin Mary Became the World's Most Powerful Woman." *National Geographic* 8 Nov. 2015. https://www.nationalgeographic.com/magazine/2015/12/virgin-mary-worlds-most-powerful-woman/.

Pagels, Elaine H. *The Origin of Satan*. New York: Random House, 1995.

Patel, Shailja. *Migritude*. New York: Kaya, 2010

Perera, Victor. *The Cross and the Pear Tree: A Sephardic Journey*. New York: Knopf, 1995.

Pineda, Cecile. *Apology to a Whale Words to Mend a World*. San Antonio: Wings, 2015.

Putnam, Robert D., David E. Campbell, and Shaylyn Romney. Garrett. *American Grace: How Religion Divides and Unites Us*. New York: Simon & Schuster, 2012.

Reade, Julian. *Assyrian Sculpture*. London: British Museum, 1983.

Relph, Edward. 1976. Place and Placelessness. London: Pion.

Roberts, Alison. *Hathor Rising: The Power of the Goddess in Ancient Egypt*. Rochester, VT: Inner Traditions International, 1997.

Santana, Debra. *Silence Always Answers*. Berkeley: Quelquefois, 2015.

Savage, Candace Sherk. *Crows: Encounters with the Wise Guys of the Avian World*. Vancouver: Greystone, 2005.

Sax, Boria. *Crow*. London: Reaktion, 2003.

Sheldrake, Philip. 2001. Spaces for the Sacred: Place, Memory, and Identity. Baltimore: The John Hopkins University Press.

———. 2002. "Interpreting texts and traditions." Sewanee Theological Review 46 (1): 48–68.

———, ed. 2005. The New Westminster Dictionary of Christian Spirituality. Louisville: Westminster John Knox Press.

Sidman, Joyce, and Pamela Zagarenski. *What the Heart Knows: Chants, Charms & Blessings*. New York: Houghton Mifflin Harcourt, 2013.

Simonini, Carla A., Carol Bonomo Albright, John Paul Russo, Christine Palamidessi Moore, and Maria Terrone, eds. *Italian Americana Cultural and Historical Review*. 1st ed. Vol. 34. Youngstown: Youngstown State U, 2016. Winter.

Sitrin, Marina, and Dario Azzellini. *They Can't Represent Us! Reinventing Democracy from Greece to Occupy*. London: Verso, 2014.

Talbot, David. *The Devil's Chessboard*. New York: Harper Collins, 2015.

Viscusi, Robert. *An Oration Upon the Most Recent Death of Christopher Columbus*. West Lafayette, IN: Bordighera, 1993.

Wyman, Nona Mock. *Chopstick Childhood (in a Town of Silver Spoons): Orphaned at the Ming Quong Home, Los Gatos, CA*. China Books & Periodicals, 1999.

Endnotes

1 Vivian Deziak, "The Cone of Power: Visions and Manifestations of a Symbol in Western Culture" in *She is Everywhere: An Anthology of Writing in Womanist/Feminist Spirituality* (Berkeley: Belladonna, 2005), 116.

2 Louisa Calio, "Signifyin Woman" in Venera Fazio and Delia De Santis, ed. *Sweet Lemons 2, International Writings with a Sicilian Accent* (Legas Publications, 2010). This poem won 1st Prize in Canicatti Sicily at the Il Parnasso Angelo La Vecchia 2017 competition.

3 Jan Parker, "Culture of Rape. Classical Greece to Hollywood USA" (PhD diss., California Institute of Integral Studies doctoral dissertation, 2016).

4 Perry Miller, *Errand in the Wilderness* (Cambridge, MA: Belknap Press, 1956).

5 Henry Farnham May, *The End of American Innocence* (New York: Columbia University Press, 1994).

6 Robert Brentano, Two Churches: England and Italy in the Thirteenth Century (Berkeley: UC Press, 1988).

7 *American Quarterly*, 1965.

8 See Bernini's statue Teresa in Ecstasy; and read Garcia Lorca's poetry conveying Teresa as soul of baroque art.

9 Pronounced "eeblah."

10 See all of my books; subsequent chapter on gift journey to Sicily in 2014; conferences of American Association of Italian Studies; Irene Shaland and Bianca Del Bello, "Rediscovering Jewish Palermo," New York Times, July 8, 2015.

11 Antonio Gramsci, *Prison Notebooks* (London: ElecBook, 1999).

12 For contemporary transformative studies, see The Mago Work. The Mago Work is committed to connecting peoples and cultures of the pre- and proto-patriarchal world: www.magobooks.com and www.magoism.net.

13 See works by Ronald Takaki for a view of USA and Japanese relations.

14 See Lawrence W. DiStasi's Branded: How Italian Immigrants Became "Enemies" During WWII (Sanniti Publications, 2016).

15 For USA culture of rape see Jan Parker, "Culture of Rape. Classical Greece to Hollywood USA" (PhD diss., California Institute of Integral Studies doctoral dissertation, 2016).

16 Sinclair Lewis, *It Can't Happen Here* (Signet Classics, 2014).

17 George Orwell, *1984* (Signet, 1961).

18 See writings by William Appleman Williams, *The Tragedy of American Diplomacy* (W.W. Norton & Company, 2009); David Talbot, *The Devil's Chessboard: Allen Dulles, the CIA, and the Rise of America's Secret Government* (Harper Perennial, 2016); Noam Chomsky, *Requiem for the American Dream* (Gravitas Ventures, 2016).

19 See Cecile Pineda, "Devil's Tango; Bulletin of Concerned Scientists."

20 See novels of Isabel Allende.

21 See the back cover image of a contemporary Sicilian banner of resistance to MUOS, gifted to me by midwife Clare Loprinzi, shows three women's legs walking across a yellow triangle (death) and a red triangle (life) at whose center is Medusa with three legs and regenerating pine cones in her hair.

22 See Antonio Mazzeo, *il muostro di Niscemi*. Florence, editpress, 2013.

23 See Democracy Now television program, October 18, 2016.

24 See map of Hawaii by Christina Blakey, Malu Aina, Center for Non-Violent Education & Action, Kurtistown, HI 96760.

25 Listen to the music of Benny Goodman.

26 See May Elawar's doctoral dissertation from California Institute of Integral Studies.

27 See writings of H. L. Mencken lambasting the "Booboisie" of USA.

28 See Deborah Grenn-Scott, *Lilith's Fire: Reclaiming Our Sacred Lifeforce* (Universal Publishers, 2000)

29 Note: It is June 2017, and I have just learned that this Lucy, a close cousin of my sister Joie and me, has died at the age of 91. See below for more on my cousin Lucy, whose unconventional life story, in my view, tapped subversive Celtic, Cathar, and Sicilian traditions. Always forthright, at the end, Lucy described her life as "one hell of a ride."

30 See research of California Institute of Integral Studies librarian, Eahr Joan.

31 See contemporary books, *White Trash: The 400-Year Untold History of Class in America* (Nancy Isenberg) and *Hillbilly Elegy: A Memoir of a Family and Culture in Crisis* (J.D. Vance), which help explain why some marginalized poor people tiring of liberal elites telling them what to believe—while calling poor people "racist" and "ignorant"—voted for Trump in 2016.

32 See discussion of Pagan Studies group in January 2017 conference of the American Academy of Religion, "The Controversy of the 'Old Religion' the Necessity of Intrafaith Dialogue" reprinted in the refreshingly inclusive e-magazine founded by an Asian woman teaching in eastern Missouri. Also see Return to Mago, January 28, 2017.

33 See Max Dashu, Suppressed Histories Archives (www.suppressedhistories.net); research of Sandy Miranda on world music (hear her on KPFA "Music of the World."); and listen to music of Woody Guthrie and Bob Dylan.

34 June 2017, I have just learned that this cousin Lucia has died . . . at the venerable age of 103.

35 See Katherine Bolger Hyde, *Lucia: Saint of Light* (Chesterton, Indiana: Ancient Faith Publishing, 2009].

36 See the novels of Dacia Maraini.

37 See the novel *Il Gattopardo* (*The Leopard: A Novel*) by Giuseppe Di Lampedusa (Pantheon: 2007) for Sicily; see movie, *The Butler*, directed by Lee Daniels (2013) for slave-holding south of USA.

38 See Lucia Chiavola Birnbaum, *Liberazione della donna. Feminism in Italy* (Middletown, CT: Wesleyan University Press, 1986).

39 E-mail April 2017.

40 See writings of Jean Rosenthal Harris.

41 See below for Joie's grandchild—daughter of her son Lance—who names herself Cat Joie.

42 See the movie, *Il Postino*, directed by Michael Radford and Massimo Troisi.

43 See the last chapters of Lucia Chiavola Birnbaum, *The Future Has an Ancient Heart: Legacy of Caring, Sharing, Healing, and Vision from the Primordial African Mediterranean to Occupy Everywhere* (Bloomington: iUniverse, 2013).

44 See Jan Parker, "Culture of Rape. Classical Greece to Hollywood USA" (PhD diss., California Institute of Integral Studies doctoral dissertation, 2016).

45 Noam Chomsky, *Requiem for the American Dream* documentary (Gravitas Ventures, 2016).

46 See clips of me in *Women's Spirituality in Higher Education*, directed by Deborah Santana (2015).

47 See David Talbot, *The Devil's Chessboard: Allen Dulles, the CIA, and the Rise of America's Secret Government* (Harper Perennial: 2016).

48 See George Orwell, *Homage to Catalonia* (Houghton Mifflin Harcourt: 2010).

49 See Ms. Magazine "She Persisted. Against all odds: Central American Women at the Border. Women in Greek Refugee Camps" (Summer 2017).

50 See the torrent of books from 2017-18-19 telling the truth as well as Amy Goodman's television show, "Democracy Now"; also my books.

51 See "Bernie Sanders: Democrats Need to Wake Up", The Opinion Pages, *The New York Times*, June 28, 2016.

52 Jan Parker, "Culture of Rape. Classical Greece to Hollywood USA" (PhD diss., California Institute of Integral Studies doctoral dissertation, 2016).

53 "Behaviorism. John Broadus Watson and U. S. Social theory, 1913-1930" (University of California, Berkeley, 1964).

54 See Chapter 1 of this book.

55 See Lucia Chiavola Birnbaum, *Liberazione della donna. Feminism in Italy* (Middletown, CT: Wesleyan University Press, 1986) and *Black Madonnas: Feminism, Religion, and Politics in Italy* (Boston: Northeastern UP, 1993).

56 See Lucia Chiavola Birnbaum, *Liberazione della donna. Feminism in Italy* (Middletown, CT: Wesleyan University Press, 1986).

57 See Max Dashu, *Witches and Pagans in European Folklore 700-1100 Secret History of Witches* (Veleda Press, 2017).

58 See writings of Marion Dumont.

59 See the back cover of my book, *Dark Mother: African Origins and Godmothers* (San Jose: Authors Choice, 2001).

60 See Lucia Chiavola Birnbaum, *Black Madonnas: Feminism, Religion, and Politics in Italy* (Boston: Northeastern UP, 1993).

61 See I Fenici, a catalog of the Italian exhibit under the supervision of Sabatino Moscati. This large tome was hand-carried home by Wally after we saw the exhibit in Italy.

62 See bulletins from the Union of Concerned Scientists, www.ucsusa.org

63 See the writings of Bill McKibben, author, educator, and environmentalist.

64 See writings of Genevieve Vaughan and Heide Goettner Abendroth.

65 For a significant sidewise view of this story from an African perspective and fluid view of sexuality, see my discussion of Bernadette in *Weighing the Cost of Pin Making: Ulli Beier in Conversation* edited by Remi Omodele (Africa World Press: 2012).

66 The stories of Jean Rosenthal Harris brilliantly convey this.

67 See Naomi Klein, *No Is Not Enough: Resisting Trump's Shock Politics and Winning the World We Need* (Haymarket Books, 2017).

68 See writings of Marguerite Rigoglioso.

69 See Lucia Chiavola Birnbaum, *The Future Has an Ancient Heart: Legacy of Caring, Sharing, Healing, and Vision from the Primordial African Mediterranean to Occupy Everywhere* (Bloomington: iUniverse, 2013).

70 See account of spontaneous helping of others during mass murder, "Bronx-Lebanon is More Than a Hospital to Neighbors. A sense of Duty Amid the Chaos", *New York Times*, July 5, 2017.

71 See *The Sniper*, directed by Gabriel Fowler, 2015.

72 See Umberto Eco's books.

73 In February 20, 2019, Sandy & Rob left for Sardinia, meeting their tour guide, Davide, who inspired us in this ancient African site nearly two decades ago.

74 See Lucia Chiavola Birnbaum, *Black Madonnas: Feminism, Religion, and Politics in Italy* (Boston: Northeastern UP, 1993), which won the Valetutti award in 1997.

75 See story of early Christian virgin martyr Barbara migrating from Tunisia, Libya, Africa, to Sicily.

76 See my discussion in *Weighing the Cost of Pin Making: Ulli Beier in Conversation* edited by Remi Omodele (Africa World Press, 2012).

77 See Moses Maimonides, *Guide for the Perplexed* (Digireads.com: 2018).

78 Lucia Chiavola Birnbaum, *Black Madonnas: Feminism, Religion, and Politics in Italy* (Boston: Northeastern UP, 1993).

79 Lucia Chiavola Birnbaum, *The Future Has an Ancient Heart: Legacy of Caring, Sharing, Healing, and Vision from the Primordial African Mediterranean to Occupy Everywhere* (Bloomington: iUniverse, 2012).

80 See Eduardo Galeano, *Open Veins of Latin America. Five Centuries of the Pillage of a Continent* (New York, 1973, 1997).

81 See account in Lucia Chiavola Birnbaum, *Black Madonnas: Feminism, Religion, and Politics in Italy* (Boston: Northeastern UP, 1993).

82 See the opera of Italian peasant life, *Cavalleria Rusticana*.

83 See Carlo Ginzburg, *Ecstasies: Deciphering the Witches' Sabbath* (University of Chicago Press, 2004).

84 See *The Sniper*, directed by Gabriel Fowler, 2015.

85 See Mary Saracino, *Heretics: A Love Story* (Pearlsong Press, 2014).

86 See the story in the last chapters of this book.

87 See Leonard Chiarelli, *A History of Muslim Sicily* (Midsea Books, 2018), a story of Sicily written by a contemporary Sicilian of Muslim inheritance who lives at Ricalmuto on the island's coast facing Africa to the south and Asia to the east.

88 Leonard Chiarelli, *A History of Muslim Sicily* (Midsea Books, 2018), 177.

89 Leonard Chiarelli, *A History of Muslim Sicily* (Midsea Books, 2018), 179.

90 Louisa Calio, Journey to the Heart Waters (Amazon Digital, 2015).

91 See Lawrence DiStasi, *Mal Occhio [Evil Eye]: The Underside of Vision* (North Point Press, 1981).

92 See Alison Lingo's monumental 2017 study of a woman healer, influenced by popular healing beliefs, who became midwife to the French queen. See Max Dashu, *Witches and Pagans in European Folklore, 700-1100 (Secret History of Witches)* (Veleda Press, 2017).

93 See Lucia Chiavola Birnbaum, *Black Madonnas: Feminism, Religion, and Politics in Italy* (Boston: Northeastern UP, 1993).

94 See Lawrence Di Stasi's *Family Matter: a novel.*

95 See dramas of Luigi Pirandello.

96 See the back cover of this book.

97 See the cover of Lucia Chiavola Birnbaum, *The Future Has an Ancient Heart: Legacy of Caring, Sharing, Healing, and Vision from the Primordial African Mediterranean to Occupy Everywhere* (Bloomington: iUniverse, 2013).

98 Princess Bari is the first shaman woman of Korea. She is able to travel to the underworld. A group of Korean shaman women offer ritual for "comfort women."

99 Yellow butterflies symbolize the resisting spirit of "comfort women" and of the movement for justice for victims and survivors of the sex slavery